MW00851515

In Pursuit of English

OXFORD STUDIES IN SOCIOLINGUISTICS

General Editors:
Nikolas Coupland
Copenhagen University, University of Technology, Sydney, and Cardiff University
Adam Jaworski
University of Hong Kong

IN PURSUIT OF ENGLISH

Language and Subjectivity in Neoliberal South Korea

Joseph Sung-Yul Park

OXFORD
UNIVERSITY PRESS

OXFORD
UNIVERSITY PRESS

Oxford University Press is a department of the University of Oxford. It furthers
the University's objective of excellence in research, scholarship, and education
by publishing worldwide. Oxford is a registered trade mark of Oxford University
Press in the UK and certain other countries.

Published in the United States of America by Oxford University Press
198 Madison Avenue, New York, NY 10016, United States of America.

© Oxford University Press 2021

All rights reserved. No part of this publication may be reproduced, stored in
a retrieval system, or transmitted, in any form or by any means, without the
prior permission in writing of Oxford University Press, or as expressly permitted
by law, by license, or under terms agreed with the appropriate reproduction
rights organization. Inquiries concerning reproduction outside the scope of the
above should be sent to the Rights Department, Oxford University Press, at the
address above.

You must not circulate this work in any other form
and you must impose this same condition on any acquirer.

Library of Congress Control Number: 2021942145
ISBN 978–0–19–085574–1 (pbk.)
ISBN 978–0–19–085573–4 (hbk.)

DOI: 10.1093/oso/9780190855734.001.0001

9 8 7 6 5 4 3 2 1

Paperback printed by Marquis, Canada
Hardback printed by Bridgeport National Bindery, Inc., United States of America

CONTENTS

ACKNOWLEDGMENTS

The past decade saw the emergence of a large number of scholars working on issues of language, neoliberalism, transnationalism, and globalization in the Korean context. In my research presented in this book, I benefited tremendously from their work, and in some fortunate cases, opportunities to speak with and work closely with them, including Choi Jinsook, Choi Lee Jin, Elaine Chun, Jang In Chull, Chris Jenks, Agnes Kang, Kang Mia, Kang Yoonhee, Jenna Kim, Stephanie Kim, Jerry Lee, Shin Hyunjung, Sohn Bonggi, and Song Juyoung. Special thanks go to Adrienne Lo, who not only took the time to read and comment on the manuscript, but always challenges me with brilliant insights about Korean society and helps me expand my vision into new directions. I also thank Bae Sohee, with whom I had the great privilege of working together on Korean transnationalism in Singapore; without her help, much of the research reported in this book could not have been carried out. Nancy Abelmann and her work remains an inspiration to me, as it does for many others working on contemporary Korean society.

There are others who helped me broaden my thinking by providing comments, questions, and criticisms, or more generally by sharing rich conversations with me on language and political economy, including David Block, Christian Chun, Alfonso Del Percio, Mi-Cha Flubacher, Gao Shuang, Monica Heller, Marnie Holborow, Miyako Inoue, Angie Reyes, Ruanni Tupas, and Cécile Vigouroux. In particular, Mary Bucholtz, Ryuko Kubota, and Ingrid Piller provided tremendous support and mentorship over the past years through their guidance and encouragement. Claire Kramsch and Rick Kern gave me a much-needed stimulus for developing this book by hosting me at the Berkeley Language Center in 2016. My colleagues Peter De Costa, Mie Hiramoto, and Lionel Wee have been a steady and reliable source of new ideas and feedback.

I cannot thank enough the editors of the Oxford Studies in Sociolinguistics series, Adam Jaworski, Brook Bolander, and Nikolas Coupland for believing in this project, and for the anonymous reviewers who provided very helpful critical comments on the proposal and manuscript. I also thank the editors at Oxford University Press, Hallie Stebbins and Meredith Keffer, who guided me with great patience during the long process of this book's writing. It would have been impossible to write this book without the many jogi yuhak families and Korean managers in Singapore who agreed to be a part of my research. Though their names will remain anonymous, I am deeply grateful for the trust and openness they extended to me through their participation.

My mother and my sister Victoria passed away during the final stages of this book's writing. They would always inquire how the book was coming, and I am sad that I can no longer show it to them in its final form. But I am happy to have Junghee, Jungin, and Jungwu with me, always comforting me and giving me hope. I thank all of them for their love.

This book's chapters build and expand upon earlier works I have published elsewhere. I thank the following for permission to reuse these materials:

- Chapter 4 is a substantially revised version of Park, Joseph Sung-Yul. 2016. "Language as Pure Potential." *Journal of Multilingual and Multicultural Development* 37 (5): 453–66, used with permission from Taylor & Francis (https://www.tandfonline.com).
- Chapter 5 is revised from Park, Joseph Sung-Yul. 2010. "Naturalization of Competence and the Neoliberal Subject: Success Stories of English Language Learning in the Korean Conservative Press." *Journal of Linguistic Anthropology* 20 (1): 22–38, used with permission from American Anthropological Association.
- Chapter 7 synthesizes sections from the following publications: Park, Joseph Sung-Yul. 2014. "'You Say Ouch and I Say Aya': Linguistic Insecurity in a Narrative of Transnational Work." *Journal of Asian Pacific Communication* 24 (2): 241–60, used with permission from John Benjamins (https://www.benjamins.com/catalog/japc); and Park, Joseph Sung-Yul. 2017. "Transnationalism as Interdiscursivity: Korean Managers of Multinational Corporations Talking about Mobility." *Language in Society* 46 (1): 23–38, used with permission from Cambridge University Press.
- Chapter 8 partly draws from Park, Joseph Sung-Yul. 2011. "The Promise of English: Linguistic Capital and the Neoliberal Worker in the South Korean Job Market." *International Journal of Bilingual Education and Bilingualism* 14 (4): 443–55, used with permission from Taylor & Francis (https://www.tandfonline.com).

The Romanization of Korean in this book follows the Revised Romanization System, except for names of individuals whose preferences are known.

CHAPTER 1

Introduction

THE WORLD IN PURSUIT OF ENGLISH

All across the world, transformations in the global economy have elevated English to the status of a language to be pursued with the utmost urgency. In Mexico, the ambitious National English Program for Basic Education was implemented in 2009, providing English instruction through public schools in an attempt to strengthen the English language competence of the whole population and enhance the competitiveness of the nation in the global economy (Sayer 2015). In Slovakia, referring to how English has become indispensable for survival in the postsocialist economy characterized by active recruitment of foreign direct investment and loosening of labor laws, a manager of a biotech firm explains, "I don't know who can change it. [English] will be the international language or second language for everybody" (Prendergast 2008:84). In Taiwan, the state's active push for market openness and international competitiveness resulted in greater promotion of English in the education system, triggering explosive growth of English language *buxiban*, or private education centers, through which parents seek to equip their children with competence in this global language (Price 2014). In India, the booming economy that was fueled by the liberalization of the national market led to widespread perceptions of the connection between English and individual success, as "call center jobs or positions in multinational corporations that required a certain amount of fluency in English have become the face of globalization-related linguistic mobility aspirations" (Proctor 2014:300).

No reader will find any of these examples strange. The fact that an increasing number of states, communities, and individuals are pursuing English does not surprise anymore. Not only has this lost the status of news, but for many, the explanation is also obvious: people flock toward English because it is the language of economic opportunity. The examples above demonstrate

In Pursuit of English. Joseph Sung-Yul Park, Oxford University Press. © Oxford University Press 2021.
DOI: 10.1093/oso/9780190855734.003.0001

their point. Governments want citizens to have competency in English because they want to boost the national economy; workers learn English in order to get good jobs; parents seek English language education for their children so that they can live a successful life; communities promote their ties with English as a way of securing economic wealth. Quite simply, as a taxi driver in Lima observes, "English is like the dollar" (Niño-Murcia 2003:121). One does not need to agree with this statement; one does not need to be happy about it; regardless of whether one considers English a blessed key to prosperity or disguised imperialism that only gives out false hopes, one thing seems certain—the world is driven toward English because it is believed to bring better jobs, better pay, and economic success.

But is this worldwide pursuit of English really just about economic value? This book says no. The argument I present here is that the way English is sought after in the global economy, despite its obvious connections with the material benefits it is supposed to bring, is mediated in important ways through the perceptual, moral, and affective dimensions of how we, as human beings, understand ourselves as actors in the world—in other words, through aspects of *subjectivity*. I also argue that considering this dimension of subjectivity serves as an important way of critiquing this promotion of English in the global economy.

A closer look at the political-economic conditions reflected in the examples above tell us why it is problematic to attribute the global pursuit of English to a purely economic motivation. All of these contexts are examples of a shift toward what we call *neoliberalism*—the belief in market-oriented freedom as the ideal organizing principle for all domains of life. Neoliberalism can be characterized by a range of practices, including deregulation, financialization, privatization, flexibilization of labor, and elimination of welfare, all of which are meant to uphold the reign of the free market in which capital can seek profit without restriction by state and society. This condition, of course, facilitates an understanding of the value of language in economic terms, and for this reason, the co-occurrence of neoliberal transformations and heavy emphasis placed on English may seem unsurprising. However, neoliberalism is not simply an economic doctrine. Its impulse to maximize the reach of the market necessarily means it has implications for the way we see and understand ourselves as subjects. In this sense, neoliberalism is also about the formation and transformation of subjectivities. This means that people's choice to pursue English in the context of neoliberalism cannot be understood as a result of some rational calculation of material benefits, but as action that is grounded in emotionally charged and politically intense qualities of subjecthood.

The case of South Korea can be a useful illustration of this point. South Korea is one of the countries which has experienced a massive neoliberal transformation. In fact, it is one of the countries that most faithfully adhered to the program of restructuring and austerity prescribed by the International

Monetary Fund (IMF) in the wake of the Asian financial crisis of 1997. Liberalization and financialization of markets, reorganization of corporate governance, and flexibilization of labor were carried out at a fast pace, transforming the very fabric of everyday life in Korean society. Coinciding with this social transformation was a heated pursuit of English, often called the English fever (*yeongeo yeolpung*; Park 2009). Koreans were suddenly making huge investments in English language learning. For university students, studying for TOEIC (Test of English for International Communication) became of prime importance; white-collar workers spent their precious time after work acquiring conversational skills in English; parents paid for expensive English language kindergartens for their children to give them a head start in learning the language. The co-occurrence of Korea's neoliberalization and the English fever only seems natural, for the country's neoliberal transformation created conditions in which English came to be closely tied with economic benefits. As corporations and the state were pressured to more actively engage in the global economy, English became an important criterion for the evaluation of workers, and given the harsh climate of the job market, this led Koreans to perceive English as a key to economic survival. In this sense, Koreans' investment in English comes as no surprise. Indeed, communication scholar and critic Kang Junman (2007) has argued that the Korean English fever is perfectly "rational behavior," in the sense that Koreans cannot but respond to the social system in which English serves as a key to valuable economic opportunities by scrambling to study and acquire the language.

Yet, to say that Koreans pursue English simply because of the economic opportunities it opens up fails to capture important realities about the way Koreans relate to English. While English is certainly associated with better jobs and economic privilege in Koreans' beliefs, when Koreans choose to study English they do not simply do so based on a detached, rational calculation about which language will bring one maximum profit. For Koreans, English conjures much, much more than that. Korean discourses about English are replete with dense expressions of feelings, longings, and imaginings. These include a desire for the different self that one might become through the learning of English; a sense of moral responsibility of carefully managing one's time and resources to invest in acquiring English; anxieties about failing to achieve their self-ascribed goals of English language learning; insecurities about their English being constantly measured and assessed against that of others; the frustration of the seemingly endless journey they trudge, in which the final destination of being a perfect English speaker is always just out of reach. Any account of why Koreans pursue English cannot be complete without making sense of these rich, intense, and visceral emotions and perceptions that define how Koreans understand English. Not only are they part of the material and bodily reality through which Koreans encounter English, they are also an important way through which the English language comes to be integrated into the logic of neoliberalism in Korean society, transforming it into a language that serves as one of the most important links in the structure of inequality, control, and endless competition that characterizes the political economy of contemporary Korea.

This, then, is the topic of this book. It presents subjectivity as the key for understanding the relationship between English and neoliberalism—and more generally, between language and political economy—using the case of South Korea as an example. By tracing the multiple ways in which aspects of subjectivity were involved in rationalizing and reifying the place of English in Korea's neoliberal transformation, it argues that the heated pursuit of English in Korea was shaped by the anxieties, insecurities, and moral desire that neo-liberal Korean society inculcates among Koreans, leading English to be seen as an index of an ideal neoliberal subject, who actively adheres to the prevalent pressure to engage in constant self-management and self-development under the changing conditions of the global economy. For this purpose, this book proposes a framework of analysis that investigates language users' experiences as thinking, feeling, and acting subjects (Kramsch 2009) in order to understand and critique formations of the political economy. In doing so, it aims to contribute to the expanding sociolinguistic research on language and political economy (Block 2014, Block, Gray, and Holborow 2012, Holborow 2015, Martín Rojo and Del Percio 2020), language and materiality (Cavanaugh and Shankar 2017), and commodification of language (Cameron 2005, Duchêne and Heller 2012, Heller 2003, 2010), suggesting how our exploration of language in political-economic relations should be grounded on the analysis of the subjective dimensions of human experience.

RESEARCHING ENGLISH IN THE GLOBAL ECONOMY

This book takes a critical perspective on the power of English as a global language and the neoliberal context in which it emerges. In this sense, it builds upon previous research on the global spread of English—that is, how English has advanced from being a language of the British Isles to an international language that is picked up and appropriated in complex ways by an increasing number of speakers across the world. This body of earlier work was for a large part developed as a critique of the relations of power and inequality behind the spread of English, investigating the cultural politics of imperialism that shape the local adoption of English in postcolonial contexts around the world. For instance, Phillipson's (1992) influential framework of linguistic imperialism uncovered the material and ideological processes that sustain and reproduce British and US hegemony through the promotion of English around the world, while Pennycook's (1994, 1998, 2007a) focus on performativity highlighted how local appropriations of English both are shaped by and reshape historical conditions of colonialism and imperialism, and Canagarajah (1999) emphasized how the global level hegemony of English may be resisted by learners in the periphery through local practices of hybridity that renegotiate colonial implications of English. The postcolonial and postimperial perspective adopted by these studies produced powerful analyses of how English as a global language comes to be taken up in local cultural context, with critical reflections on politically loaded yet seldom questioned concepts such as that of the native speaker or standard English.

Recently, however, with the expansion of English beyond the previous British or American colonies, and the prominence of English in the context of neoliberalism, a small but notable number of studies have started to take aspects of the political economy as their central concern for analysis (Ricento 2015). Instead of foregrounding the cultural practices of local appropriation of English as informed by a postcolonial perspective, an increasing number of studies is turning to the material and economic conditions and constraints that surround the global spread of English, with a focus on issues of class (Price 2014, Proctor 2014), labor (Kubota 2011a, Lorente 2012, 2017), and consumption (Gao 2012, 2019, Kubota 2011b), and how they intersect with conditions of global migration, which often impact traditional English-speaking countries as well (Allan 2013, Warriner 2016). These works, in turn, are informed by the burgeoning body of sociolinguistic research on the commodification of language (Cameron 2005, Duchêne and Heller 2012, Heller 2003, 2010, Muth and Del Percio 2018, Tan and Rubdy 2008), which tries to understand how shifts in the modes and conditions of production have led to new ways of conceptualizing language—that is, how language is increasingly seen as a resource that can be flexibly mobilized for economic profit, rather than an emblem of an enduring sense of identity.

In this sense, these political-economically oriented studies make a major contribution of bringing the research on the global spread of English into the domain of mainstream sociolinguistics and linguistic anthropology. Prior to this, critical study of the global spread of English was mostly understood as belonging to applied linguistics. It was often envisioned as a critical response to the hegemonic ideologies and practices of TESOL (Teaching English to Speakers of Other Languages) and most of the prominent researchers came from the field of English language teaching. Also, sociolinguistic research that engaged with this issue tended to be positioned within a highly specific subdiscipline, such as sociology of language (Fishman, Conrad, Rubal-Lopez 1996) or world Englishes (Kachru 1985, 1997). By highlighting its relevance to a major theoretical concern within sociolinguistics, the new body of research on the global spread of English brings the attention of the field to a key issue of our time, urging sociolinguistic research to more directly engage with the prominent position language takes in the changing global economy.

However, there still remains much room for deeper theorization of the relationship between English and neoliberalism. For instance, while many studies note and criticize how English is actively promoted within neoliberalism, it is often overlooked that there is nothing about neoliberalism that inherently privileges English over other languages. Neoliberalism certainly does not depend on English to operate. The discourse of neoliberalism can be, and is being, spoken in many different languages (Kramsch 2006). And it is also not the case that neoliberalism means a world where monolingualism in English prevails. Neoliberalism happily promotes multilingualism in so far as it allows capital to respond to demands of different markets across the globe in a flexible and efficient way. For example, global capital does not wait for the world to learn English so that it can do business in new locales; the neoliberal vision of a boundless market means that capital is always ready to learn and incorporate local languages if it allows maximization of profit (Dor 2004, Kubota 2013). Insistence on English-only, in fact, may conflict with the ideals of neoliberalism; as neoliberalism valorizes endless competition and self-development, the ideal neoliberal subject would constantly be acquiring new languages as skills to maximize her own marketability, rather than believing the single language of English would suffice. Yet, as we have seen above, English is flourishing under neoliberalism in many national contexts, widely perceived to be the language of neoliberalism to the exclusion of others. Current research that focuses on the economic value of English as a key for explaining its status in neoliberalism does not sufficiently address this problem.

Likewise, the notion of commodification, which often serves as the theoretical foundation for the perspective that views the neoliberal promotion of English in terms of economic value, has also received much criticism. Many scholars have called for a more careful discussion of what exactly do we mean by commodification of language, given the clear difference that language has from more typical forms of commodities that are products of human labor (Block 2014, Holborow 2015, 2018a, McGill 2013, Simpson and O'Regan 2018). These scholars caution that, without deeper reflection on the place of language in the political economy, there is danger of simply treating the neoliberal condition as a natural state of affairs, overlooking the interests and inequalities upheld by discourses that promote languages such as English as a key for economic prosperity. May (2014), for instance, points out how the notion of English as an economic resource is uncritically embraced in the arguments of political theorists such as Archibugi (2005) and Van Parijs (2011), who valorize English as a global lingua franca that can foster economic advancement and social mobility for linguistic minorities, ignoring the conditions of social class that constrain who can economically benefit by acquiring the language (see also Ives 2010). Likewise, the popularity of what Kubota (2016) calls the multi/plural turn in language research, in which fluidity and dynamism of multilingualism is celebrated as challenging essentialist perspectives on language and identity, also risks obscuring inequalities reproduced through English, as it tends to emphasize creative agency of individuals over historical and material conditions of power. This underlines the need for a deeper theorization of the relationship between English and neoliberalism that moves beyond a focus on economic value to question how English comes to be valorized in the neoliberal economy in the first place.

An orientation to the subjective experiences of English rooted in the materially specific conditions of neoliberalism can be one way of moving the discussion forward. The affective, emotional, and moral dimensions of how we pursue, acquire, and value English in the political economy reminds us that underneath the processes of neoliberalism lie our thoughts, actions, and struggles as human beings—that we are not merely calculating participants in the market driven by profit, even as we are constrained by structural forces beyond our immediate control that condition our actions. A focus on subjectivity, then, can help us develop a more grounded perspective on neoliberalism, through which its true effects and contradictions may be laid bare. Indeed, dimensions of subjectivity have received much attention in current studies of commodification. For instance, one of their key findings is the anxieties and dissonance that workers experience as they are pressured to put on "authentic" performances to enhance the value of customer service regardless of how they actually feel inside (Cameron 2005, Mirchandani 2012). The way in which language and authenticity is commodified in the process of work, in turn, evidences how the neoliberal condition of labor represents an ever-expanding system of exploitation that treats workers' selves and bodies as expendable resources (Piller and Takahashi 2013).

However, developing a serious theory of the relationship between English and neoliberalism requires us to attribute an even more fundamental role to subjectivity in the political economy. In order to theorize the unique position English occupies within neoliberalism, we would need to consider the anxieties, desires, insecurities, and moral burdens that people experience in relation to English not only as a consequence of the commodification of language, but as elements of our constitution as subjects in the neoliberal economy. In other words, it is crucial to consider how the ideological construction of language as a commodity in itself may be shaped by the way we are molded as subjects, if we are to historically and ideologically interrogate the prevalent discourse of English as an economic resource. For this reason, this book's exploration of the nexus between English and neoliberalism through the lens of subjectivity does not simply contribute to the study of the global spread of English. It offers a challenge to the existing body of work on language in political economy, by suggesting an expansion of what constitutes the materiality of language—that it should not only include the raw economic aspects of class, labor, and relations of production, but also the broader semiotic and experiential conditions through which language users, as human subjects, engage with the realm of the economic.

SUBJECTIVITY AS A CRITICAL PERSPECTIVE ON NEOLIBERALISM

Subjectivity, quite literally, can be understood as the experience of being a subject. Following numerous recent works (Ortner 2005, Luhrman 2006, Biehl et al. 2007, Blackman et al. 2008), I highlight through this term aspects of affect, morality, and desire that characterize our lives as agents in social context—the range of feelings, sentiments, perceptions, impulses, and values that shape and condition our sense of who we are, and serve as the basis for our acting upon the world.

Our definition above might conjure up the conventional opposition expressed by the terms *subjective* and *objective* (i.e., with *objective* concerning the factual, impartial, and reliable; and *subjective* the impressionistic, imprecise, and biased), in the sense that feelings, desires, and values are normally seen as residing beyond that which can be positivistically studied. However, to consider subjectivity as the unreliable residue of the objective is misleading, for such conception is based on a false opposition that sees the 'external' world as fundamentally dissociated with the realm of the 'personal.' The subjective dimensions of our lived experiences are inextricably bound with material and social relations, in what Raymond Williams (1977) called 'structures of feeling.' To focus on subjectivity, therefore, is not to retreat into the individual's inner mental world, looking away from the political realities of society. On the contrary, it is to confront the relations of power that shape ourselves into particular social beings, and the way we react against them.

To appreciate this, it is helpful to consider the significance of the term *subject*. As opposed to related ideas such as *individual*, which implies a free, autonomous being with its own attendant consciousness as well as rights and responsibilities, or *self*, which presumes a unique and coherent psychological inner essence of a person, *subject* posits a much more conflicted and constantly shifting entity, a social agent that engages with the world, yet is continuously conditioned and shaped by it as well—which is reflected in the dual meaning of the term, simultaneously denoting something that acts upon (as in the 'subject' of a grammatical sentence) and something that is being acted upon (as in 'subject of the law'). For this reason, the subject is not a naturally existing entity, but produced through the political process of *subjectification*. Foucault's work shows how the subject does not simply interact with power, but is in fact an effect of power; that is, the way we are shaped as particular kinds of subjects is precisely how power operates—through our constitution as social beings (Foucault 1980). According to this perspective, the way we view ourselves as free, autonomous individuals or internally coherent selves, for instance, is in itself an outcome of subjectification, tied with discursive and material conditions of a modernist rationality that serves as the basis for today's everyday institutions of power, ranging from the state to schools and the workplace.

Subjectivity, then, as the lived, embodied experience of the subject, is both a window for understanding our constitution as agents (who are not always coherent and rationally explainable, interacting with the world in a politically and emotionally charged way) and a perspective for critiquing the conditions of power that constrain us (by instilling in us particular feelings, beliefs, desires, fears, and hopes, which in turn permeate our thoughts, bodies, and behaviors). It helps us find a well-grounded vantage point for theorizing the tension between structure and agency, pointing to the fictitiousness of the presumed gap between an overarching structure that exists beyond our control and the unassailable independence of our will as human beings (Giddens 1984). As Ortner points out, "agency is not some natural or originary will; it takes shape as specific desires and intentions within a matrix of subjectivity—of (culturally constituted) feelings, thoughts, and meanings" (2005:34). Tracing such dimensions of subjectivity therefore can reveal the complexity of our social life, which exceeds what any dichotomy can characterize, pulsing with intersecting emotions, desires, and moral concerns that defy a logic of consistency yet are nonetheless deeply conditioned and guided by systems of power.

For this reason, subjectivity has recently emerged as a critical perspective on neoliberalism (Walkerdine 2011, Allison 2012, Wilce and Fenigsen 2016). The principles of the free market as valorized by neoliberalism have deep consequences for subjectivity on multiple levels. On the one hand, neoliberalism presses us to adopt a particular mode of subjectivity, as it views welfare and solidarity as outdated and sees society as a collection of individuals who each act as an entrepreneur with moral responsibility of carefully managing his or her own potential, now assessed in terms of 'human capital' (Sennett 2006). As this human potential includes our entire being, one of the most important aspects of our lives that we are asked to cultivate for the neoliberal market is our very affects, emotions, and feelings, leading to the prominence of emotional labor (Hochschild 2003). On the other hand, the endless competition and increasing precarity of work introduced by neoliberalism means our experience of neoliberalism is necessarily characterized by a deep sense of anxiety, insecurity, and frustration. As work becomes increasingly flexible and short-term, we are treated more and more as disposable and fungible components in the capitalist labor machine, working more for less, with little or no job security, inevitably leading to deepening anger, suffering, and depression (Berardi 2009).

In other words, neoliberalism is not simply a state of the market in which pursuit of economic value becomes the ultimate motive, but a condition of subjectivity, in which we are led to take on particular subject positions that are more consonant with the demands of intensified capitalism, and whose experience is inextricably tied with subjective responses. In this context, a subjectivity-based critique of neoliberalism may be accomplished on two levels. First, highlighting the subjective dimension of neoliberalism, particularly the intense sense of insecurity and anxiety associated with increasing precarity, can provide evidence of the violence of neoliberalism, debunking celebratory narratives of neoliberalism which present it as a gospel that promises opportunities for success to all. Second, on a deeper level, a focus on the subjective can uncover the process by which neoliberalism is rationalized and reproduced, for the anxieties and insecurities we experience under neoliberalism are not merely an outcome of neoliberalism, but the very process by which we are driven to become neoliberal subjects, through which the logic of neoliberalism comes to penetrate the most fundamental fabric of our own humanity.

Based on this insight, this book approaches subjectivity as a channel through which the study of language can contribute to such a critique of neoliberalism. In this sense, this book builds upon the broad range of existing work that explores the intersection of language and subjectivity. In particular, it draws much guidance from studies that focus on the role of affect and emotion in the cultural constitution of subjects by refusing to consider the subjective as isolated from the structured dimensions of linguistic practice (Besnier 1990, De Costa 2015, Hiramoto and Park 2014, Lutz and Abu-Lughod 1990, Ochs and Schieffelin 1989, Pavlenko 2005, Wilce 2009). However, this book also aims to move beyond the frameworks of those studies by foregrounding the way in which affect, desire, and morality are mobilized in the political economy. In this book, I argue that the heated pursuit of English in Korea was shaped by the anxieties, insecurities, and moral desire that neoliberal Korean society inculcates among Koreans, leading English to be seen as an index of an ideal neoliberal subject. That is, I claim that subjectivities of Koreans as users and learners of English were one of the key sites through which the logic of neoliberalism was propagated and rationalized. By highlighting subjectivity as the link between English and neoliberalism, I therefore give language and subjectivity a more explicitly embodied, materialized, and politicized role within the neoliberal economy.

Language does not simply encode or express different emotions. As Kramsch (2009) shows, being a speaker of a language is in itself a subjective experience. Learning, using, and living with a language is never a purely cognitive matter of picking one abstract communicative code over another, but has profound implications for our perception, judgment, and feelings about ourselves as language users. Kramsch's study is full of narratives of multilingual speakers and foreign language learners who struggle with, seek comfort in, agonize over, or place their hope in being a speaker of a language. It is precisely this dimension of language that neoliberalism engages with, reaching deep into our souls by reshaping and remolding us into subjects of capitalism. As the intensification of capitalism calls for even more intense control over our minds and bodies, subjectivities of language become a powerful channel through which such control takes shape. In the case of Korea, neoliberalism latches onto the historical significance of English as a language of power and the insecurities Koreans have about speaking this language of the powerful Other, to instill within them a complex set of feelings, emotions, and desires that compel them to align themselves to the order of neoliberalism. This book aims to outline this process, by tracing the multiple aspects of subjectivity that constitute the way Koreans experience and relate to English under the new conditions of political economy.

ENGLISH, NEOLIBERALISM, AND SUBJECTIVITY IN SOUTH KOREA

South Korea is a context where the complex relationship between language, neoliberalism, and subjectivity becomes salient, making it an extremely productive site for the theorization of that relation. Despite the fact that Korea is a country with a relatively strong degree of monolingualism with the Korean language being used throughout virtually all domains, the English language casts an enormous shadow over Korea. South Korea has been under the strong influence of the United States since it occupied the southern half of the Korean peninsula immediately after the end of the Second World War, and English has been widely recognized as a language of power and economic success throughout Korea's modern history, even as the language rarely played a major role in everyday communication. For instance, many English-speaking, US-educated elites occupied important positions in the US military government that operated until the establishment of the South Korean government in 1948. The continuing political, economic, cultural, and military dependence of South Korea on the United States throughout the rest of the 20th century meant that English was widely associated with power and social status.

This power attributed to English was greatly enhanced when Korean society went through rapid neoliberalization since the mid-1990s. Shifts in the material conditions of the job market played a significant role in this enhanced hegemony of English. With Korea's neoliberalization, Korean corporations needed to actively respond to the new conditions of the global economy, where growth of other developing Asian countries led to greater competition and risk, and where short-term emphasis on maximizing shareholder value became a prominent goal, trends that were solidified through the IMF-mandated structural adjustment in the aftermath of the 1997 Asian financial crisis (Ji 2011). One major response to such conditions was the flexibilization of work. Retrenchment became routine; stable, life-time employment was replaced with short-term, irregular contracts; and constant pressure was put on workers to work harder for less, or face joblessness. Competence in English emerged as an important criterion for the evaluation of white-collar workers in this context. English language skills, as part of a range of soft skills that served as a new index of the ideal worker, was seen both as a practical competence that enabled the worker to successfully deal with global challenges, and as evidence of the worker's preparedness for the job market. In a highly precarious job market, there was little room for workers to question such positioning of English, and this led university students and white-collar workers to spend much time and money on developing and refining their English skills. It was such specific material conditions that gave rise to the boom in English language learning under neoliberalism, presenting English as a valuable economic resource that everyone should pursue in Korean society.

The resulting English fever (*yeongeo yeolpung*), in which English was pursued as a crucial necessity for Korea's survival in the new global economy by corporations, the state, and individual Koreans, was manifest in multiple forms. On the level of state policy, the Korean government, seeing English as a crucial necessity for boosting the country's global competitiveness, promulgated revisions to the national curriculum to lower the age of introduction of English and emphasize communicative competence (Kwon and Kim 2010). Regional governments also played a major role in establishing 'English villages' where Koreans can immerse themselves in supposedly authentic English-only environments to practice their English (Park 2009). Many Korean universities also introduced English as a medium of instruction to enhance their global competitiveness in the context of reducing state support and pressure toward internationalization (Piller and Cho 2013). The corporate emphasis on English language skills pressured many white-collar workers and university students to make investments in English language learning a priority, and the English language teaching industry grew phenomenally in this context, as people flocked to classes that can help them prepare for tests such as TOEIC or OPIc (Oral proficiency Interview by Computer) (Nam 2012). Zealous parental investment in their children's English is another highly discussed aspect of the English fever, with parents actively seeking out English-only kindergartens, afterschool English classes, and private tutoring that can give their children a head start in English over others (Bae and Park 2020). Widely discussed in relation to this was the boom in early study abroad, or *jogi yuhak*, in which middle-class pre-university age children are sent abroad to study in English-speaking countries, with the hope that they may grow up as a native speaker of the language—the popularity of which led observers to identify it as 'South Korea's educational exodus' (Lo et al. 2015).

Though material conditions of the neoliberal economy, particularly the emphasis on endless competition and growing precarity of work, serve as an important context for the Korean English fever, another important aspect that we must consider in understanding its nature is that of subjectivity. Multiple strands of subjectivity can be seen as making up the fabric of the English fever. As English is often associated with chances of success in competition with others and better economic opportunities, Koreans' pursuit of English often constitutes a desire, in which they long for the different self they may become through acquiring the resource of English. With English being increasingly emphasized as an index of an ideal neoliberal worker, learning English also comes to be imbued with a sense of moral responsibility, driving Koreans to willfully invest in English language learning despite the recognition that not everyone will be able to benefit from learning the language. Koreans' active investments in English, particularly those of middle-class parents for their children, reflect an intense anxiety about not being able to pass down their class position to the next generation, and about wishing to make the most of the 'human capital' inside the malleable minds and bodies of youth. Despite the enormous investments they make in English language learning, though, Koreans still are unsatisfied with their competence in English, and this is reflected in their deep linguistic insecurity, in which Koreans continue to see themselves as illegitimate speakers of English and defer linguistic authority to native speakers of English, leading to intensifying cycles of further investment in English.

The context of South Korea, where rampant neoliberalization of society, heated pursuit of English, and intensification of subjectivities simultaneously take place, then, becomes a particularly useful context for our investigation of how subjectivity mediates the relationship between English and neoliberalism. This book therefore traces the multiple strands of subjectivities that illustrate different aspects of Koreans' experiences of English in the changing political economy—that is, the aspects of *desire, morality, anxiety,* and *insecurity*—in order to explore how such dimensions of feelings and affect contributed to the valorization of English as an index of ideal neoliberal subjecthood in South Korea. The extensive nature of Korea's neoliberal transformation and the divergent facets of the Korean English fever mean that addressing this question necessarily requires a multidimensional and multisited approach. For this reason, the argument to be presented in this book draws from multiple and diverse data sources; they include language ideological debates on government and corporate language policies, media representations of English language learners, ethnographic fieldwork on the *jogi yuhak* phenomenon, and interviews with transnational Koreans engaged in the global workplace. In particular, the analysis focuses on *metapragmatic discourse*—that is, discourse about speakers and their ways of speaking (Agha 2007, Wortham and Reyes 2015)—as a window for understanding how English comes to be associated with an image of a neoliberal subject. By tracking how metapragmatic discourse that circulates across multiple sites of the English fever layered Koreans' images of themselves with affective and emotional meaning, this book demonstrates how subjectivity allows English to serve as a key linchpin in the logic of neo-liberalism that permeates Korean society.

OUTLINE OF THIS BOOK

This book, then, explores how the dimension of subjectivity mediates the re-lationship between English and neoliberalism, by presenting an analysis of the process by which English gained prominence in South Korea as an index of the ideal neoliberal subject. In this chapter, I introduced the main issue to be investigated in this book: the question of how to understand the relation-ship between English and neoliberalism, and how subjectivity may serve as a potential answer to that question. I discussed the significance of this question in relation to previous research on the global spread of English and commod-ification of language, and presented an outline of what I mean by subjectivity and why it can be relevant to the study of language in political economy. I also introduced South Korea as a unique site for highlighting the importance of subjectivity as a key link that mediates English and neoliberalism.

Chapter 2 establishes the theoretical and methodological basis for our in-quiry. It first provides a detailed overview of the theoretical frameworks for understanding neoliberalism and how they might be adopted for the study of language and subjectivity. In particular, it contrasts Marxist approaches to neoliberalism, which emphasize its class-based political-economic condi-tions, and Foucauldian approaches, where technologies of government are foregrounded; and considers how we might build upon the strengths of both approaches to investigate the working of subjectivity in the political economy. It also discusses how analytic constructs from sociolinguistics and linguistic anthropology, in particular resources for the analysis of metapragmatic dis-course, might be fruitfully applied to the study of subjectivity in neoliberalism.

Chapter 3 provides a more in-depth picture of our ethnographic context by presenting a brief historical account of neoliberalism in South Korea, and the role the English fever played in it. South Korea's neoliberalization advanced throughout the 1980s and 1990s, as democratization of Korean society and transformations in the global economy led to an increasing ide-alization of the free market, a trend that was solidified in the aftermath of the 1997 Asian financial crisis. This chapter traces this process, focusing on the role of the United States, major corporations, and the state to high-light how Korea's neoliberalism closely aligned with a growing emphasis on English as a crucial skill in education and the job market. It also discusses how historically grounded subjectivities of English in Korea provided an ideological and semiotic basis for the Korean English fever, situating Koreans' subjective self-positioning in relation to English in historical and political-economic context.

Chapter 4 begins the main analysis of this book by outlining how a desire for English provides a particular articulation for neoliberal ideologies of language, linking economic value of English with images of the ideal neoliberal subject. It focuses on a key language ideology in neoliberalism—the ideology of language as pure potential, or a view of language as a transparent medium of communication that allows a speaker to realize her potentiality in an unadulterated way—and argues that the way in which English is desired in Korean society as a means of self-realization in the global world provides a bodily and experiential basis for this ideology, facilitating the neoliberal promotion of English in Korea. This chapter illustrates various manifestations of this desire, demonstrating how they work to reproduce and support the neoliberal discourse of human capital development.

Chapter 5 discusses the way in which neoliberalism reframes English language learning as a moral project, a technology of the self (Foucault 1997) through which we mold ourselves as ethical subjects engaged in careful management of one's self. One effect of this reframing of English language learning as moral responsibility of neoliberal subjects is its obscuring of class-based inequalities that are reproduced through English. This is illustrated through an analysis of how successful learners of English were represented in the Korean conservative press during the early years of the Korean English fever. Such learners, who are mostly privileged elites, are represented as subjects who demonstrate their moral caliber through endless investment in English language learning. Through such representations, English language learning comes to be understood as an ethical way of being in neoliberalism, instead of a site for reproduction of social inequality.

Chapter 6 explores how the strong sense of anxiety that permeates Koreans' experience of English allows neoliberalism to extend its reach into their bodies. The figure of the ideal English language learner presupposes anxieties about English—fears that one's own English is not yet sufficient for fully engaging in the global market, that whatever skill one has acquired can be easily lost, that one cannot be fully recognized as a legitimate speaker of English, and so on. This chapter argues that such anxieties transform bodies into a site of intense management, or a target of biopolitics (Foucault 2008), and focuses on the case of *jogi yuhak* to show how this project of early study abroad is driven by parents' anxieties about wasting the human capital inherent in their children's malleable bodies, as indexed by their ability to acquire English with greater ease than adults.

Chapter 7 focuses on the notion of linguistic insecurity to illuminate the processes by which essentialist conceptions of language, race, and ethnicity contribute to the hegemonic status of English in neoliberalism. In particular, it highlights how conflicting ideologies about English in neoliberalism—one in which English is valorized as a valuable economic resource and one in which the legitimate speaker of English is defined in ethnonational terms—jointly create a sense of insecurity in Korean speakers of English, leading them to rationalize the inequalities they are subjected to in neoliberalism. To illustrate this, this chapter turns to the case of Korean mid-level managers working at multinational corporations in Singapore, whose efforts at neoliberal self-development through English are thwarted by colonial ideologies of nativeness, and analyzes how the managers' linguistic insecurity leads to further valorization of English language learning.

Chapter 8 considers the consequences of the subjectivities of English discussed in the previous chapters, exploring how they contribute to the conditions of extreme precarity prevalent in contemporary Korean society. In the unstable conditions of the Korean job market brought about by neoliberalism, where irregular and insecure employment has become the norm, anxieties and insecurities of English that workers experience naturalize the way their English language skills are constantly devalued. The shift in the preferred mode of English language assessment in the Korean white-collar job market since the 1990s is illustrative of this point. Through an account of TOEIC's rise and fall in popularity as an instrument for English language assessment preferred by major corporations, this chapter discusses how constantly evolving regimes of assessment of English language skills lead Korean workers to internalize a neoliberal subjectivity which treats precarity as an ordinary mode of life.

Chapter 9 closes this book by considering the implications of the arguments made in previous chapters for the study of language in neoliberalism. It calls for an approach to political economy that foregrounds people's subjective experiences permeating their sociolinguistic choices in the material world, suggesting that it can help open up new directions for sociolinguistic research on language and political economy that speaks to our deep-seated feelings that define us as humans.

CHAPTER 2

Language and Subjectivity in Neoliberalism

DEFINING NEOLIBERALISM

In this chapter, I outline the theoretical and methodological framework to be followed in this book, centering on the question of what is neoliberalism, and how can we understand it in relation to subjectivity. This book's premise that the relationship between English and neoliberalism must be explained through the lens of subjectivity requires us to take a closer look at neoliberalism, for how we understand its nature and characteristics will have many implications for the way we theorize its link with language and subjectivity. Neoliberalism is now a widely discussed and researched topic, yet there is still much debate and confusion about how to conceptualize it, in part due to its multifacetedness and in part due to the politicized ways in which the term is used. For this reason, it is worth spending some time here to clarify what stance this book will take toward neoliberalism as a concept before we move onto our main discussion in the following chapters.

In this book, I understand neoliberalism as an ideological condition in which market-based freedom is promoted and rationalized as the ideal principle for all aspects of human life. Actual manifestations of neoliberalism encompass an extremely wide range of phenomena that have become increasingly prevalent across the world since the 1970s. All of these phenomena are driven by the assumption that endless, unfettered competition among individual social actors will naturally and most efficiently maximize wealth and happiness for everyone, and involves undoing of various constraints that restrict such competition, thereby extending and intensifying the logic of the market across multiple domains. In terms of actual practice, this often takes

In Pursuit of English. Joseph Sung-Yul Park, Oxford University Press. © Oxford University Press 2021.
DOI: 10.1093/oso/9780190855734.003.0002

the form of a reduction of state control over the market, as can be seen in the following examples:

- *Deregulation*: removal of restrictions on the free movement of capital, such as lowering of trade barriers, reduction of taxes, elimination of regulations on industries, based on the assumption that such restrictions are inefficient and run counter to the working of the market. This ensures greater freedom for capital to pursue its interest in an uninhibited way.
- *Privatization*: opening up to private interests fields that are traditionally considered to be in the domain of the public. State-owned enterprises and state-controlled services such as transportation, health, education, and security are handed over to private investors, subjecting their operation to market-based principles.
- *Financialization*: deregulation in the domain of finance leads to growing investment of capital in the finance market instead of industrial production and trade of goods, maximizing shareholder value as a key for corporate governance. New forms of financial instruments, particularly financial derivatives, open up more diverse ways for capital to profit from a volatile market.
- *Flexibilization of labor*: restrictions on the hiring, deployment, and firing of workers are relaxed, as stable, long-term employment comes to be seen as detrimental to the ability of capital to quickly adapt to market demand. As a result, precarious labor, such as contract-based and contingent work, becomes normative. Workers are also expected to continuously develop new skills, flexibly adapt to new tasks, and constantly compete with each other, actively embracing their own precarity in the name of resilience.
- *Retreat of welfare*: in societies where systems of social welfare functioned as a safety net for workers struggling under adverse conditions of labor, such provisions are seen as undermining workers' desire to actively function as an agent in the market, as well as a burden for the state and society. Reduction or elimination of welfare leads workers to fend for themselves as they face increasing precarity.

These structural transformations are frequently accompanied by particular discourses that work to rationalize and naturalize them. For this reason, these discourses also become important characteristics of neoliberalism:

- *Individualism*: in neoliberalism, a particular mode of individualism that emphasizes the individual's market-based freedom and property rights becomes dominant. This leads to a general deterioration of a communal spirit, as traditional foundations of solidarity, such as those characterized by community and organized labor, are eroded.

- *Entrepreneurship*: individuals are encouraged to take up mindsets as an enterprise, actively seeking opportunities for greater profit in the market, and willingly taking risks while being responsible for their own actions. Values such as resilience, innovation, initiative, and creativity come to be seen as desirable characters of individuals, regardless of whether they are actual entrepreneurs or not (Keat and Abercrombie 1991).
- *Self-branding*: in relation to the above, individuals are expected to continuously develop and market themselves in a way that corporations market their products and themselves. This involves careful and reflexive management of one's own self through continuous development of skills and competencies that may be marketable, rather than being content with one's past achievements and qualifications (Gershon 2016, Wee and Brooks 2010).
- *Accountability*: rollback of state expenditure on public services comes to demand greater market-oriented productivity and accountability of organizations and individuals. Audit cultures, in which quantificational and statistical technologies of auditing serve as a new mode of governing workers, lead to greater orientation to quantitative measures such as key performance indicators and rankings (Strathern 2000, Shore and Wright 2015)
- *Commodification*: expanding the logic of the market leads things or domains that are not subject to economic exchange to be increasingly be perceived and treated in market-based terms. The value of individuals, cultures, natural resources, and human interaction, for instance, come to be understood primarily in economic terms (Ertman and Williams 2005, Comaroff and Comaroff 2009).

This brief overview of the range of policies, practices, and discourses that are commonly associated with neoliberalism shows that neoliberalism is in fact a highly complex phenomenon. This provides several challenges for clearly defining neoliberalism. First, since the characteristics observed above operate on different levels, there is the question of whether neoliberalism should be understood as a specific set of policies, a more general model for economic development, an ideology that provides the basis for such a model, or a broader way of life centered around the ideal of the free market (Ganti 2014). Second, 'actually existing neoliberalisms' (Brenner and Theodore 2002) rarely, if ever, display the above characteristics in pure form; rather, neoliberalism always emerges in 'variegated' forms (Brenner, Peck, and Theodore 2010), reflecting the uneven pathways along which different societies move toward neoliberalism. In particular, neoliberal policies and practices are often incorporated into societies that do not position themselves as 'liberal', such as socialist or authoritarian states (Ong 2006), showing how the above characteristics constitute malleable technologies rather than a fixed system. Finally, some features discussed above are not necessarily unique to neoliberalism—for instance, Kipnis (2008) notes how emphasis on self-management and self-cultivation is not necessarily foreign to socialist China or traditional Chinese culture—which makes it problematic to treat them as defining characteristics of neoliberalism. In this sense, the concept of neoliberalism is often considered to be slippery and fuzzy (Ferguson 2009, Venugopal 2015). The matter is further complicated by the fact that the term neoliberalism is frequently used as a pejorative label that indexes a commentator's critical stance toward contemporary political economic realities, and therefore often serves not only as a purely analytic term but also as a political one. This has led some commentators, such as Dunn (2017), to go so far as to suggest abolishing the term altogether. Indeed, while it is certainly imperative that we highlight and criticize the destructive consequences of neoliberalism for human and social life, the force of our critique will suffer if neoliberalism becomes an easy label for attributing all the problems of contemporary society without careful reflection and analysis of the political economic conditions behind them (Peck 2013:139, Boas and Gans-Morse 2009).

In this book, however, I do not consider the broad scope and divergent characteristics of neoliberalism as a problem that proscribes us from talking about it. The issues above remind us that our understanding of neoliberalism should be based on careful consideration of the unique historical and material conditions of different societies that can ground our engagement with neoliberalism in their specific mechanisms and realities. But at the same time, I take the position that the fuzzy quality of neoliberalism is something that we should embrace and investigate, rather than attempt to limit and constrain through a narrower definition. The divergent forms and hybrid configurations in which neoliberalism emerges are in themselves evidence of neoliberalism's deep impact on wide-ranging aspects of our social lives. They tell us that neoliberalism is not simply a fixed set of policies or arguments whose impact can be measured within a neatly defined domain along a given number of parameters. Instead, the nature and significance of neoliberalism can only be fully understood when we pay attention to its complex effects and outcomes as they intersect with and transform our social lives. For this reason, understanding and investigating neoliberalism requires us to adopt a broad and flexible perspective that considers the interconnections and dynamics among the myriad processes and consequences of neoliberalism taking place across multiple planes of social organization and crosscutting dimensions of human experience—simultaneously as specific institutional policies, as concrete subjective experiences that arise as an outcome of such policies, and as a general form of rationality that pervades and justifies such experiences (Dardot and Laval 2013).

Such a perspective is particularly crucial when we consider the role that language occupies within neoliberalism. Since language itself is a highly complex social phenomenon, its intersection with neoliberalism must also be sought through multiple dimensions of social life. On the one hand, a key link between language and neoliberalism lies in the way in which language gains prominence as a resource for economic exploitation in various contexts. Such contexts are well explored by studies on the commodification of language, which has focused on the technologization of language in the service industry (Alarcón and Heyman 2013, Cameron 2000, Muth 2018, Rahman 2009); language as a resource for authentication of tourist destinations (Gao 2012, 2019, Heller et al. 2014, Johnstone 2009); framing of language as skill for branding of individuals (Flubacher 2020, Flubacher, Duchêne, and Coray 2018, Gray 2010, Martín Rojo 2020, Urciuoli 2008); and promotion of heritage and foreign language learning as a basis for economic competitiveness (Bernstein et al. 2015, Kubota 2011a, Leeman and Martínez 2007). By accounting for the shifting patterns of language use at such sites, these studies shed light on the specific political economic forces and the material interests that drive this shift—including the increasing competition in the market that motivates corporations to seek more minute control over workers' labor (Block and Gray 2016, Gee, Hull, and Lankshear 1996, Iedema and Scheeres 2003, Urciuoli and Ladousa 2013), weakening state support that leads ethnic minorities to commodify their language and culture as an alternative source of profit (Duchêne and Heller 2012), and demands of accountability that reframe education as inculcation of marketable skills and development of human capital (Urciuoli 2011, Flubacher and del Percio 2017).

On the other hand, the nature of language as socially embodied and ideologically mediated practice means that changing material practices and policies regarding language have much deeper consequences than just economic ones. Thus, research on the commodification of language has highlighted the subjective experiences of language users who are inserted into this shifting regime of language, uncovering, for example, the dissonance they feel as they perform 'authentic' identities that they are required to take up as part of scripted work routines (Cameron 2005); their frustration toward the rosy promise of language work as a new opportunity for economic advancement (Heller 2003); and the moral imperative to develop language skills as human capital that is imposed by institutions of education and labor (De Costa, Park, and Wee 2016). These studies thereby also point out that, since conceptions of identity, community, belonging, and social relations are profoundly shaped through the mediation of language, the incorporation of language into neoliberal practice constitutes a deep ideological shift in the way we experience and understand the world around us, a transformation whose implications reach far beyond the realm of the economy. In fact, it is the location of language at the intersection of material practices, subjective experiences, and ideological processes that makes it a powerful fulcrum for the expansion of neoliberal rationality into the everyday fabric of our lives (Martín Rojo and Del Percio 2020, Shin and Park 2016). Thus, in order to appropriately account for the role language plays within neoliberalism, a broad and flexible perspective on neoliberalism that encompasses its multiple characteristics and manifestations is absolutely crucial.

However, our review of the difficulties in defining neoliberalism also reminds us that such a perspective must be grounded on a firm understanding of the political economic processes of neoliberalism, lest an appreciation of neoliberalism's fuzziness slips into analytic muddiness. The charges that the term neoliberalism is often used in a loose way also apply to language-focused research. For instance, Block, Gray, and Holborow (2012) note how neoliberalism is often used in applied linguistic and sociolinguistic research interchangeably with terms such as 'globalization' and 'capitalism', as a label that crudely characterizes some economic conditions of our time but without a clear account of why those conditions should be identified as 'neoliberal'. McGill (2013) also points to a similar imprecision when he notes how studies on the commodification of language tend to ignore the need to explain the process of commodification in robust political economic terms—that is, in exactly what sense may language be seen as a 'commodity' or 'economic resource,' particularly if the way language functions in the process of production and circulation clearly differs from the way other commodities (e.g., material goods produced through human labor for exchange in the market) behave. A perspective that aims to holistically bring together the material, ideological, and subjective dimensions of neoliberalism under critical analysis, then, can be meaningfully accomplished only when it is sustained by a careful orientation to the specific political economic processes that distinguish neoliberalism. In this book, I therefore aim to situate neoliberalism in historical context, as part of the broader flow of capitalism, and seek to account for it by paying attention to the specific conditions that make neoliberalism a distinct phase in the expansion of capitalist power relations. To consider how this may be theoretically articulated in relation to subjectivity, let us turn to the next section.

THEORIZING NEOLIBERALISM: POLITICAL ECONOMY OF SUBJECTIVITY

In seeking ways to understand the complex realities of neoliberalism, we may consider two broad theories of neoliberalism: Marxist and Foucauldian approaches. Here I review the different ways in which these two approaches understand neoliberalism and, based on the insights these approaches offer, consider how we might construct our own approach for studying the role of subjectivity in the neoliberal appropriation of language.

As a perspective established as a critique of capitalism and as a theoretical foundation for class struggle, Marxism views neoliberalism in terms of historical continuity of capitalist accumulation. The fundamental insight of classic

Marxism is that capitalism is a system based on exploitation of labor power; it derives profit by extracting surplus value from the work of wage laborers—workers who are deprived of their own means of production and therefore have no choice but to sell their labor to capitalists for survival. As a system of exploitation—of labor, of social relations, of nature—capitalism is also a constantly evolving system, as it must continuously seek new modes and targets of exploitation to maintain its drive for profit. Marxism also recognizes the facilitating role of the state in this process; capitalist accumulation was certainly not possible without the support offered by the state through mobilization of labor, legalization of private ownership, and global expansion of the market through colonialism and imperialism.

According to this perspective, then, neoliberalism is a new stage in this system of exploitation, a response to the crisis in the capitalist system of accumulation in the 1970s (Duménil and Lévy 2004, Harvey 2005). The post-World War II global economic order was a time of stable economic growth, during which Fordist and Taylorist management of work was coupled with Keynesian state concessions to labor made following the recessions of the 1930s. For advanced capitalist states, this led to high rates of growth and expansion of markets during the 1950s and 1960s, providing strong profits for capital, which was nonetheless put in check by regulations on global capital flow as well as steady public expenditures and provision of welfare. This system started to show its limits during the 1970s, however, as rising inflation and unemployment took a significant toll on the world economy, resulting in a crisis in capital accumulation, with the political and economic power of the upper class being increasingly restrained. The upper class thus sought to recoup their diminishing profits and asset value by reasserting the freedom of capital accumulation without state control, paving the way for the emergence of neoliberalism as a political project during the 1970s and 1980s. Duménil and Lévy (2004) show that neoliberal economic reforms in this period have in fact resulted in a sharp increase in the concentration of the world's wealth in the hands of the top 1% of income earners, which lead them to identify neoliberalism as a project for the restoration of capitalist class power.

Therefore, in Marxist-oriented analyses, what distinguishes neoliberalism is the new strategies of capitalist accumulation that it promotes under the guise of greater 'freedom'. The shift away from Fordist and Taylorist management of work toward a more flexible mode of labor does not mean liberation and empowerment of workers but a more efficient strategy of controlling productivity by holding the workers accountable for their output; and the 'roll back' of state power is not a retreat of state from control over the market but a more dispersed form of governance that allows for greater responsiveness to the demands of the market (Jessop 2002, Peck and Theodore 2012). This is indeed what is emphasized by the term neoliberalism as opposed to designations such as 'late capitalism'; if the latter may be read as implying a neutral temporal period that might naturally emerge as a stage in the evolution of capitalism, 'neo'-liberalism emphasizes how the liberal rationalization of capitalist exploitation is taking place in new and more intense ways, how it is a political project, a 'thought collective' (Mirowski and Plehwe 2009) that seeks to provide ideological and philosophical ground for reasserting the interests of capital through a rearticulation and reinterpretation of liberalist ideals (Ganti 2014).

The Foucauldian perspective on neoliberalism, in contrast, focuses more on the micro-operations of power that are realized through technologies and discourses that govern the conducts of people and thereby constitute them as subjects, instead of highlighting the specific class-based and material foundations of neoliberalism. Foucault's early work highlights how power is not something that is located within specific individuals or groups but is immanent in social relations, not only exercised through oppression and coercion but more fundamentally through discourses that produce knowledge and techniques that work upon bodies, thus constituting them as subjects. Therefore, rather than positing specific classed interests as the driving force for neoliberalism and locating neoliberalism in the macro-level transformations of the political economy, this discourse-centered approach asks how neoliberalism works in terms of *subjectification*—that is, how neoliberalism consists of various practices, strategies, and rationalizations that make possible particular subjects and senses of 'self'.

What plays a central role here is the notion of *governmentality*—often explained as 'the conduct of conduct,' or 'a form of activity aiming to shape, guide or affect the conduct of some person or persons' (Gordon 1991:2). As Foucault himself clarifies, "to 'conduct' is at the same time to 'lead' others . . . and a way of behaving within a more or less open field of possibilities" (1982:789); governmentality thus underlines how power is exercised not only through coercing others into action but through guiding others to conduct themselves and manage their own actions. In this view, neoliberalism can be understood as a mode of governmentality, in which people are guided to modulate their own behavior to align themselves with the ideals presumed by the capitalist social order even in the absence of overt coercion, as an effect of discourses and policies that posit a particular relationship between the state, market, and individuals. The broader social transformations that characterize neoliberalism are thus analyzed primarily in terms of how they give rise to particular 'technologies of the self'—practices that allow individuals "to effect, by their own means, a certain number of operations on their own bodies, their own souls, their own thoughts, their own conduct, and this in a manner so as to transform themselves, modify themselves" (Foucault 1997:177; see also Chapter 5).

For instance, conditions of neoliberalism such as increasing emphasis on market-based competition, accountability, and entrepreneurship are not only significant due to their immediate economic effects (including the way it allows retraction of state control over the market and greater flexibility for movement of capital) but also due to the way they guide workers to modulate their own behavior and thoughts—for example, taking up responsibility to make sure one has up-to-date skills relevant to the workplace, viewing oneself as 'human capital' that does not need social support to make a living, and blaming oneself for not having developed one's own potential when one is faced with layoffs—thereby internalizing the logic of the market and becoming an entrepreneur of one's own self (Foucault 2008:226). By tracing the specific operations of governmentality, manifest not only in broader policies on the state level, but also in micro-level practices of management in the workplace (Rose 1990, Brown 2009) and systems of knowledge generated across disparate domains ranging from psychology (Rose 1996) to biomedicine (Adams, Murphy, and Clarke 2009), Foucauldian analysis of neoliberalism offers an account of how neoliberalism is more than a political and economic configuration, but a site through which new kinds of subjectivities are constituted.

For the purpose of this book, which aims to foreground subjectivity as a key for understanding the relationship between language and neoliberalism, the Foucauldian perspective of governmentality offers a useful theoretical basis. This is not only because the notion of governmentality has already been actively embraced by scholars concerned with questions of language in neoliberalism (Martín Rojo and Del Percio 2020, Shin 2018a, Urla 2019), but also because its explicit focus on neoliberalism as formation of subjectivities allows us to develop an analysis that centers on speakers' subjective experiences of language. Rather than treating the anxieties, desires, and insecurities about English that Koreans experience as a mere psychological reaction to the global spread of the language, through the perspective of governmentality we can view such affects as deeply implicated in the multiple discourses and technologies that construct Koreans as neoliberal subjects.

However, our comparison of the Marxist and Foucauldian approaches to neoliberalism also underlines the need to situate this governmentality-based perspective more firmly within political economic context. Studies of neoliberalism by Foucault and those inspired by him have recently been criticized for their tendency to overlook the specific interests underlying neoliberal transformations (Rehmann 2013, Zamora and Behrent 2015). That is, such analyses often stop short of uncovering the material realities of inequality and exploitation that the logic of neoliberalism obscures, and often fail to develop into a full-fledged critique that challenges the claims and assumptions of neoliberalism and exposes it as a system that rationalizes capitalist exploitation. Simply describing the discourses and technologies of neoliberalism— for example, how we are now inclined to see ourselves as human capital, how the pressure of competition leads us to make endless investments in self-development, how language is now seen as an important skill that can serve as an economic resource, etc.—is not sufficient as a critique of neoliberalism, unless it is accompanied by an analysis of how such discourses and technologies work to naturalize the new social conditions of neoliberalism and to serve specific interests.

For this reason, it is essential for our purposes to balance the governmentality-based perspective with a political economic viewpoint inspired by Marxism. That is, we need to ask: What implications do formations of subjectivities through governmentality have for capitalist relations? More specifically, how are the discourses and technologies that constitute neoliberal governmentality put to use within broader political economic processes of labor, production, and consumption? With what consequences? And what underlying contradictions of capitalism does this reveal? Keeping these questions in mind would force us to maximize the critical potential of the notion of governmentality, reminding us that neoliberal government of the self must always take place within specific political economic relations.

This eclectic perspective is in fact not only useful for refining our analysis of Foucauldian governmentality, but also for highlighting the subjective grounding of Marxist political economy. While Marxist studies of neoliberalism that focus on macro-level political economic relations tend to overlook the role of subjectivity in this process, subjectivity is in fact not foreign to classic tenets of Marxism. For instance, the notion of alienation, by which workers come to experience the objectification of their humanity due to the commodification of their labor power, was a fundamental contradiction that highlighted the exploitative nature of capitalism in Marx's (1964) analysis. Such insight is further extended into critiques of neoliberalism by several Marxist scholars, such as Berardi (2009), who outlines how pervasive precarity brought about neoliberalism has destructive effects on workers' souls.

Similarly, a focus on the subjective experiences of neoliberalism would help us better understand the contradictions inherent in the logic of neoliberalism, by revealing the struggles, frustrations, anxieties, and desires that fill the everyday experiences of people in neoliberalism. Indeed, many studies that adopt a governmentality-based approach have been productive in exposing the problematic and devastating consequences of neoliberalism. Ethnographic work that traces the frustration, anxiety, despair, and struggle of working-class women (Walkerdine 2006, 2011) and disenfranchised youth (Allison 2012), for instance, has powerfully demonstrated how analyses of the subjectivities generated by conditions of precarity can expose the false promises of neoliberalism and the inequalities it exacerbates. As Williams (1977) emphasized, understanding the lived experiences of social life is a crucial key for overcoming the false opposition between the 'personal' and the 'social'. In this sense, the minute gaze that the governmentality perspective directs toward micro-level operations of power and their consequences for subjectivity can be a useful resource for triangulating our investigation of the political economy.

Therefore, in this book, instead of considering the Marxist political economy approach and the Foucauldian governmentality approach to be incompatible, I aim to draw from the strengths of each approach—the former's focus on structural relations of exploitation that are being intensified through neoliberalism and the latter's emphasis on micro-operations of power that lead to the government of selves—to build a synthetic approach that can highlight the way in which subjectivity mediates the material conditions of life under neoliberalism. Such theorization of neoliberalism as governmental rationality that reveals the contradiction of capitalist political economic relations is indeed appropriate for the broad scope of neoliberalism that I aim to account for (as outlined in the previous section), for it allows us to grasp how neoliberalism is simultaneously driven by political economic interests that underlie market-oriented policies and experienced through specific discourses and technologies that guide our feelings, thoughts, and behaviors. This approach also offers an important reminder for research on language in political economy—that it must critically interrogate the way in which language is increasingly hailed as an economic resource, assessing the implications this has on our own subjective experiences in social life as well as how such transformation of subjectivities rationalize the political economic conditions that lead to the commodification of language in the first place.

LANGUAGING SUBJECTIVITY: METHODOLOGICAL NOTES

Given our definition and theorization of neoliberalism as outlined above, how might we methodologically approach our goal of investigating the way subjectivity mediates the relationship between English and neoliberalism? In this section I briefly discuss what theoretical and analytic constructs from sociolinguistics and linguistic anthropology may be usefully adopted for our purposes, and explain the method I use to deploy them in the analysis presented throughout this book.

We may begin by recognizing that the specific dimensions of subjectivity that we are considering cannot be treated as positivistically analyzable phenomena. As I have defined subjectivity (in Chapter 1) as the lived and embodied experience of being a subject, the aspects of feelings, sentiments, and thoughts that form that experience must also be understood as culturally and socially embedded, reflecting the multiplicities and tensions that are endemic to everyday life. Indeed, sociolinguistic and linguistic anthropological work has actively contested the perspective that views affects, emotions, and feelings purely as an individual's inner psychological response to the outside world, arguing instead that, through the mediation of language, such psychic dimensions of our being actively play a part in our constitution as cultural and social agents (Besnier 1990, De Costa 2015, Lutz and Abu-Lughod 1990, Ochs and Schieffelin 1989, Park 2020a, Pavlenko 2005, Wilce 2009). Thus, in this book, I adopt the basic assumption of those studies that language does not merely encode or express our inner feelings but actively works to shape and transform our subjective experiences, both as discourse (i.e., through which we talk about affect and emotion) and as semiotic resource (i.e., as signs in themselves through which we negotiate affective meaning).

But at the same time, since our goal is not merely to recognize the significance of subjectivity for language but to account for its role in shaping the place of language within the political economy, we also need a more precise way of operationalizing our analysis of language and subjectivity. As McElhinny (2010) suggests, this requires a more historicized and material approach, for we need to be able to explain precisely how language becomes promoted as a key aspect for the constitution of neoliberal subjectivity and why this has become such a prominent issue at this particular historical juncture. For this, then, we must equip ourselves with an analytic strategy that can trace the ideological and semiotic processes by which specific conceptions of language and subjecthood emerge, solidify, circulate, and evolve through chains of social interaction. Such an approach will allow us to trace the political and material interests that lie behind the construction of neoliberal subjectivities of language, and to sketch out the specific technologies that operate to guide us into such subjectivities.

In this book I propose the analysis of *metapragmatic discourse* as an approach appropriate for this task. For the past couple of decades, scholars working at the intersection of sociolinguistics and linguistic anthropology have been developing models to account for the way interdiscursive chains of language use contribute to the negotiation and transformation of indexical meaning (Agha 2007, Wortham and Reyes 2015). This body of work has outlined how indexical meaning of a linguistic form is never stable, and evolves continuously through the way the form is put into use, its meaning being reified or negotiated depending on the social and discursive context into which it is inserted. In particular, metapragmatic discourse—that is, discourse about language use—plays an important role in this process, as it juxtaposes linguistic forms with specific social situations, images of speakers, sociocultural values, and other linguistic forms, adding new layers of highly contextualized meaning onto the form in question. For instance, the hegemony of standard forms of English such as Received Pronunciation was historically constructed and reproduced through interdiscursive chains of metapragmatic discourse including etiquette manuals, novels, classroom interaction, and news reports, as a locally prestigious sociolect was imbued with images of class, refinement, and distinction to be repositioned as a national standard (Agha 2007). Metapragmatic discourse is thus a site for the generation and reproduction of language ideologies, which rationalize and naturalize language structure and use (Silverstein 1979, Schieffelin et al. 1998, Kroskrity 2000), therefore a powerful locus of the social structuredness of language.

It is important to note that metapragmatic discourse is not about abstract circulation of signs. Because metapragmatic discourse does not simply assign indexicals to abstract categories of value (e.g., 'standard,' 'regional,' 'women's language,' etc.) but juxtaposes them with highly specific social contexts and personae, it intervenes in material processes in an important way as well. For instance, a particular way of speaking, such as a standard dialect, might not just be linked with an abstract category of socioeconomic class, but a range of demeanor indexicals, including the ease and comfort with which one speaks it, the posture and gait of its speaker, the way in which the speaker dresses, etc., to establish a highly embodied relationship between a language variety and its speaker—which, as Bourdieu (1991) shows, powerfully naturalizes the class-based distinction of speakers. Conceptualized in this way, analysis of metapragmatic discourse can offer a specific way for engaging with Bakhtin's insight that language is a site of political contestation, where dialogicality of language inevitably involves negotiation and tension between competing ideological positions in society. As Bakhtin puts it: "The utterance is filled with *dialogic overtones* . . . After all, our thought itself—philosophical, scientific, and artistic—is born and shaped in the process of interaction and struggle with others' thought, and this cannot but be reflected in the forms that verbally express our thought as well" (1986:92; emphasis in the original). Analysis of metapragmatic discourse aims to lay bare such "dialogic overtones" by identifying traces of "interaction and struggle" through the semiotic, ideological, and stylistic resources employed in the way we talk about language, speakers, and speakerhood.

A crucial concept here is *figure of personhood*, or socially recognizable personae that can be performed through semiotic enactment (Agha 2005, 2011). Metapragmatic discourse centers around such figures in a substantial way. We never experience linguistic difference as an abstract, decontextualized difference. Linguistic differentiation always takes place in an interactional context, where linguistic form is linked with particular speaker roles and social positions. When sets of linguistic features recur with particular social, behavioral, and characterological traits in interactional context, figures of personhood come to be linked with language varieties. Metapragmatic discourse consists of such recurrent juxtapositions of speaker models with linguistic forms that make us recognize those forms as constituting a linguistic variety with particular social meaning.

Figures of personhood are an important key for locating subjectivity within metapragmatic discourse, because dimensions of affect, sentiment, and morality are central elements of what makes up such figures (Park forthcoming). Those traits that define and establish the subjective character of figures of personhood are the fundamental, if not always consciously recognized, basis for our interpretation of different person types. Is the speaker a morally responsible character? Is the speaker emotionally excitable or calm? Is the speaker cooperative and kind? Is the speaker feeling upbeat, sad, upset, or nervous? Is the speaker confident and well poised? What does the speaker desire, loathe, fear, or cherish? Innumerable elements like these make up the characterological shade of the figure of personhood we attribute to speakers, including ourselves, coloring our interpretation of their behavior and social action. More importantly, such figures of personhood serve as building blocks for our socialization process, as they are constantly invoked and highlighted in the way we interact with society (e.g., "don't speak like that to your teacher," "how would that make them feel?," "that's so kind of you," etc.) and we learn to embody those affects, moralities, and desires that are associated with the figures we are supposed to play (Lo 2004, 2009). In this sense, figures of personhood circulated and reproduced through metapragmatic discourse are not mere conceptual placeholders for different identities, but semiotic material for the constitution of subjectivities.

In this sense, metapragmatic discourse and figure of personhood can be powerful resources for analyzing the ideological and material processes through which neoliberal subjectivity comes into being. Neoliberal subjecthood, or the ideal image of a person who is fully aligned with the principles of neoliberalism, may be understood as a particular figure of personhood, with particular social, behavioral, and characterological traits, including particular ways of feeling, thinking, and conducting oneself. By tracing how that figure is constructed through the metapragmatic articulation of specific policies, practices, and ideologies, then, we can identify the processes by which neoliberal subjectivity emerges, and use it as a basis for our critique of neoliberalism. Since metapragmatic discourse intersects with neoliberalism on many levels—ranging from hegemonic promulgations of policy goals and dominant characterizations of the ideal worker, to everyday accounts of one's struggles in enduring the harsh economic climate (Chun 2017)—the figures of personhood resulting from such analysis allow us to consider neoliberal subjectivity in its full complexity, simultaneously as an idealized prescription of how we are expected to live our lives under neoliberalism and as the actual emotions, anxieties, desires, and hopes we experience under the material conditions of neoliberalism. The gap, or the tension between the two, then, highlights the contradictions of neoliberalism, allowing us to uncover and confront its false premises and promises.

Therefore, in this book, I aim to outline how English was involved in this process in Korean society of the past two decades. Through an analysis of various strands of metapragmatic discourse about English circulating in Korean society, I try to show how subjectivities of English—the desires, moralities, anxieties, and insecurities about English—served as an important semiotic and embodied element for figures of personhood associated with the Korean speaker of English; I then consider how those figures of personhood became the basis for rationalizing the neoliberal order and the image of ideal neo-liberal subjecthood that so deeply penetrated everyday life in Korea. In this way, I argue that the question of English in neoliberal Korea was more than just a matter of language; through the mediation of metapragmatic discourse that gave rise to a particular configuration of subjectivities, it had a much more fundamental and wide-reaching impact on Korean society and political economy.

This book draws upon metapragmatic discourse from multiple sources for its data; they include media reports on the Korean English fever, articula-tions of language policies of the state and the workplace, and interviews con-ducted with transnational Koreans, collected over the past decade through my ongoing research on the ideologies of English in neoliberal South Korea (I explain the sources and circumstances of data collection at relevant places throughout the book). The divergent sources of data are meant to provide a multisited glimpse of the figure of the Korean English speaker, illuminated from various nodes along which that figure is circulated interdiscursively, showing us how the material and ideological conditions surrounding the speakers and agents located at those various nodes imbue that figure with complex layers of affect, desire, and morality, guiding them to mold them-selves into neoliberal subjects. Our tracing of these flows of metapragmatic discourse about English thereby offers a concrete picture of how the forma-tion of subjectivities becomes a key basis for the significance of language in neoliberalism.

CONCLUSIONS

In this chapter, I discussed how neoliberalism might be defined, empha-sizing in particular how complex and multifaceted neoliberalism is as a phenomenon, and suggesting a broad perspective that recognizes neolib-eralism simultaneously as a material, ideological, and subjective condition. I then considered different ways of theorizing neoliberalism, contrasting the Marxist perspective that views it as an intensification of capitalist exploitation and the Foucauldian perspective that understands it as gov-ernmental rationality, proposing to draw from the strengths of both approaches, foregrounding the Foucauldian focus on governmentality and the Marxist emphasis on political economic relations. In terms of method-ology, I suggested the analysis of metapragmatic discourse as a way of oper-ationalizing this theoretical approach in relation to language, highlighting the figure of personhood as a semiotic juncture for studying the formation of neoliberal subjectivity. In the chapters that follow, I put this theoretical and methodological framework to work, showing the various dimensions of subjectivity that penetrated Koreans' relation to English under neoliberalism. But such analysis must be grounded in an understanding of Korea's political economic and historical context, so in the next chapter, I present an ethnographic overview of neoliberalism and English in Korea to offer a more detailed picture of that background.

CHAPTER 3

English and Neoliberalism in South Korea

NEOLIBERAL SOUTH KOREA: A PORTRAIT OF HELL

Since its neoliberal transformation in the 1990s, South Korea has become a prominent player in the global economy. Having risen up dramatically from the rubble of the Korean War through its state-led economic development in the 1960s and 1970s, the country once again dazzles the world with its sleek and trendy products in the global market, from smartphones and automobiles to music videos of popular idols. It might thus seem that Korea's embrace of neoliberalism over the past decades has paid off well, allowing it to reinvent itself again after the traumatic days when it had to ask the International Monetary Fund (IMF) for funds to bail itself out of the Asian financial crisis of 1997. Yet such an image of success only masks a much darker reality that is experienced on the ground, the deep sense of alienation, frustration, despair, and fatigue that confronts everyday lives of Koreans.

One scene that captures this feeling of desperation is the "aerial protests," in which Korean workers protest mass layoffs and illegal hiring practices by climbing power transmission towers, outdoor billboards, or tower cranes, isolating themselves there for many days to have their voice heard (Y. Lee 2015a). In May 2014, for instance, Cha Gwang-ho, a worker at Star Chemical, camped out on top of a 45-meter-high chimney of the factory when the company was sold off in pieces and 228 workers lost their jobs. He then spent 408 days there all by himself, exposed to the scorching summer heat and freezing winter air of Korea. When Italian theorist and activist Franco Berardi visited Seoul, he noted, "in other countries, members of environment organizations occasionally climb trees in protest, but hardly anywhere else workers climb up transmission towers for indefinite sit-ins" (Berardi 2013). The drastic measures

In Pursuit of English. Joseph Sung-Yul Park, Oxford University Press. © Oxford University Press 2021.
DOI: 10.1093/oso/9780190855734.003.0003

that these workers must take in order to get any attention to their cause are both a reflection of the marginalization and oppression of the labor movement under neoliberal Korea and a testament to the harsh social conditions that Korean workers must endure to defend their human dignity.

Contemporary Korea is indeed a weary and disconsolate place. South Korea is a country with one of the highest suicide rates in the world. The World Health Organization's report shows that in 2012, 36.8 people out of 100,000 committed suicide in Korea, surpassing all other countries in its survey (WHO 2016). Many argue that the precarity and social isolation arising from recent socioeconomic transformations as the reason. Korea's suicide rate has more than doubled since 2000 (Ryu 2014) as the country's relentless neoliberalization dismantled traditional social safety nets and brought about atomization of social relations. A large part of this increase comes from the elderly, with a suicide rate of 116.2 per 100,000 for people over 70, a number 10 times higher than the same age group in other countries (Yu and Nam 2016). Nearly half of Koreans older than 65 years live below the poverty line (OECD 2017), many of them living alone, and amidst the absence of social security and a deteriorating sense of community, they are being left behind to die a lonely death in the fast-paced Korean economy that preys on fresh, lively labor.

The younger generation has a no less depressing reality of their own to face. The official unemployment rate for Koreans in their twenties has reached 12% in 2016, but some argue that the real rate should be as high as 34.2% when one takes into account the fact that large number of those youths work in undesirable temporary jobs and many delay entering the job market because of bleak employment prospects (J. Lee 2016). In 2015, over 60% of newly employed Koreans in their twenties and below were various forms of insecure and contingent employment—commonly called irregular employment (*bijeonggyujik*)—for which they receive no employment benefits or job security and are paid only half compared to those with stable employment (Kim and Jeong 2016). Such precarious conditions of work threaten their basic rights, including their right to adequate housing (Song 2014). The living conditions of Korean youth are typified by (*ban*)*jiha*, dark and damp (semi)basement units; *oktapbang*, rudimentary rooms built on rooftops of buildings exposed to heat and cold; and *gosiwon*, cramped boarding houses with rooms barely large enough to spread one's legs—collectively referred to as *jiokgo*, which incidentally also means 'suffering of hell.' In fact, for many Korean youths, Korea is simply *hell Joseon*, an infernal place where inequality, injustice, and fiendish devouring of the weak prevails. The fact that they use the name of the premodern kingdom of Joseon to characterize today's Korea speaks to their disillusionment toward the supposedly 'modern' advances the country has made through its globalization.

When we consider these grim and dreadful snapshots of Korea under neoliberalism, the pressure that Koreans receive to learn English may seem like a relatively benign problem. If Korea's neoliberalization brings about drastic consequences of inequality, exploitation, isolation, and death, then having to learn a language, particularly one that supposedly has much utility in this globalizing world, does not sound very high on the list of evils that we must fight. Wouldn't securing fair employment, equal pay, adequate housing, and dignity of human life be more pressing issues than questioning why one should learn English? This is certainly true. However, it is also important to note that Korea's emphasis on English is not just about learning the language. English in Korea has played a prominent role in advancing Korea's neoliberalization itself, through the way it was symbolically employed in the rationalization of neoliberal logic. In this sense, English is not separable from the dark consequences of Korea's neoliberalization, and a critical understanding of how English came to occupy such a position is indispensable for contesting such consequences. To appreciate this point, it is necessary to situate our discussion within the historical and material context of Korea's neoliberal transformation and the country's English fever. In this chapter, we take a short tour of this background. First, I present a brief history of neoliberalism in Korea, highlighting the key actors that played a major role in the process of neoliberalization and their interconnected interests. Then, I turn to an account of Korea's English fever, explaining how its unfolding was intertwined with the country's neoliberal transformation. Finally, I shed light on the affective dimension of the English fever as a foundation for the discussion to follow, emphasizing how this subjective aspect is not merely something that can be attributed to an essentialist sense of Korean 'culture,' but closely tied to the political economic context of Korea's history in the modern world.

KOREA'S NEOLIBERAL TRANSFORMATION: HISTORY, ACTORS, PROCESSES

South Korea's economic ascent into an industrialized country in the 1960s and 1970s, commonly attributed to Park Chung-hee's military dictatorship (1963–1979), was made possible by a range of global, regional, and local political economic conditions. The post-World War II global economic order, characterized by the Bretton Woods agreement that pegged the value of member state currencies to the price of gold, facilitated a relatively stable international market that allowed the Korean state to place sustained emphasis on an export-oriented industrial development strategy. The cold war geopolitics of the East Asian region also offered unique opportunities. The United States provided strategic economic and military support for South Korea as an advanced base in its contest against communism, tolerating Korea's protectionist development strategy. South Korea's participation in the Vietnam War was rewarded with "preferential access to US markets" as well as South Vietnam's (Pirie 2008:67), jump-starting Korea's economic development. South Korea's rebuilding of ties with Japan, the former colonizer which had emerged as the regional industrial leader, allowed for import of crucial technologies for industrialization as well as Korea's integration into the regional production network. Domestically, the military dictatorship's firm grip on politics and economy created conditions favorable to capitalist accumulation. Through its control over banks and credit allocation, the state facilitated the growth of *jaebeol*s, family-owned conglomerates which profited massively by playing a major role in the country's export drive. Brutal oppression of labor movements kept the cost of labor low, while silencing voices that called for democracy and justice (Lie 1998). As a result of these conditions, the South Korean economy achieved remarkable growth, with its GDP growing from 2.41 billion US dollars to 65 billion US dollars between 1961 and 1980.

By the late 1970s, however, these conditions for high economic growth started to break down. The dissolution of the Bretton Woods system in 1971 led to the emergence of the 'Dollar-Wall street regime' (Gowan 1999), in which the US dollar unpegged from gold allowed the financial capital of Wall Street to promote its interests in the world economy. Shifting US policy demanded that South Korea relax its protectionist strategy of economic development and open up its market. Japan, similarly facing pressure from the United States to raise the value of the yen, went into a long recession, which led the country to stop its technology transfer to Korea and to divert its investments toward emerging Southeast Asian economies. In 1987, the Korean democratization movement ended the long period of military governments and facilitated a massive labor uprising, which strongly challenged the authoritarianism of the establishment sustained by anti-communism and developmentalism. This not only led to growing wages but also questioning of corrupt ties between the government and the jaebeol. These changes signaled a new age where the developmental state model could no longer serve as a reliable engine for South Korea's economy.

According to Ji (2011), the origins of Korea's neoliberalism can be sought in the group of technocrats who received their PhDs in economics in the United States, who believed that the state-led, development-oriented model of Korea's economy should be shifted toward a market-based framework focusing on monetary policy. Positioned in the government's financial departments and the national think tank, Korea Development Institute, these US-educated economists initiated various reforms that expanded the role of the market, such as the 1979 plan for economic stabilization, which pushed for liberalization of the finance industry through lifting of state control over commodity prices, reduction of state investment in heavy-industry development, cutting incentives for exports, and liberalizing imports (Ji 2011:114). These reforms promoted market-centered principles as the basis for the

Korean economy and aimed to strengthen Korean corporations for greater competitiveness in the global stage.

This move toward neoliberalism was invigorated on a greater scale during Kim Young-sam's presidency (1993–1998). Kim's government highlighted *singyeongje* ('new economy') and *segyehwa* ('globalization') as its catchphrases, aiming to boost the Korean economy by replacing state-led development with market principles and by actively participating in the global economy. In particular, the state's retraction from bureaucratic control of banks was signaled through the 1993 blueprint for financial liberalization, which was developed in response to the mounting pressure from the United States to open up and liberalize the Korean financial market. The blueprint, which was submitted to and approved by the US treasury department, outlined a plan to liberalize foreign exchange, capital transfer, interest rates, and securities trading, offering foreign financial capital significant access to the Korean market (Ji 2011:138). It was on the condition of such reforms that South Korea was able to join the Organization for Economic Co-operation and Development (OECD) in 1996, which was celebrated by Kim's government as the country's making it into the rank of rich, developed countries. The government's globalization drive was also accompanied by the rapid global expansion of the jaebeol. During the 1990s, the jaebeol actively moved their production abroad and made new investments in overseas markets as a way of countering mounting competition from the region and rising cost of labor. This was made possible by Korea's financial liberalization, which allowed the jaebeol to secure short-term loans from foreign capital to fund their costly and aggressive expansion and investments that were no longer supported by the state's assistance.

The cost of such accelerated liberalization, however, was an unstable economy incapable of checking the volatile flow of global capital. With the government no longer controlling the banks, there were no mechanisms for monitoring and supervising financial capital. The jaebeol, still comfortable in its developmental spirit in which they never had to exercise self-restraint, recklessly borrowed money to fuel its overinvestment, and persisting corrupt ties between jaebeol and political power led banks to approve unsound loans. In January 1997, one of the jaebeol companies, Hanbo corporation, went bankrupt with over 5 billion US dollars in debt. This led to a string of other bankruptcies, including that of Sammi, Jinro, and automobile manufacturer Kia, throwing the Korean economy into a downfall, including the banks that had lent money to those collapsed companies. Such mounting problems led foreign investors to lose confidence in the Korean market, and this was particularly dangerous as Korea's short-term foreign debt had risen spectacularly through its liberalization.

And the situation exploded with the Asian financial crisis of 1997. In May, the Thai baht was rapidly devalued as speculative global capital started to pull out due to fears of a bursting bubble and the rise of interest rates in the

United States. As the crisis quickly spread to other countries in the region, the short-term loans from global capital that Korean companies had made started to mature, causing Korea's foreign reserves to deplete. The Korean won started to plunge by October, and mounting bankruptcies caused the country's credit rating to be downgraded. As foreign investors withdrew their funds in masses, Korea faced a full-blown crisis as it had no way to repay its immediate debt, which was estimated to be around 65 billion US dollars by official figures, but later turned out to be much larger, at least by 50 billion dollars (Blustein 2001). With no time to deal with the crisis, the Korean government was forced to turn to the IMF for its bail-out package, which required strict reforms as a condition for a 58 billion US dollar loan. An agreement was signed on December 3, 1997.

The subsequent reforms accelerated Korea's shift to neoliberalism. The course of action agreed between the IMF and Korea focused on strong austerity measures, such as raising interest rates in order to balance the country's deficit; greater financial liberalization, which removed restrictions on foreign exchange transactions and provided foreigners access to the Korean equity and real estate markets as well as ownership of financial institutions; restructuring of corporate and financial institutions, including merging of weak banks and companies into more competitive ones, and enhancing transparency in management structure; and privatization of public enterprises (Shin and Chang 2003, Lee and Han 2006). The state-centric framework of national development was now officially abandoned. Securing short-term financial interest based on fast flow of capital became the key goal for the economy. Attempts to defend the borders of the national market were now regarded as outdated, as the Korean economy strove to open itself up to the flow of foreign capital and the logic of the Dollar-Wall Street regime. The state's strategic protection of industries was now formally withdrawn, and market-based 'competitiveness' of corporations became the ultimate measure of their value.

The Korean people—as opposed to global and domestic capital—suffered inordinately under this transformation. Restructuring of the economy resulted in 1.27 million people losing their jobs in 1998, tripling the number of the jobless. Many more had to take deep cuts in wages and work for longer hours, while the plummeting value of the Korean won also led to rising cost of living. To this day, the 1997 crisis remains a traumatic memory for the Korean people, as the 'IMF age' is frequently referred to as one of the darkest periods in modern Korean history. But the crisis had much more enduring effects, including a massive precarity of work (see also Chapter 8). Even before the crisis struck, in 1996 and 1997, new labor laws were being passed in response to capital's demand for deregulation since the late 1980s, allowing employers to implement mass layoffs and to actively rely on contingent and subcontractual labor. These changes were further solidified in subsequent revisions of the laws in 1998, significantly transforming the scenery of the Korean labor market (Kim 1998, Koo 2000). While Koreans had enjoyed relatively strong job stability through traditional expectations of lifetime employment until the early 1990s, such expectations were now completely shattered. The seniority-based wage system was abolished and replaced with a merit-based, yearly renegotiation of contracts; people worked for longer work hours for less pay, constantly worrying about keeping their jobs; and irregular employment became the dominant mode of labor across all sectors (Y. Lee 2015b).

In contrast, foreign capital benefited hugely. The reforms, while ostensibly prescribed as a strategy to help Korea overcome the crisis, barely concealed the fact that they were designed to protect the interests of global capital represented by the financial institutions of Wall Street. Indeed, specific terms of the IMF loan were practically dictated by the US treasury department, which insisted on a clear plan toward Korea's financial liberalization and persuaded major American banks to extend the deadline of their loans to Korea (Ji 2011:190–94, 208–9). Because Korea never actually defaulted on its loans, creditor banks and foreign capital suffered no loss due to the Korean crisis; instead, they profited enormously through the high interest rates and by taking over Korean banks and companies for a cheap price. The reforms established the Korean economy as a new financial market that offered foreign investors multiple ways to profit.

The fate of the jaebeol turned out to be not too terrible, either, even though their reckless expansion and unsound practices were among the immediate causes of the crisis. While some of the largest jaebeol groups, such as Daewoo and Ssangyong, fell and broke down into pieces, many others, including Samsung, SK, and LG, as well as some companies that branched out from former jaebeols, such as Hyundai Motors, emerged as stronger than before, thanks to the business restructuring, financial adjustment, and flexibilization of labor mandated by the reform. In particular, focused investment in areas such as semiconductors, automobiles, wireless communication, and computers lead to greatly increased export, propelling many jaebeol groups into the status of veritable global conglomerates. This resulted not only in greater profit for the companies, but also in a greater concentration of political power in the hands of the families that own and run the jaebeols. Using this clout, the jaebeols were able to pressure the state system to work for their benefit, and exploit small and medium enterprises through unfair subcontracting. Despite the high concentration of wealth in the hands of the jaebeol-owning families—the top 10 jaebeols in Korea account for more than half of the country's market capitalization, half of which belongs to Samsung (Oak 2016)—the jaebeols' contribution back to the Korean economy is limited; for instance, they employ only about 12% of workers in the Korean job market where unemployment and underemployment is widespread (B. Park 2017). It is by providing such conditions for the jaebeol's exploitation of the Korean market that the restructured Korean economy after the crisis enabled these conglomerates to reconsolidate their power.

Korea's escape from the financial crisis itself was relatively quick. The foreign reserve shortage was resolved early during the crisis. The country was able to repay the IMF by 2001 ahead of schedule, and the Korean economy, which had shrunk by 6.7% in 1998, achieved a 10.9% and 8.8% growth in 1999 and 2000, respectively (Lee and Han 2006). As Pirie notes, the Korean case was exceptional in "both the strength of the macroeconomic recovery and, more importantly, the speed with which the microeconomic weaknesses that beset the economy have been addressed and a new relatively stable growth regime established" (2008:147). That new regime was neoliberalism—firmly established as a new logic of capital accumulation, now serving as a fundamental doctrine for the organization of Korean society. More importantly, neoliberalism was no longer just a macro-level policy of the state that affected large corporations or international trade, but a basic maxim that structured everyday social life. With the financial crisis strongly etched into the cultural memory of Koreans as a period of pain, suffering, and humiliation, neoliberal principles of individualism, competition, and entrepreneurship were promoted and accepted as the only way in which one can survive in the harsh new economy.

Corporate culture was one of the sites through which the spirit of entrepreneurship was made prominent. During the mid-1990s, even before the crisis, in their effort to embrace globalization and more liberal corporate governance, jaebeol corporations were envisioning a new model of an ideal employee. For instance, in a process informally called 'creative destruction of hiring practice' (*chaeyong pagoe*), they introduced new technologies of assessment to scrutinize and evaluate the range of practical and demonstrable skills possessed by job applicants. This served to bring corporate culture more in line with the neoliberal imagination of the worker as a 'bundle of skills' (Urciuoli 2008). For instance, written exams of 'general knowledge' (*sangsik*) and one's major area, which used to form a central element of the evaluation process, were abandoned by most companies, as such tests came to be seen as reflecting stilted academic knowledge rather than being connected to practical, job-related skills and competence. Instead, alternative modes of assessments, such as interviews which seek to identify the applicant's character (*inseong*), aptitude (*jeokseong*), creativity, leadership and teamwork skills, etc. (i.e., what are commonly referred to as 'soft skills'), started to take on a central role (see also Chapter 8).

An effect of such practices was to shift the image of the ideal employee from a bookish, elite school graduate to a flexible worker who can effectively adapt to the changing demands of the workplace. That is, the ideal worker came to be understood as an entrepreneur of one's own self, constantly striving to make oneself relevant to the workplace and the job market by acquiring new skills and competencies (Shin 2018a). On the managerial level as well, a newer managerial figure that emphasized technical expertise, professional adaptability, horizontal communication was promoted, displacing the traditional image of the manager as an authoritarian, inflexible, older male figure, who was increasingly perceived as unproductive and oblivious to the changing social and professional trends (Prentice 2017). Such changes also led to a booming popularity of self-development (*jagigyebal*) and self-management (*jagigwanli*) literature. From Stephen Covey's *The Seven Habits of Highly Effective People* and Robert Kiyosaki's *Rich Dad Poor Dad*, to works of local authors such as Gong Byeongho and Goo Bonhyeong, a wide range of self-help books provided inspiration as well as practical advice for Korean workers to reimagine themselves as entrepreneurs, brands, and human capital, and to subject themselves to responsible and continuous practices of self-improvement (Seo 2009, Yi 2013).

State policy also promoted this notion of self-help through a reformulation of welfare. The welfare policy of the Korean government launched in the aftermath of the financial crisis centered on the notion of productive welfarism or "workfare," which prioritized nurturing employability of the poor and jobless and their capacity for self-rehabilitation as a means of minimizing the cost of welfare (Hwang 2006, Song 2009). In this way, citizens were expected to become deserving subjects of state support by adopting a neoliberal mindset of individual economic responsibility. Financialization also became a principle for the household economy. Relaxation of the finance market extended lines of credit for Korean citizens as consumers. With a drop in real wages and insecurity of employment, workers were enticed to make purchases on credit and invest in financial products such as equity funds, chasing fantasies of becoming an agentive consumer and productive managers of their own wealth. In 2002, a major credit card company's television commercial, in which the catchphrase *buja doeseyo!* 'become rich!' was packaged as a heartwarming New Year's Day blessing, became a huge hit, illustrating how prevalent the dream of economic prosperity through financial self-management had become—though such dreams would be belied by the large number of delinquencies and personal bankruptcies that erupted in the following years (Choi 2013).

Another domain that was heavily reconfigured was that of education. The Korean education system, which had traditionally been characterized by a standardized, national curriculum that minimized the effects of class-based difference in educational outcomes (commonly referred to as the equalization, or *pyeongjunhwa*, policy), became the subject of intense debate throughout Korea's neoliberal transformation (Lim 2012). The state's globalization drive reframed education as a site for human capital development, a key foundation for enhancing Korea's national competitiveness in the knowledge-based economy. The corporate sector and the jaebeols demanded that the Korean education system produce flexible and creative workers with soft skills and entrepreneurial spirit that can spearhead the companies' global expansion. The

Korean middle class, who realized through the traumatic experience of the financial crisis how fragile their class standing was, sought to find educational opportunities for their children that can endow them with a sense of distinction so that they may pass down their classed position to the next generation. As a result, various educational reforms took place, reconceptualizing education as a space that should be organized according to neoliberal principles of competition, individual excellence, and inculcation of commodifiable skills.

For instance, revisions to the national curricula announced throughout the 1990s emphasized English and computer skills as an important basis for molding students into global citizens (Kang 2014; see also Chapter 6). Liberalization of the education system led to the opening of specialized schools that were allowed to develop their own curricula and select their own students (such as special purpose high schools, autonomous private high schools, and international middle schools), which emerged as new elite schools that provided strong advantage in university admission. This effectively dismantled the equalization policy and injected a spirit of competition and excellence into the field of education (Park 2013a). Higher education was also reimagined in market terms, as harsh conditions of the job market elevated development of employable skills to the foremost goal of university education. The research function of the university was also absorbed into the logic of neoliberalism, as national initiatives such as Brain Korea 21 (BK21), introduced in 1999, distributed funding for university research according to a competition-based model.

In short, Korea's neoliberal transformation was a process of increasing expansion of market-oriented principles, deployed to defend the interests of specific actors in the changing conditions of the global economy. Our brief historical overview reveals several important characteristics of Korea's neoliberalization. First, the strong influence the United States had over the country's transition toward neoliberalism shows how the country's political economic transformation was an integral part of US-centered geopolitics and the Dollar-Wall Street regime. Second, the active role of the state and US-trained technocrats in driving and guiding the process of neoliberalization indicates how, even after the authoritarian developmental state regime was dismantled, government policy and state control continued to shape the course of Korea's political economy. Third, the way in which the advent and unfolding of neoliberalism in Korea was deeply intertwined with the economic activities of the jaebeol points to the prominent position those corporations occupy in the Korean economy and their influence in propagating the logic of neoliberalism. Finally, the relatively faithful and rapid manner in which Korea carried out neoliberal reforms across all scales of society demonstrates the extent to which neoliberalism as a guiding principle of economic and social life was internalized in the minds of Koreans, particularly through the collective memory of the financial crisis. In the next section, I turn to an account of how these characteristics of Korea's neoliberal transformation gave rise to a veritable "English fever" that was arguably unprecedented in anywhere else in the world.

KOREA'S ENGLISH FEVER AND ITS NEOLIBERAL GROUNDING

It is important to consider Korea's English fever in the context of neoliberalism, not only because it was contemporaneous with the country's neoliberal transformation, but also because it was an integral part of that neoliberalization process itself. In what sense was the Korean English fever 'neoliberal'? To answer this question, it is not enough to point to the fact that English language competence was increasingly associated with economic profit and opportunities. As noted in previous chapters, it is problematic to identify neoliberalism with mere expansion of profit-seeking behavior. Neoliberalism as an ideological configuration is a much more specific condition than a general orientation to profit, even though relentless capitalist pursuit of profit is indeed one of its important driving forces. To identify a particular context as neoliberal, we would want to consider how such maximization of profit is embedded within specific political economic relations (such as shifts in the state's control over the market) and ideological justifications (such as rationalizing enhancement of one's competitiveness in the market as an ethical imperative for responsible subjects).

Indeed, the association between English and material profit predates Korea's neoliberal transformation. English in South Korea has always been linked with economic wealth and privileged opportunities throughout its modern history, particularly since the US military's occupation of the southern half of the Korean peninsula following the end of Japanese colonialism in 1945. The enormous political, economic, cultural, and military influence that the United States exerted over South Korea meant that the ability to speak good English was a means of securing profit and privilege, as evidenced by the powerful positions that US-educated intellectuals enjoyed in postcolonial Korean society (Choi 2014). English has always been one of the most important subjects in the Korean education system since the introduction of the national curriculum in 1954 (Kwon and Kim 2010). This made English language learning a crucial matter for anyone who sought valuable academic degrees or profitable white-collar jobs.

How was Korea's English fever different from the historical valorization of English as a key for economic profit, then? The answer to this question can be sought in how the English fever constituted a radical transformation in the way Koreans understood their relationship to English and the way they understood themselves. In neoliberal Korea, competence in English is not so much an advantage one has over others, than a basic requirement without which one cannot survive. If speaking English well in Korea's developmental state period was a valuable skill that can bring one great opportunities, it was nonetheless not an absolute requirement for such opportunities; despite the importance of English, one could still choose not to invest in acquiring English language skills, instead strategically deciding to distinguish oneself through other means, such as a degree from an elite university or fluency in a foreign language other than English. Since the 1990s, however, English came to be considered a practical, basic skill for everyone, a language that, regardless of one's line of work, level of education, or career aspirations, one must master if one is to become competitive in the job market. And in this sense, English took on meaning as a moral imperative; to ignore English was to neglect one's responsibility to cultivate and develop the value of one's own human capital (see also Chapter 5). Lack of English skills was no longer a mere risk one may choose to take, but a transgression—a telltale sign that one did not heed the neoliberal message that everyone should constantly work to enhance their relevance to the market for society's and their own good. It was this shift in the way English was understood that led to widespread investments in English across all domains of Korean society, distinguishing the English fever from the older orientations to English as a language of opportunity. And it was this reconceptualization of English that made the English fever a crucial element of Korea's neoliberalization.

One major aspect of Korea's neoliberal transformation that triggered such reconceptualization of English was the state's education policy that emphasized English as a key for enhancing the country's economic competitiveness in the global market. The revisions to the national curricula, carried out during the peak of Korea's globalization drive, emphasized preparing students for the dawning 21st century, which the policy defined as an age of globalization and information technology (see also Chapter 6). Changes in English language education were the most prominent aspect of this new focus, as the revised curricula presented spoken communicative skills in English as an indispensable competence for the new globalizing world (Ahn 2013, Kwon and Kim 2010). The shift in emphasis toward oral competence was also reflected in the College Scholastic Ability Test, the national college entrance examination, which adopted listening comprehension as a new component of its English section in 1993. At the same time, the reforms lowered the age at which English was introduced into the curriculum, in order to expand the students' hours of exposure to English and to make the most of younger children's malleability in language acquisition. The government also initiated schemes to bring in native speakers of English (in this case defined as nationals of Kachruvian inner circle countries of the United States, United Kingdom, Canada, Australia, New Zealand, etc.) to teach English in Korean schools—EPIK (English Program in Korea) and TaLK (Teach and Learn in Korea), introduced in 1995 and 2008, respectively (Jeon and Lee 2006, Jeon 2012a)—building upon the pervasive ideology in Korea that spoken competence in English is best acquired through interaction with native speakers. Higher education was also affected by these trends. Under pressure to transform themselves into internationally competitive institutions, universities in Korea aggressively expanded the presence of English on their campuses, recruiting staff and students internationally and establishing international colleges (S. Kim 2016, 2018), pressing researchers to publish in English (Lee and Lee 2013), and adopting English as a medium of instruction (Cho 2012, J. Choi 2016, Kim, Choi, and Tartar 2017, J. S. Park 2017, Piller and Cho 2013).

Another aspect of Korea's neoliberal transformation that instigated the English fever came from the corporate sector. As discussed in the second section above, global expansion of jaebeol groups made good communicative competence in English an important quality they sought in their employees. Corporations did not valorize English just for its practical need in conducting international business; the symbolic value of English in indexing the global orientation of the employee was just as important. Regardless of whether using English was required in an employee's daily routine of work, good competence in English came to be seen as evidence that the employee had the right mindset befitting the global corporation—a sensitivity to changes in the globalizing market, a willingness to take on challenges beyond one's own cultural zone of comfort, and the ability to flexibly adapt to new ideas and new situations.

Communicative skills in English were emphasized in a shifting job market where competition and precarity were becoming new norms. As corporations moved away from traditional systems of personnel management in which lifelong employment at one workplace could normally be expected, corporate workers and job seekers could no longer rely on their past achievements such as an academic degree from good schools to prove themselves as worthy employees, and were forced to invest in continuous development and accumulation of new skills, particularly soft skills that could allow easy adaptation to fluctuating demand of labor. In this context, English language competence emerged as the most important soft skill. Corporate employees or anyone seeking a white-collar job was placed under enormous pressure to respond to this new emphasis on English. Preparing for TOEIC (Test of English for International Communication) or honing one's skills in conversational English became a major task for university students (see also Chapter 8). In the harsh economic climate that followed the financial crisis, there was a sense of desperation in the way Korean workers turned to studying English; securing good competence in English was now elevated to a matter of life and death, as not equipping oneself with the skills that the corporate job market was demanding could now easily mean loss of employment and income.

The enhanced importance of English in the job market also led to a great boom in English language teaching for children—which became one of the most prominent aspects of Korea's English fever. The emphasis on English in the school curriculum and in the corporate workplace led Korean parents to make zealous investments in their children's English language learning. South Korea has always been a country known for its educational fever in general (Seth 2002), with parents typically considering provision of good education for their children an important part of their parental responsibility. In the aftermath of the financial crisis, in which many members of the Korean middle class experienced a significant fall in their class position, investment in the English language education of children became particularly important. With a great sense of urgency, middle-class parents sought opportunities for their children to acquire good English from an early age, so that they may stay ahead in the competition with other children in school and the job market. Ultimately, for these parents, investing in their children's English language learning was a way of passing down their class standing—or, protecting them from falling further down on the class ladder.

This "fear of falling" (Ehrenreich 1989) of the Korean middle class gave rise to a huge education market that offered a wide range of educational arrangements purporting to inculcate in the student good competence in English. The educational market for early childhood was particularly heated (under the name of *yeongeo jogi gyoyuk*, commonly translated as "early English education"; see Chapter 6). For instance, English-only kindergartens and private English language institutes (*hakwon*) that offered an immersion education environment with native-speaker English teachers became highly popular among the middle class, despite their high cost of attendance and selectivity (Bae and Park 2020). In the secondary education sector, new elite schools that emerged due to the dismantling of the equalization policy, such as special purpose high schools and international middle schools, became highly popular, not only because they were considered a necessary step for entering prestigious universities, but also because of their strong association with English. Many of such schools used English as a medium of instruction, and required proficiency in English as part of their admission criteria (Jeon 2012b). The growing importance of these elite schools triggered even more early investment in English.

Efforts to strategically develop good competence in English at an early age led to another prominent phenomenon of the Korean English fever: the trend of sending pre-university children to study overseas, commonly called *jogi yuhak*, which is typically translated as "early study abroad" (H. Lee 2010, M. Lee 2010, Lo et al 2015, Park and Bae 2009, H. Shin 2012, Song 2010; see also Chapter 4). Driven again by the belief that immersion in an English-speaking environment is necessary for acquisition of good English, middle-class parents used short-term study abroad as a strategy for having their children learn English and also gain valuable educational credentials for further competition back in Korea. For example, a child might spend a couple of years of her primary school education abroad in the United States, during which she develops native-like competence in English, and then return to Korea, using the

English language skills and transnational educational experience to enter a special purpose high school back in Korea, and in turn move on to a prestigious university in Korea or in the West. The *jogi yuhak* phenomenon is perhaps the most apt demonstration of how Korea's boom in early English education was a project of strategic management of youth as a human resource (see also Chapter 6). This is because early study abroad not only involves huge deployment of material resources and effort, but also constant re-assessment of how the linguistic and cultural capital acquired by the child will be valued under the changing conditions of the market and across transnational space (Bae 2014a, 2014b, Park and Lo 2012, Kang 2018).

Our discussion of Korea's English fever shows how the intense pursuit of English was deeply grounded in the logic of neoliberalism. On the one hand, English was framed as an indispensable skill in the global economy that everyone should strive to acquire, a resource that a responsible citizen should invest in so as to ensure their own and society's well-being. On the other hand, English became a key element of a new, competition-oriented social order, in which one must make continuous and strategic management of their English language learning to stay ahead of others. In this sense, the Korean English fever was simultaneously a process driven by neoliberalism and a phenomenon that facilitated the penetration of neoliberalism into Koreans' everyday lives.

As is typical of neoliberal processes, such incorporation of English into neoliberalism contributed to the exacerbation of inequalities. The gap between the English "haves" and "have nots" became more prominent than ever, as the wealthy middle class made increasing investments in costly opportunities for English language learning that were also considered to be efficacious in inculcating valuable English language skills (Shin and Lee 2019). More fundamentally, the specific trajectory of Korea's neoliberal transformation outlined in the previous section enabled the English-speaking elite to consolidate and expand their power. Korea's industrialization was a process by which the traditional middle class (consisting of agriculturalists and small business owners) was gradually displaced by the newer middle class (the professional and managerial class), a process that was further intensified by neoliberalism (Cho 2006, Jang 2013). The US-centric, export-oriented, and jaebeol-driven character of Korea's neoliberalization attributed more value to the symbolic and cultural capital of the newer middle class, who were more likely to possess familiarity with and competence in English. In this way, the historical privilege that the English-speaking elites enjoyed in Korea came to have a more robust classed foundation in neoliberal Korean society.

This neoliberal grounding of the English fever did not go unnoticed in Korea, and much criticism has been made of the overheated emphasis on English in Korean society. To some extent, such criticism has resulted in a backtracking of several policies promoting English. For instance, attempts to introduce English as a medium of instruction for all public schools (as proposed by the presidential transition committee of the president-elect Lee Myung Bak in 2008) had to be withdrawn after intense criticism, which complained that the proposed policy will bring even greater exacerbation of class-based inequalities and heavy burden on students. Such moments suggest that the neoliberal valorization of English is not a unilateral process and must be understood in the context of competing political interests that intersect in complex ways (Byean 2015, Park 2013a). However, in general, resistance to the neoliberal emphasis on English in Korean society has been weak, with few voices contesting the very premise of the English fever—that English is a valuable resource that must be cultivated to maximize the value of one's own human capital. Despite change of government administrations throughout the two decades of the Korean English fever, the notion of English as a crucial skill for human capital development and the anxious pursuit of the language driven by competition have remained a constant. And this should not be surprising if we see the English fever as a neoliberal project, given that the drive of neoliberalism has persisted throughout that same time period as well.

More than two decades since its beginning, what has become of the Korean English fever now? On the surface, one might say that the frenzied zeal with which Koreans pursued English has somewhat subsided. At the time of this book's writing, for example, we no longer see endless strings of new measures being introduced to boost the English language competence of Koreans as we did during the heydays of the English fever. In fact, some of the strategies that previously characterized Korea's heated pursuit of English are now in seeming decline. For instance, the relative importance of standardized exams of English such as TOEIC has diminished, as major corporations move away from such quantifiable measure of English proficiency. Also, jogi yuhak, once the quintessential symptom of the early English education boom, is not as popular anymore; while the number of jogi yuhak students showed rapid growth during the years 1998–2006 (from 1,562 to 29,511; Kang and Abelmann 2011), that number has dropped to 18,118 in 2009 and to 10,907 in 2014 (J. Lee 2015).

However, this hardly means that Koreans have moved on from English. Instead, we may read the above examples as an illustration of how the neoliberal pursuit of English has become a completely mundane and unremarkable aspect of Koreans' everyday life—what we may call a *normalization of English* in Korean society. In other words, the idea that English is a language that must be pursued at all costs is fully internalized, no longer a trendy idea that represents the change of times, but a normal, mundane statement that represents a timeless truth, with the infrastructure of Korean society having evolved to take this for granted. As we will see in Chapter 8, the decline of standardized tests such as TOEIC in fact reflects the expectations of corporations that white-collar job applicants should have much greater English language proficiency than just an ability to score well on a test (Kim, Choi, and Kim 2018). The diminishing popularity of jogi yuhak is also likely a result of the phenomenal growth of the domestic private English education market, which now offers such a diversified range of services (at least for the middle class who can afford them) that going abroad purely for the purpose of acquiring good English language skills is no longer useful or attractive (Bae and Park 2020). In other words, the above examples merely indicate a shift in the technologies through which English is pursued, rather than a fundamental decline in the significance of English. On the contrary, English continues to be clearly recognized as a "base" upon which other skills should be acquired in the project of neoliberal self-development (Abelmann, Park, and K 2009). This is why, even as Mandarin has also become an increasingly popular language in Korea due to the growing power of China in the region and around the world, the hegemony of English in Korean society is hardly challenged (Curran 2021, Kang 2017).

In this sense, we may say that even though Korean society has moved out of its phase of English "fever," the neoliberal significance of English as a language of continuous self-development and self-realization has been fully normalized, now completely established as Gramscian "common sense." And we might argue that that two decades of the Korean English fever has been a long process through which such normalization took place. The rest of this book will take a deeper look at this process, focusing on how this was an outcome of the political economic conditions that gave rise to particular subjectivities of English, which led Koreans to reconceptualize their relationship to English and how they understand themselves. Why is it necessary, then, for us to study the Korean English fever from the perspective of subjectivity? What makes Korea an ideal context for considering the relationship between English and neoliberalism in terms of constitution of subjects? To answer these questions, in the next section I turn to a discussion of one crucial characteristic of the Korean English fever that we did not address in our account above: how strong feelings, emotions, and affects about English rooted in Korea's historical relationship to English served as a foundation for the country's English fever.

SUBJECTIVE FOUNDATIONS OF THE ENGLISH FEVER: A HISTORICAL PERSPECTIVE

The Korean English fever was not simply a process of material and social transformation through which English acquired a hegemonic position in society; it was also a time-space in which a range of intense feelings and affects pervaded Koreans' experiences of English. The various phenomena discussed in the previous section already point to this. For instance, the heavy investments that parents made in the English language learning of their children reflected their hopes for the children's better future; anxieties about their children falling behind in competition with others; the sense of moral responsibility that drove them to seek out the best opportunities for their children's English language learning; and the passion and zeal with which they endured the heavy economic and psychological burden that comes with such efforts. For university students and white-collar workers, striving to improve their TOEIC scores and conversational skills in English represented their desire to secure a (even if minimally) better position in the increasingly competition-oriented job market; the frustration of having to continuously subject themselves to ever evolving regimes of testing and assessment; dreams of becoming a person well prepared for the global times; and the jadedness that comes with the constantly deferred fulfillment of such dreams. Discourses of the government, jaebeols and the media, which emphasized the importance of English in a globalizing world, circulated nationwide amidst feelings of great crisis, as lack of good English was presented as a significant liability for Korea in the new economy; they also appealed to buoyant aspirations and pride about the amazing things the Korean people could achieve in the world only if they managed to master the global tongue of English.

These affects, feelings, and emotions were not merely epiphenomenal to the social and material conditions of the English fever. For instance, parental zeal for their children's English was not a passive reflection of changes in the national curricula or the job market; rather, it formed a co-constitutive relationship with such social transformations, serving as an integral element of the English fever itself. On the one hand, such dimensions of subjectivity drove the heated pursuit of English, by guiding Koreans to desire, seek out, and long for English; on the other hand, the broad emphasis on English across society inculcated such subjectivities, by setting up the conditions in which these affects, feelings, and desires can take root. The pervasiveness and intensity of such affects and emotions, in fact, is why the neoliberal pursuit of English in Korea was called the English *fever* in the first place. That is, these subjectivities *were* the English fever—the very nature of the Korean English fever was a configuration of subjectivities.

That dimensions of subjectivity had a fundamental role to play in the unfolding of the English fever can be seen from the fact that strong affects, emotions, and feelings associated with English were not something that was introduced into Korea in the 1990s, but had a longer history in Korea's engagement with English throughout its process of modernization. Korea's initial encounter with Western modernity in the late 19th century and the subsequent periods of modernist development was mediated in part by how Koreans came to see their own position in the world through the lens of English, forming subjectivities of English that would articulate Koreans' relationship to English in affective terms. Such subjectivities served as the foundation upon which the Korean English fever could unfold, and were further reproduced to guide Koreans into becoming ideal neoliberal subjects through English.

We can think about this issue through another highly salient aspect of Korean subjectivities of English: a debilitating sense of anxiety and inadequacy called *junuk*, which overwhelms Koreans when they need to speak in English (Park 2012, 2015). Generally speaking, junuk refers to a strong feeling of inferiority one experiences when facing a powerful figure; how one feels small, weak, insignificant, incompetent, and helpless in the presence of a superior other. When applied to the case of English, that powerful other is the figure of the racially defined (white) native speaker, whose linguistic authority serves as a reminder of the illegitimacy of Koreans as speakers of English. Koreans' talk about English frequently references this sense of junuk. For instance, situations in which one has to speak in English are frequently presented as triggering intense feelings of embarrassment, fear, and nervousness, as well as psychosomatic responses such as palpitations, sweating, and sudden loss of words, often described by the term *yeongeo ulleongjeung* 'English nausea.' The image of a Korean who freezes with embarrassment when a foreigner approaches and asks for directions in English is a highly common trope that is circulated in many jokes, stories, and complaints, which shows how strongly Koreans associate English with the feeling of junuk (Park 2009).

One recent example of this is a series of commercial advertisements for Speakingmax, an online service for English language learning (Park forthcoming). In each advertisement in this series released in 2015, a young, attractive-looking Korean is shown engaging in various common English language learning activities—listening to English language audio recordings, taking the TOEIC test, reading an English language newspaper, or listening to the news in English—implying that they are good and successful learners of English. Yet, when a foreigner (played by an actor who would be perceived as racially white in Korea) approaches them speaking in English, they are unable to say a word; their facial expression becomes stiff with fear and embarrassment, and they start to sweat profusely (in a highly exaggerated and humorous manner) as they desperately try to avoid eye contact with the foreigner. The advertisements then conclude by inviting the viewers to use Speakingmax to overcome their "English paralysis" (*yeongeo mabi*). Examples like these illustrate how deeply feelings of junuk permeate Koreans' perception and experience of English. They show how such paralyzing fear and nervousness about English serves as a common reference point for Koreans. Even though the figure of the Korean English language learner shown in the advertisements is clearly an exaggeration (many Koreans, despite feeling nervous, would be able to carry out at least some conversation with an English speaker, for instance), the figure's affective experience is presented as one that all Koreans can relate to, representing a feeling with which they will immediately identify, for it is a feeling that they live with and live through, as they continue to struggle with being an illegitimate speaker of English.

It is important to recognize that such anxieties about English should not be seen as reflecting an actual incompetence in English that Koreans have as non-native speakers of English. Rather, it is a manifestation of the more general ideology of *self-deprecation*, in which Koreans see and talk about themselves as inherently lacking good competence in English (Park 2009, 2017). The feeling of junuk is not considered to be a feeling that is experienced only by a subset of Koreans who lack good competence in English (e.g., people who did not have adequate opportunities for English language learning, such as the working class [Curran 2018] or elderly [J. S. Lee 2016]), but something that all Koreans in general are supposed to be familiar with. The Speakingmax advertisements, for instance, feature and target contemporary young Koreans, who have grown up during the English fever and would have had more intense exposure to English than any other generation of Koreans before them. In fact, the Korean characters in the advertisements are presented as being diligent and successful in their English language learning, yet still experiencing junuk about English. Indeed, highly educated Koreans with relatively good competence in English also speak of struggling with junuk (Park 2012, see also Chapter 7). In contrast, one rarely encounters reports of Koreans experiencing junuk about languages other than English, such as Mandarin or Japanese, even when their competence in those languages is minimal (Park 2009). This suggests that junuk is not an instantiation of a general language learner anxiety that will disappear as the learner acquires more proficiency and confidence in speaking the language. Instead, it is an ideological condition that leads Koreans to view and perceive themselves as illegitimate speakers of English who forever remain inferior to the authority of the racialized native speaker.

Indeed, the ideological and subjective positioning of Koreans that underlie feelings of junuk toward English was formed over a much longer time period of Korean modern history, through which English came to be imagined as a language of the modern Other. In the late 19th and early 20th centuries, for instance, a group of well-educated reformers (*gaehwapa*) sought to modernize Korea as a way of countering the imperial powers that were descending upon Korea, including those of Japan, Russia, and the United States. These reformers argued that Korea needed to move away from what they saw as the backwardness of traditional Korean ways of life, and instead embrace Western-style enlightenment, so that Koreans could join the ranks of modern nations to gain power and respect on the global stage. Their view of modernization was based on a binary opposition between the East and West; the West was understood as the rational, civilized, superior Other whose values and practices represented modern ideals that all nations needed to follow, while the East was cast as its ignorant, barbarous, inhumane mirror image. As the reformers circulated their visions of an enlightened Korea through modern newspapers they published for the general public, such binary oppositions were also articulated in terms of affect. The articles they wrote in their publications sought "to inculcate shame and anger into the readers"—for instance, to have them feel upset about "Korea's lowly place on the ladder of civilization and the resulting humiliating treatment" by the imperial powers, and be embarrassed of fellow Koreans who "without any sense of shame, urinate and defecate in the streets" (Schmid 2002:43). While English was not yet being taught or learned widely among the populace, several of the reformers, such as Seo Jaepil and Yun Chiho, were passionate learners and users of English, projecting their strong desire for Western ideals and resentment toward Korean society and culture through their linguistic preferences (Cho 2017). In this way, Korea's initial encounters with English were being situated within a complex configuration of affects, between colonial longing and shame, between feelings of admiration and inferiority toward the Western Other.

In the years following Korea's liberation from Japanese colonial rule, these subjectivities were further reinforced through the dependent relationship that the southern half of the Korean peninsula entered with the United States. The political, military, and cultural influence that the United States wielded over South Korea led English to be seen as a highly desired language of wealth, power, and opportunity, an image supported by the US-educated elites who occupied important positions in the post-independence and postwar Korean governments (Choi 2014). The linguistic authority of those figures of power established English as the language of the powerful Other, invoking much insecurity among Koreans and demanding their submission. Discourses of English in popular culture that circulated between the United States and Korea further enhanced such insecurity. For instance, American films and television serials that were widely viewed in Korea depicted Asians as incompetent speakers of English who spoke in broken, pidginized English (Kim 2008, Lo and Kim 2012). In particular, such images of native and non-native speakers were constructed in terms of race, with American English and the United States being identified with whiteness, and Koreanness seen as inherently non-native and illegitimate—a racializing hierarchy of authority that was also reproduced and reified through dominant practices of English language teaching, such as the privileging of native-speaker teachers over non-native ones (Jenks 2017, Jenks and Lee 2020). The construction of English as a language to be desired, yet legitimate mastery of which is constantly out of reach, served as fertile ground for feelings of junuk, as it placed the Korean English language user in a perpetual state of inferiority (Park 2012).

Our brief review of the historical context of subjectivities of English in Korean society shows that the range of salient affects and feelings that permeate the Korean English fever—from the deep desire and longing for English, to the feelings of insecurity and inadequacy about speaking English—have deeper roots in the political and ideological conditions of Korea's process of modernization and the subjective relations to English that were formed through that process. The Korean English fever built upon those feelings, emotions, and affects, thereby extending the historical significance of English in Korea into the present, but at the same time, rearticulating and reframing such subjectivities in a way that aligns with the ideals of neoliberal subjecthood.

This also shows why it is important for us to consider the Korean English fever from the perspective of subjectivity. Not only are subjective experiences of English a salient aspect of the English fever that must be accounted for, but they also press us to situate the contemporary neoliberal valorization of English within broader historical context and to understand it within the continuities of the geopolitical and political economic conditions of Korean society. If affects and feelings that permeate Koreans' experience of English today are rooted in more fundamental social positioning of Koreans forged throughout modern history, this also means that neoliberalism's promotion of English is neither just about English, nor just about neoliberalism. Rather, it is about making of subjects—or, the process of subjectification—through which material and historical conditions of capitalism and colonialism extend their reach into Koreans' bodies and selves, by crafting the way they feel, experience, and act in the world. Just as the Korean English fever is one particular extension of how Koreans come to position themselves within the global world, the celebration of English as the language of neoliberalism is one particular juncture in the broader process of subjectification, which must be understood in terms of material conditions and interests in historical context.

Our approach that considers subjectivity from a historical and political economic perspective also helps us address some questions regarding to what extent can the subjectivities of English discussed in this book be seen as reflecting unique and essential aspects of Korean culture. That is, could it be that the particular affects and moralities that characterized the English fever derived from traditional Korean cultural values or sentiments that can be traced back to the country's premodern times? For instance, the intense parental zeal for their children's English language learning is often interpreted as a reflection of Korea's status-oriented culture, which in turn can be attributed to the country's Confucian tradition, in which expansion of knowledge through education is valued as a means of 'cultivation of self' (as emphasized in classics of Confucianism such as *Great Learning*) and in which providing a good education for one's children is seen as an important moral responsibility of parents (Song 2011). Korean culture is also often characterized by outsiders as displaying "extreme emotionalism" (Huer 2009), particularly in relation to the cultural notion of *han*—the pathos of melancholy, bitterness, and grief that is considered to flow from collective and individual experiences of injustice and victimization, which all Koreans are supposed to share (S. Kim 2017). The pervasive feelings of longing, frustration, and resentment that permeate the way Koreans account for their experiences of English may then seem to have some affinity with such emotionalism. In these views, the salient affectivity of the English fever might be considered a manifestation of an essential Korean cultural trait, which may lead us to question the generalizability of the role of subjectivity in linking English and neoliberalism.

The position I adopt in this book takes critical distance from such perspectives, for the following reasons. First, it is generally problematic to account for social phenomena by referring to a unified "culture." This would risk positing an essentialist view of culture and society, treating historically and materially constituted social relations as a matter of some inherent essence of a people. While cross-cultural difference in values and practices is certainly important to notice and account for, whether such difference can have explanatory power in itself or whether such difference can be accounted for in terms of a fixed set of values or religious traditions is questionable. For instance, attributing what goes on in contemporary Korean society to something like the influence of "Confucianism"—as if Confucianism is a unitary, readily available explanatory concept—not only is overly simplistic but also not something we would attempt in explaining social phenomena in Western societies. Second, to the extent that such cross-cultural differences exist, it would make sense to understand them as discursively constructed and reproduced through interactional and social practices, rather than as a preexisting cultural essence. Linguistic anthropological studies of how Koreans place moral significance in attending to each others' feelings and affects (through what is often called *nunchi*), for instance, show that such values are inculcated through specific interactional practices of socialization (Lo 2004). Similarly, Korean cultural orientation to social hierarchy and collective social harmony is also demonstrated to be something that is discursively brought about through participants' negotiation in interaction (Kang 2003). Such an approach, which considers cultural difference as interactionally accomplished effects of sociality, rather than as an explanatory factor that needs no account in itself, would be a much more productive approach for understanding the nature of such difference. Third, in relation to the second point above, invoking an essential cultural concept as explanation for social phenomena overlooks how such concepts may in fact be part of the politics of subjectification, as they are naturalized and reified to the status of a cultural essence. Sandra Kim (2017), for instance, points out how the concept of *han* discussed above derives from Japanese colonial discourse that sought to rationalize its conquest of the Korean people by constructing them as "docile, ignorant, naïve, and complacent subjects of empire" (p.260), which was later incorporated into Korean ethnonationalism as a "biologistic badge of Korean uniqueness" (p.266).

This book's approach, which locates subjectivities of English within historical and political economic context, enables us to overcome these problems. By identifying the affects, feelings, and desires associated with the Korean English fever as rooted in longer historical trajectories of Korea's relationship with the West and the material conditions of Korean society, we can avoid accounting for such dimensions of subjectivity in terms of a cultural essence, instead locating them in terrains of the political economy to properly understand subjectivity as a socially, politically, and materially constituted aspect of our lives. But this approach is important not only for avoiding essentialism, but also for a more incisive account of the role of English in Korea's neoliberal transformation. Our discussion above has already shown how the conditions that gave rise to subjectivities of English in Korea were also the same ones that shaped the structures of power, class, and inequality in modern Korea. As will be shown in the chapters to follow, the Korean English fever extrapolated those subjectivities, extending yet taking them in new directions—as a foundation for reconsolidating the power of the new neoliberal elite represented by the jaebeol and the new middle class, as a basis for rearticulating the existing moral order of Korean society to befit a neoliberal vision of entrepreneurship, and as a way of sustaining the unequal relations between Korea and the racially defined West in a postcolonial world. In this sense, moving beyond an essentialist view of subjectivity toward one that finds subjectivity's basis in political economic relations is crucial for understanding the historical and material effects that subjectivities of English produce in the context of neoliberalism.

While the following chapters are organized in terms of specific aspects of subjectivities of English—desire, morality, anxiety, and insecurity—this book does not treat them as isolable, comparable affects. For instance, it is not my intention to determine whether the specific articulations of the desire for English in the Korean case are similar or different to those manifest in other countries, or what factors allow us to explain such similarity or difference. Rather, by studying the locally specific process through which Koreans are guided to become neoliberal subjects through English, this book aims to show that subjectivity plays a key role in mediating the relationship between English and neoliberalism, even though specific manifestations of that subjectivity are expected to vary significantly across national contexts. While this book ultimately makes a general claim about the centrality of subjectivity in the neoliberal promotion of English, I do not rely on a positivistically comparative approach in doing so. Rather, this book's discussion is based on a conviction that aspects of subjectivity call for an analytic perspective that appreciates their local specificity, ethnographic embeddedness, and complex fluidity. For this reason, it strives to ask what can we learn when we do justice to the salience of the affects, feelings, and sentiments that fill Koreans' experience of living with English in neoliberal Korean society, by making those aspects of subjectivity the central focus of our investigation of the relationship between English and neoliberalism.

CONCLUSIONS

This chapter provided an overview of the ethnographic context of this book's study, presenting a brief historical account of neoliberalism in South Korea, the role the English fever played within it, and the salience of affects, feelings, and sentiments in Koreans' experience of English in this historical juncture. Our review of Korea's neoliberalization focused on the role of various actors that played a critical role in driving this process, including the United States, major Korean conglomerates, and the state, clarifying how the heated promotion of English since the 1990s was connected in important ways with the interests of these actors. This chapter also emphasized the neoliberal nature of the Korean English fever: how it was more than just a pursuit of the supposed economic value of the language, but a process by which the logic of human capital development insinuated itself throughout Korean society through the way English was valorized as a sign of good management of one's own self. Finally, highlighting the pervasiveness of intense feelings and affects about English as an important characteristic of the Korean English fever, the chapter argued for the importance of attending to the historical and political economic groundedness of such dimensions of subjectivity. This background information sets the stage for our discussion to follow, where we explore in greater detail how specific aspects of Koreans' subjective experiences of English contributed to the naturalization and internalization of the logic of neoliberalism in Korean society. In the next chapter, we begin that exploration with a consideration of how a desire for English was inculcated through ideological and material conditions of Korea's changing political economy under neoliberalism.

CHAPTER 4

Language as Pure Potential

Crafting a Desire for English

WHO DESIRES ENGLISH?

The Korean English fever can be depicted as a massive display of desire for English. Many aspects of Korea's pursuit of English conjures up an image of intensive longing and yearning for the English language. The sheer variety of English study books that fill up entire sections of bookstores, the swarm of people signing up for English language classes at private language institutes, the endless movement of young students traveling abroad to study English, the number of corporations that proclaim they want employees with better competence in English, and the string of new initiatives and curricular revisions with which the government reformed the education system to highlight English language skills—all of these seem to evidence a huge zeal for English on the level of the state, individuals, and corporations: Koreans want English, and they want it bad.

This image of people outside of English-speaking societies enthusiastically seeking English has been a common element of celebratory narratives of English as a global language. A publication by the British Council titled *The English Effect* (2013), for instance, attributes the contemporary global spread of English to the huge "demand" for English from outside of the traditional developed world, and forecasts "at least double digit growth—in some cases up to 40%—in demand for English in Indonesia, Pakistan, Brazil and Mexico, as well as the large African countries, particularly Nigeria, Ethiopia and Sudan" (p.8). In narratives like these, the overflowing desire for English is explained as a natural outcome of the practical benefits that English brings. The same publication continues: "One of the strongest incentives for learning the language is the use to which it

In Pursuit of English. Joseph Sung-Yul Park, Oxford University Press. © Oxford University Press 2021.
DOI: 10.1093/oso/9780190855734.003.0004

can immediately be put, socially, economically and culturally . . . it also helps economies overseas to prosper. English language skills provide life-changing opportunities, and promote prosperity and security around the world" (p.10).

However, of course, the desire for English is more than a matter of rational and economic logic, and ultimately points to the deep entanglements of hopes, dreams, frustrations, and yearnings that constitute desire. After all, what terms such as "English fever" intend to capture is not simply the volumetric growth of the English language teaching industry or the relative importance given to English as opposed to other languages, but the affective intensity and emotional immediacy that characterizes a society's engagement with English. The British Council publication mentioned above indeed alludes to such deep-seated desires for English when it cites the voices of several successful English language learners:

> English language skills are an indispensable tool for daily communication with most of the outside world, either in my professional or personal life. Through English I was not only able to assemble a vast professional network spanning around the globe, including China and Japan, I was also able to meet and get to know very inspiring personal friends around the region and in other, very different countries in Europe. It is vitally important that I am able to speak English; as important as being able to speak at all.
>
> Vladimír Vano, Chief Analyst, Volksbank Slovensko AS, Slovenia

> If I have to summarise the meaning of the English language in one word then it has to be freedom. Freedom to relate to others, explore new cultures, freedom of information, to do what I want to do for a living and live in a place I love . . . English has opened my horizons in every sense of the words and I owe who I am today to the ability to speak the language.
>
> Francisco Rodriguez-Weil, set and costume designer, Venezuela

> (British Council 2013:9–10)

Quotes like these not only foreground the economic and material opportunities that English provides by highlighting the professional status of the speakers to whom they are attributed (chief analyst at a financial institution, set and costume designer), but strongly suggest an underlying desire that drove these speakers to pursue English. In these quotes, the speakers articulate, in exultant words, how English served them as an "indispensable tool for communication with most of the outside world," offering them "freedom" and "open[ing] horizons in every sense of the words." As they proclaim that English is "as important as being able to speak at all," they display their passion for English and their will to hold on to the language. These quotes show that desire for English, attributed to English language learners from around the world, is an integral part of celebratory accounts of the global spread of English. Particularly in the context of neoliberalism, the desire for English often indicates a desire for unbridled realization of the self. Neoliberal promotion of English is thus often justified on the grounds that it is a much-needed response to the desire of people, who strive toward a better life for themselves, and who yearn to make the best of themselves in a global world of opportunity.

Such framing of desire can be critiqued in many ways. For instance, it does not account for where such a desire for English comes from in the first place: Does it derive from the promise of economic and material benefits through which English is supposed to lead individuals to a path of self-realization and freedom? If so, how does English come to be associated with such promises to begin with? It also presents a misleading picture of whether such promises actually deliver, for it overlooks the historical and political economic conditions by which English translates into material benefits and opportunities in the educational and job market (more on this in the following chapters). But more fundamentally, as I will elaborate in this chapter, it is premised on an impoverished model of desire. In these celebratory narratives, desire is seen as a natural response to a lack: many people in the non-English-speaking world lack English and access to the positive values and opportunities the language represents, and therefore they desire it. And this view, in turn, works to naturalize the resulting pursuits of English such as the Korean English fever ("who can blame Koreans if they want English for their better future?"), rather than viewing them as processes that are driven and shaped by political economic conditions. An alternative perspective, deriving from recent theorizations of desire, would be to consider it instead as a socially constituted force through which desiring subjects and desired objects come into being. That is, desire may be approached not as a negative term, defined by an absence and yearning—which already presupposes distinctions between subject and object—but as a process by which we come to see the world in terms of what is desirable and what is not, and who we are as ones that desire what we desire. My argument in this chapter is that such a conception of desire is crucial for critically engaging with the desire for English, for it allows us to link the subjective experiences of those who desire English to the political economic conditions according to which English is valorized under neoliberalism.

Thus, this chapter takes desire as a starting point for this book's exploration of subjectivities of English in the neoliberal promotion of English in Korea. Rather than considering desire as a want that naturally emanates from subjects encountering English in the world, it looks at the processes by which neoliberalism crafts a desire for English, thereby crafting particular subjects who desire English. For this, I focus on how desire articulates a specific neoliberal ideology of language which I call the ideology of *language as pure potential*. Grounded in the conception of the modern, rational subject, the ideology of language as pure potential works to rationalize the neoliberal view of individuals as "human capital" (Lemke 2001, Foucault 2008, Holborow 2018b)—as subjects with latent capabilities that have inherent economic value, which only needs to be fully realized in the external world via the transparent medium of language. English is particularly valuable, according to this ideology, because due to its perceived global currency, it comes to be seen as a language that is most capable of serving as such a medium. Through a discussion of manifestations of desire in the Korean English fever, I show in this chapter how Koreans' desire for English not only builds upon this ideology of language as pure potential, but at the same time, provides a specific bodily and experiential basis for it as well—that is, it crafts Korean learners of English as subjects who desire English. For Koreans who pursue English as a key to self-realization, the ideology of language as pure potential is not an abstract idea, but a natural logic of sorts that lives in their hopes and dreams about what they may achieve through English.

DESIRE, NEOLIBERALISM, AND LANGUAGE IDEOLOGY

As noted above, this chapter's approach to desire is informed by recent perspectives that consider desire as a socially productive force. The influence of Lacan's psychoanalytic theory frequently leads desire to be conceptualized in terms of alterity: that is, desire is the desire for the Other, thus characterized by a fundamental absence, lack, alienation, frustration, and negativity. However, in their discussion of desire, Deleuze and Guattari (1983) critique this view as already presupposing the desiring subject and desiring object. That is, by understanding desire as a person desiring some object, it reduces desire to a mere representation of the relationship between two things, things that by implication precede the desire that represents them. This, of course, ultimately leaves unexplained how those two things are put in a relation of desired and desiring in the first place, and therefore fails to account for where desire comes from. To overcome this problem, Deleuze and Guattari instead imagine desire as flow of life itself—for instance, the intensity of life that draws an infant's mouth to the mother's breast, in which the mouth and the breast are not distinct terms, but "the expression of a flow of life from which extended terms can then be abstracted" (Colebrook 2002:103). In other words, desiring subjects do not precede desire as a life force, but happen only as an outcome of the abstraction of desire under social conditions, such as the binaries of sexuality that attribute femininity vs. masculinity to distinct bodies.

This perspective has several benefits for theorizing the desire for English as a global language. First, it allows us to avoid reifying the object of that desire, English, as an already existing entity that dwells out there independently of the discursive and material forces that serve as its conditions of possibility. Instead, it reminds us that the object of English as a desired entity cannot exist apart from the discourses and practices that call it into being and associate it with qualities that make it desirable (Pennycook 2007b, Park and Wee 2012). Second, it tells us that desire for English does not necessarily have to be seen as oppressive in itself, enabling us to imagine a politics of English in which desire for English not only serves as a foundation for rationalizing the imperialist spread of the language but also may be redirected to dismantle the very assumptions of such rationalizations. If desire can be seen not in terms of blind pursuit of material and social benefits reflecting pre-given structures of inequality, but in terms of a force that is harnessed within political context for the crafting of subjectivities, this opens up the possibility of channeling desire into "non-coercive rearrangements" (Spivak 2002, cited in Motha and Lin 2014), where the oppressive politics of English can be resisted through a conscious and critical evaluation of "just whose interests are being privileged in the context of our 'educational' practice of socializing certain desires and prohibiting others" (Motha and Lin 2014:337; see also Kramsch 2009). Third, it allows us to trace in specific terms the political, material, and discursive processes through which subjectivities of English are formed. Recognizing that desire for English is socially crafted, we are able to turn our attention to the very mechanisms by which non-English speakers and English language learners are constituted as subjects desiring English, thereby placing subjectivities of English in historical and material context—which is precisely the goal this book aims to achieve.

This chapter emphasizes the third point above in its exploration of how desire for English plays a key role in the constitution of neoliberal subjectivities in Korea. Recent studies on English as a global language have focused on desire as a window for uncovering the historically and politically situated way in which English language learners come to align themselves with a longing for English and the new identities it represents. In the large body of work on desire for English in Japan (Bailey 2006, Piller and Takahashi 2006, Kubota 2011b, Takahashi 2013), for instance, *akogare* (commonly translated as desire/longing/yearning) for English is situated within Japanese society's historical relationship with the West and the material interests sustaining the *eikaiwa* industry (the network of commercial schools/institutes and instructional activities for English language conversation). These studies point out the deeply racialized and gendered ways through which English evokes feelings of longing and desire, such as how Japanese women's talk about English language learning is often closely intertwined with romantic imaginations of the West and white Western males. In doing so, they show that such desire must be understood in relation to Japan's modernization process, in which the West served as a foundational point of reference and in which the construction of Japanese women as modern subjects played an important role (see also Kelsky 2001, Inoue 2006). Such historically constituted desires and subjectivities, in turn, are appropriated and reproduced through the way the *eikaiwa* industry represents and markets its products and services, calling into being the English language learner as a consumer who pursues English not simply as an economically valuable communicative skill, but as a way of realizing one's dreams, living out one's fantasies, and becoming a modern self who is connected with the world beyond Japanese society.

Similarly, desire for English in Korean context is heavily conditioned by the historical process of Korea's modernization, as outlined in Chapter 3. As in the case of Japan, English in Korea indexed a liberal, enlightened, and advanced social order, from early on in the country's modern encounters with the West, but particularly since the United States started to exert a direct influence on South Korean society following its independence from Japanese rule. Integral to this process was the imagination of different bodies and subjects as having different relations to English and thus embodying different degrees of desirability. Perpetuated by US mass media, development aid, and military presence, the hegemony of US imperialism in Korea in the aftermath of the Korean war led the white, racialized Other to be seen as the representative figure of an ideal modernity and a prosperous life. Since this racialized Other was also imagined to be a native speaker of English, English came to index the desirability of foreign bodies, in terms of qualities such as political power, liberalized sexuality, and cosmopolitan outlook (Cho 2017, Choi 2014, Jenks 2017, Kim 2008, Lo and Kim 2011). More crucially, we may argue that the historical conditions of postcolonial and postwar Korean society led to the formation of new subjectivities mediated by English. As the unfamiliar, foreign tongue wielded by the powerful Other, English came to signify, inscribe, and construct a distance between the racialized native speaker of English and the non-native speaker Korean, thereby naturalizing the relations of power constituted by historical conditions. In this way, Koreans were positioned as desiring subjects who yearn for the idealized values and bodies associated with English (Park 2012).

One important point that the historical and material rootedness of desires for English brings up is the role of language ideology in the formation of desiring subjects. Our earlier discussion above highlights how the desire for English is not a natural phenomenon in which one body is driven to toward another, but an ideologically constituted process whereby politically situated beliefs about English serve as the foundation for constructing certain bodies as enthralled by the dreams, promises, and opportunities that English offers. As Motha and Lin note, "desire connects identity to the role of English in securing access to material (and social) resources, and relatedly narratives that make promises (of varying degrees of veracity) about English's proximity to material resources" (2014:340–41). It is language ideologies that facilitate such connections, for language ideologies, as culturally grounded ideas about the structure, use, and users of language (Kroskrity 2004, Silverstein 1979, Woolard 1998), both link linguistic forms to particular social meanings and attribute concrete images and affects to language users, thereby providing a semiotic basis for differentiations among ways of speaking and among speaker identities (Irvine and Gal 2000). In our discussion of postwar Korea above, for instance, language ideologies that link English with images of race posit the white native speaker of English as the ideal figure of global modernity, establishing a semiotic contrast in which Koreans, as speakers who possess neither the ability nor the legitimacy to speak English, are positioned as inferior, backward social beings who are naturally drawn to desire English as a ticket for a better life.

The significance of such language ideological processes, we may further argue, becomes even greater in the context of neoliberalism. The increasing pressure to consider language as a skill and competence through which an individual can secure valuable opportunities in the job market (Cameron 2005, Heller 2010, Urciuoli 2008) has critical implications not only for linguistic differentiation along axes of legitimacy, authority, and authenticity, but also for the conception of language itself. That is, neoliberal subjectivity does not simply entail acquisition of particular resources (such as ways of speaking English that are deemed to carry more value), but more importantly a particular orientation to language and language learning itself—for instance, understanding language learning as a moral imperative for maximizing one's worth in the world (De Costa, Park, and Wee 2016). It thus becomes necessary for us to consider how desire for English in neoliberalism is not only driven by ideologies specific to English, but also broader ideologies that characterize the shifting ways in which language itself comes to be conceptualized under neoliberalism. This not only helps us address the fact that neoliberalism does not solely focus on English (as discussed in Chapter 1, neoliberalism does not demand English-language monolingualism, contrary to what is frequently assumed), but also allows us to critically examine even more intensified modes of desire for English: how the neoliberal subject is expected to not simply desire English, but also to desire *pursuing* English—that is, how endless pursuit of English in itself becomes a highly valorized index of an ideal neoliberal subject. In the rest of this chapter, I elaborate on this point by offering a detailed critique of the ideology of language as pure potential and how it has led to a new way of articulating the desire for English in neoliberal Korean society.

LANGUAGE AS PURE POTENTIAL

What I am calling the ideology of *language as pure potential* is the belief that language is a transparent medium of communication that allows its user to fully realize one's inner potential in its purest form, unconstrained by one's ethnolinguistic background or social provenance. Based on the assumption that all individuals have latent capabilities with inherent economic value— a potential—that only needs to be identified, excavated, and materialized through careful management and development, it posits that language is a crucial key for ensuring the full realization of this potential. Because, in the real world, this process of realization is necessarily constrained by distorting forces such as linguistic difference, cultural incommensurability, or socioeco-nomic conditions, language must be mobilized as a transparent tool for trans-lating one's potential against such forces. This becomes particularly important in the context of globalization, where individuals are actively encouraged to work beyond the confines of one's cultural home.

Consider, for instance, the following extract from an interview I conducted in 2010 with Mr. Noh, a Korean mid-level manager at the Singapore office of a US-based multinational corporation. In this extract, he explains Koreans' lack of success in moving into higher management positions in the global work-place by attributing it to their (supposed) incompetence in English and the problems of communication it engenders:

> 딱 영어 하나만 보자면은 진짜 어릴때 부터 상당히 좀 더 준비를 해야겠다, 상당히 능력있고 이 상당히 근면한 한국인들이 외국에 나와가지고 이 자기 능력에 비해서 과소 평가를 받는 대부분의 경우는 이 커뮤니케이션, 커뮤니케이션이 안되다 보니까 그런 불이익을 많이 당하죠. [. . .] 한국사람들은. 뭐 생각이 짧고 이래서 그런 기회를 놓치는 경우는 없다 그거죠 [. . .] 실제적으로 제가 보기에는 일반 한국 대학생들이 공부하는거 전공 부분에 있어서는 충분하게 그 경쟁력이 있다고 보거든요. 경쟁력이 있는데, 고거를 표현하고 발휘를 할 수 있는 수단, 언어라는 측면에서 막혀 버리니까 이제 제가 보기엔 능력을 발휘를 못하는거죠. 알고 머리 속에서만 빙빙 돌면 뭐하냔거죠.

> When it comes to English, I think there needs to be a lot more preparation from young age. Koreans, who are quite capable and hard-working, are often under-valued compared to their abilities, and the reason for this is usually due to com-munication. It's because of communication that they face such disadvantages.... When Koreans miss such opportunities (such as promotion to a higher posi-tion), it's never because they are unintelligent, for example. . . . I think Korean university students are highly competitive in terms of their studies and know-ledge of their major area. They are competitive, but they get stuck when it comes to the tools to show and make use of that, when it comes to language, so they are unable to realize their abilities, I think. What's the use if it's only in your head?

This is one argument that I repeatedly heard many Koreans make over the course of my research on English in Korea—that Koreans are highly capable people who display many good qualities that point to their underlying potential, such as intelligence, diligence, and willingness to work hard, but that potential is frequently undermined outside Korea due to Koreans' inability to translate that potential onto a global stage through the medium of English. Only if they had good command of English, the argument goes, they would be able to articulate their ideas, carry out their plans, build productive relations, and to truly become who they can be beyond the linguistic space of Korea; they would be able to fully realize their potential without it being sullied by problems of miscommunication, unequal relations of power, or cultural prejudice. While I will return to the case of Noh and other Korean managers working abroad in Chapter 7, for now we can note that this complaint represents language as a medium that can transparently enact, perform, and materialize what resides inside one's mind and the wonderful possibilities that inner self holds. According to Noh and many other Koreans, English is *the* language that ensures this maximum realization of potential. While the Korean language, with its limited geospatial ambit, can serve as an expression of that inner self within Korea's borders, it is English, with its status as a global language and its global reach, that would allow Koreans to realize their potential in a truly unbounded way. This argument thus presents English as a crucial resource in the context of globalization, the absence of which can make useless the most valuable of skills and abilities, leading to Noh's lament, "what's the use if it's only in your head?"

The ideology of language as pure potential is grounded in the modernist idea that language can serve as a transparent medium of communication free from social constraints. This is of course a prevalent ideology that was foundational to the imagination of western civil society. Belief in the possibility of a language that can transparently mediate abstract and rational thought gave educated European men like John Locke the confidence to speak of scientific knowledge with objectivity and authority, unimpeded by any cultural preconceptions or emotional distortion (Bauman and Briggs 2003). In Habermas's (1989) discussion of the public sphere, the idea of language as a transparent medium of communication—free from prejudice, manipulation, and sophistry and used in the open and egalitarian spaces of coffee houses—is what allowed the emergence of a new notion of the public in the 18th century, rationalizing the rise of the bourgeoisie as a political force (Gal and Woolard 2001, Gaudio 2003). In other words, this conception of language was crucial in unlocking the potential of the ideal modern subject: a cosmopolitan whose rationality, civility, and morality is made universal by his (as this subject was imagined as male) use of such transparent language.

In the context of globalization, this idea of language as a transparent medium finds a new manifestation in the domain of intercultural communication, where foreign language learning is often actively appropriated by the interests of global capital. In her critique of foreign language education in the United States, Claire Kramsch (2006) points out that the growing interest and investments in learning foreign languages during recent years have not led to greater understanding of other cultures and societies, for those languages are often simply appropriated for the purposes of promoting various corporate, military, or political goals overseas. Such disregard for culture and meaning in language learning illustrates how language in cross-cultural training is often assumed to be a medium that can translate and transmit ideas unproblematically without any recontextualization or resemanticization. In other words, languages are imagined as self-sufficient monolingual tongues, each equal in its capacity for representing meaning, and intercultural communication is considered a straightforward matter of finding semantic correspondences between those languages with no anticipated loss, demonstrating a belief in the capacity of language to mediate meaning in completely decontextualized ways (Gramling 2016, Park 2020b).

But another significant characteristic of the ideology of language as pure potential is its conceptualization of individuals as a container of potential—that is, inherent and underlying capacities, abilities, or dispositions that can be turned into economic value with the right management and development. In the context of neoliberalism, this has much affinity with *human capital theory*, which reframes specific capabilities of people as abstract "human capital" and places significant value on the realization of such potential capabilities. Grounded on the work of theorists such as Jacob Mincer (1958), Theodore Schultz (1971), and Gary Becker (1993), who argued that education and training should be seen as akin to investment in economic capital due to the fact that they lead to difference in an individual's earnings and social valuation, human capital theory redefines wages as return on capital, rather than price of labor. Within this framework, the worker is not a passive, exploited cog in the capitalist machine who is forced to sell her labor in the market, but an enterprise of herself, who actively invests in oneself through education and training, so that the skills, knowledge, and experience acquired and accumulated through such investment can provide a steady and profitable income stream long into the future (Foucault 2008, Lemke 2001). In other words, according to human capital theory, what should be identified, cultivated, and managed for profit (that is, what serves as embodied human capital) is the underlying potential of the individual—the capacity to absorb various skills and knowledge, naturally endowed aptitude that can be honed and refined, and distinct talents that can be developed to set an individual apart from others in the market.

The ideology of language as pure potential provides human capital theory with both a specific vision for implementation and a concrete foundation for rationalization. On the one hand, it spells out a practical step that needs to be fulfilled if human capital theory is to work for individuals. If one is to benefit from the development of one's own human capital, one not only needs to invest in one's underlying potential, but one's ability to communicate that potential for others to see. My brilliantly innovative business plan must be demonstrated to investors through effective presentation skills to have a chance of realization; my capacity to flexibly work with people from other areas of specialization should be proven through ability to translate expert knowledge into a language non-specialists can understand; and my eagerness to seek out new opportunities that await in the global market can only be made convincing through mastery of a global language that allows me to take up work anywhere in the world. In other words, the ideology of language as pure potential highlights that language is an essential foundation for the realization of the potential of human capital. Moreover, it suggests that language is capable of channeling that potential *without any loss*, because language is a transparent medium of communication that allows its users to transcend their cultural and social provenances, as long as it is acquired and used appropriately. In this sense, the ideology of language as pure potential completes the blueprint for human capital development.

On the other hand, the ideology of language as pure potential is an extremely powerful basis for rationalizing the logic of human capital. While the notion of human capital promotes the belief that anyone can benefit from this potential source of value that resides in all of us just by excavating and developing it appropriately, such promises are patently false. It is naive to believe that anyone can transcend one's socioeconomic, cultural, and biological positioning by simply investing in acquisition of valuable skills. To begin with, the time and resources one can invest in such acquisition will be constrained by one's social positioning. Also, how the skills acquired through such investments are evaluated is also conditioned by socially embedded relationships, such as social class, gender, race, ethnicity, and nationality. As noted by Holborow, the increasing income inequality that we are witnessing in the economy of recent years "reflects a social divide based on class rather than one based on skills possession" (2018a:63; see also 2018b). And in the context of increasing transnational and intercultural work, cultural difference can have a significant effect on how one's qualification and preparedness for employment is assessed, as classical and contemporary work in sociolinguistics and intercultural communication has repeatedly shown (Gumperz 1982, Campbell and Roberts 2007, Roberts 2012, among others). In this sense, "the idea of ability innocent of experience is . . . fiction" (Sennett 2006:120), and this reveals a major gap in the logic of human capital. If realization of one's potential is constrained by the social embeddedness of one's positioning, how can human capital be a means of overcoming such social conditions in the first place?

The ideology of language as pure potential is a perfect foundation for rescuing the logic of human capital from this impasse. Language, imagined as a transparent medium for communicating across cultural and social difference, nullifies the charges that human capital is a fantasy that conveniently ignores social inequalities and power relations. The ideology of language as pure potential coolly admits there is inequality in the world, and that it can work against you and unfairly judge the valuable effort you have made to become your very best. But it also suggests that such inequalities can easily be overcome if you have the transparent tool of language, as it will allow you to show who you really are to those who might not share the same social or cultural background with you, so that the skills and abilities that you have developed for yourself will be truly and equitably valued. In this way, the ideology of language as pure potential reduces structural inequalities rooted in the system of capitalism to the level of mere cultural misunderstandings and prejudices, defending the logic of human capital as an idea that offers hope to the underprivileged, as long as one also makes the necessary investment in the ability to use language in its appropriate, transparent mode.

What we can note from this discussion above is how this ideology's support of the logic of human capital strongly resonates with the way desire for English is articulated in neoliberal Korean society. Just like the ideology of language as pure potential, Koreans' desire for English imagines it as a language that will bring the English language learner access to economic opportunities, unrestricted information, and true realization of one's self; thus, English is desired for its power to unlock one's human capital and to open up a world of possibilities that is already inherent in oneself. And in this sense, the ideology of language as pure potential serves as a way of articulating the desire for English.

But at the same time, the ideology of language as pure potential also allows us to consider the specific way in which the desire for English gets modulated in the context of neoliberalism. As discussed in the second section above, the desire for English in Korean society has a longer history than neoliberalism, which can be traced back to the postcolonial conditions of the political economy that placed Korea under the influence of the United States. In this context, English was desired as the language of the modern, racialized Other, the acquisition of which promised an escape from the backwardness of Korea and its oppressive and restrictive conditions. However, I suggest that, the Korean English fever introduced a new articulation of this desire: English is to be desired not because speaking it allows Koreans to *emulate* that racialized Other, but because it tells them that they are *already that other*—they already hold that potential inside them, and English will enable them to activate it. In other words, even though the figure of the modern, racialized other still remains a point of reference, desire for English in neoliberal Korea turns its focus from that figure toward Koreans' own inner self, incorporating desire for English into a neoliberal project of developing one's human capital. Tracing how the ideology of language as pure potential facilitates this shift, then, becomes important for understanding the process by which desire for English contributes to the crafting of neoliberal subjectivities. In the next section, I turn to various cross-sections of the Korean English fever to explore this process in more detail.

COSMOPOLITAN DESIRE AND DREAMS OF SELF-REALIZATION

The desire for English in Korea today cannot be understood apart from Korea's globalization. The promotion of English as a necessary language for engaging with the world throughout the country's globalization drive from the mid-1990s reframed Koreans' desire for English in a new way. This renewed desire for English was rooted in its imagination as a language that allows one to go and live abroad. While English had already been desired as a language of the modern and powerful other since Korea's independence and through its years of rapid state-centric development, neoliberal transformation of Korea led English to take on a more specific, concrete image of a global language that enables Koreans to travel, work, and live overseas as a global citizen. Thus, English became a key to what Park So Jin and Nancy Abelmann called "cosmopolitan striving"—"the desire to feel at home in the larger world" (2004:664)—drawing from the work of Ann Anagnost (2000). It is important to note that the world outside of Korea, as imagined in such cosmopolitan striving, is not simply a romantic destination for travel or exotic cultural experience, but a space of possibilities: a glorious arena where one can fully realize one's own potential and become whatever one wants to be. In this way, the desire for English that had emerged out of the language's association with powerful racial Others was now rearticulated in the neoliberal vocabulary of self-realization and human capital.

Various shifts in Korean society in the 1990s led to this reimagination. For example, the liberalization of foreign travel in 1989 provided practical conditions for Koreans to consider the world overseas as a relevant space for imagining their future lives. Up until then, during the military regime that tightly controlled citizens' freedom, opportunities for traveling overseas or even having a passport issued under one's name were severely restricted. But the advancing democratization of Korean society and economic development that fostered a more positive attitude toward conspicuous consumption (Nelson 2000) led to a relaxation of the governments' control, making foreign travel for leisure and tourism something that is practically within reach for ordinary Koreans. As a result, even though foreign travel was clearly still constrained by one's economic means, the 1990s saw a significant increase in Koreans traveling abroad, particularly among younger Koreans, such as university students who went abroad for backpacking or short-term study overseas. Thus, liberalization of foreign travel provided opportunities for Koreans to imagine the outside world as actually accessible contexts, thereby opening the door to possibilities of navigating the space of the global world for strategic purposes, such as projects of early study abroad that would become popular later in the decade.

Moreover, a discourse that valorized the globally oriented subject circulated in Korean society during the 1990s. The *jaebeols'* demands that their employees also take up a global outlook and embrace the challenge of the global economy—to boldly go beyond the familiar horizon of Korea to take new risks and achieve things that a complacent worker would not be able to—was a major source of this discourse. One prominent example of such discourse was the highly popular 1989 book, *Segeyneun neolbgo hal ileun manhda* 'The world is so wide, with so many things to do' by Kim Woo-Choong, the founder and president of the Daewoo Corporation, one of the largest *jaebeol* groups at the time. Kim was known for his *segye gyeongyeong* 'world management' strategy, in which he aggressively expanded his company all over the world, and his book, which recounted his experiences and explained the principles that guided his lifetime work of establishing and running a global business, was widely read as a guide for developing a global vision and strategies for success in the international stage. While the appeal of Kim's mantra was seriously tarnished when Daewoo went bankrupt in 1999 following the Asian financial crisis (precisely due to the excessive debt it undertook to finance its worldwide expansion), the popularity of the book in the 1990s illustrates the extent to which the world beyond Korea's borders came to be imagined as a frontier full of challenges and promises that Korean workers should actively dream of conquering. In this way, Korean workers were urged to envision themselves going out to the world to seek new realms of success and to prove their true worth.

This global orientation was not only something that was expected of employees of major corporations. Expanded opportunities for going abroad gave prominence to a new class of transnational elites, who were promoted in the media as trailblazers who demonstrated new courses of success that Koreans may seek overseas. A popular subject in Korean media of the 1990s was figures who chose the bold path of going abroad to achieve success at the heart of the global world (see also Chapter 5). Depicted as cool cosmopolitans whose achievements overseas gave them wealth, prestige, and a refined transnational sensibility, such figures imbued traveling abroad for study and work with a romantic sense of fulfillment of dreams, overcoming of one's limitations, and transcending the restrictive culture of Korea. A notable example of such discourse is another bestseller, *Chilmak chiljang* 'Seven acts seven scenes' by Hong Jungwook, published in 1993. The book is Hong's account of his early study abroad experience, in which he left Korea after finishing middle school to study in the United States, enrolling in the prestigious boarding school, Choate Rosemary Hall, and then Harvard University, following the footsteps of John F. Kennedy, whom he deeply admired. As a record of the strenuous effort Hong had made to achieve his success (it outlines, for example, how he stayed up late at night memorizing entire dictionaries to master English: Cho 2017), the book is often credited with starting the early study abroad boom in Korea, setting up a cool, attractive image of a cosmopolitan elite that many parents and students came to strive for (the son of a famous actor and a good-looking man himself, Hong would later become a successful entrepreneur in Korea after further studying in Stanford and Beijing).

Such cosmopolitan striving, which penetrated Korean's imagination of the world as the country was rapidly globalizing, helps us understand how English came to be seen as a language that allows the unbridled realization of one's potential. As the world outside of Korea was increasingly seen as a space of new possibilities for pushing oneself beyond one's own limitations, English, the global language that was considered a necessity for navigating that space, also came to be seen as the essential foundation for pursuing such dreams of self-realization. In this way, the material and discursive conditions of Korea's globalization, in which Koreans were exhorted to think of the world as a glamorous space for neoliberal human capital development, served as fertile ground for rethinking English as the language of pure potential.

This reimagination of English as a language essential for the realization of one's potential in a global stage is starkly illustrated by parental desires for their children's acquisition of English, the very context in which Park and Abelmann (2004) situate their discussion of cosmopolitan striving in Korea (see also Chapter 6). Parents' zealous investments in their children's English language learning, one of the most prominent symptoms of the Korean English fever, functioned as a pragmatic and calculated choice where they attempt to give the children a head start in navigating the Korean educational and job market. But more importantly, they were couched in a trope of English as a language that allows the child to soar high beyond the space of Korea. Parents often speak of English as "wings to enable [one's] children to fly freely and high in a wider world" (Bae 2013:422). The "wider world" referred to in such statements directly indexes the global, transnational space that English allows a child to explore. At the same time, that space does not just imply greater geographical range of physical mobility, but a state where all constraints on the realization of one's potential is removed—be it the restrictiveness of the Korean public education system, backwardness of Korea's hierarchical culture, or socioeconomic inequalities that unfairly hold one back. In other words, the "wider world" that parents hope to offer to their children through English is a world of greater possibilities.

For instance, in the following interview conducted by Bae Sohee, a father of one jogi yuhak student in Singapore speaks about his belief about how English will provide his son with opportunities to realize his potential in a broader world beyond Korea:

그러니까 재민이가 그런 게 돼서 미국 서점에 가서 '어 이 책 재미있다, 오늘 이 책이나 떼야지' 이런 식이 되면... 책이 문제가 아니라 그만큼 그 쪽 문화를 이해하는 수준이 되는 거니까 주류가 아니더라도, 그 넓은 세상에서 볼 수 있는 과학, 정치, 경제 이런 것들... 은행측면에서 봐도 한국은행들은 외국은행 따라가는 것밖에 안 되는 거죠. 어려운 거 있으면 배워야하고 금융 기법도 알아야 하고 파견도 나가고 그런 것들을 주가 되서 하지 못해요. 하려면 항상 파트너 끼고서 걔들한테 배우는 건데, 내 아들은 안 그랬으면 좋겠죠. 자기가 직접 그런 것을 만들어내고 자기가 프리젠테이션도 하고 인스트럭처링도 하고 이런 거 있잖아요. [...] 저는 항상 그런 거, 영어를 자유롭게 할 수 있고 그 문화를 백퍼센트 자유롭게 이해할 수 있으면, 물론 한국인이라는 것을 잊으면 안 되겠지만 기왕 이렇게 된 거라면 여기나 홍콩보다는 미국에서 능력을 좀 펼쳐 볼 수 있는 그런.. [...] 그리고 영어를 하면 월드와이드로 할 수 있잖아요. 미국에서 한국와도 되고 홍콩, 싱가폴 심지어 일본을 가도 되고. 다 통하니까.. 그런 면에서 재민이가 좀 넓게 살았으면 좋겠어요.

So, if Jaemin (becomes fluent in English) so that he can walk into an American bookstore and say "hey, this book looks interesting, I think I'll finish this one today," then it's no longer just a matter of reading books but understanding their culture. So even if he's not a mainstream member of society there, he can understand things like science, politics, and the economy from the perspective of a wider world. Even in the field of banking, Korean banks are busy catching up with foreign banks. There's a lot of difficult things to learn, you have to know the financial techniques and go out and learn them, but we cannot take a leading role in that. We have to form a partnership and learn from them. I wish my son didn't have to do that. He could create things on his own, he could do presentations and instruct others, things like that. . . . I always wish, if he can use English freely and understand its culture 100% freely, of course he shouldn't forget he's Korean, but since he came all this way, he could realize his abilities in the US, rather than here or Hong Kong. . . . And if you can speak English you can go worldwide. He could come to Korea from the US, or he could go to Hong Kong, Singapore, or even Japan. Because English is understood. In that sense, I wish Jaemin lives his life widely. [Jaemin's father, interviewed by Bae Sohee, September 2010]

To Jaemin's father, English is crucial for allowing his son to venture beyond the limiting environment of Korea. Based on his experience working at the international department of a major Korean bank, he laments the limitations Korean bankers face in keeping up with foreign banks, implicitly attributing the dependence they have on those foreign banks to Koreans' lack of competence in English. He then envisions Jaemin's future with English as one in which he is freed from such limitations, using the language of English to fully understand foreign cultures, to work across national borders, and to express himself freely without others' mediation ("He could create things on his own, he could do presentations and instruct others, things like that"). While he considers the United States as the ideal final destination for Jaemin, what he ultimately desires for his son is the freedom to go anywhere he wants ("He could come to Korea from the US, or he could go to Hong Kong, Singapore, or even Japan"), and become anything he wants. Such freedom in fact resonates strongly with people like Jaemin's father. In his 40s during the time of the interview, he is a Korean of the generation whose early work career has unfolded during the post-Asian financial crisis period. Though he himself has been fortunate enough to maintain a reasonably successful career, he, as many other Koreans, has observed how unstable and precarious employment in contemporary Korea can be, and knows that Koreans constrained to the national job market rarely get to choose what kind of job one will take up where and when. To Jaemin's father, then, the (presumed) mobility and employability of fluent bilinguals is valuable not just because of the financial benefits it brings, but because it means being in a position to pursue what they want to do, having different options laid out for them, and living in a world of possibilities. This is what he means when he says he wishes his son "lives his life widely"—and English is what offers such potential to the Korean child.

More fundamentally, the possibilities offered by the "wider world" is not only about the child's future career trajectory, but about the kind of person the child may become. To look at the formulation of another jogi yuhak parent from Bae's research, who was living in Singapore with her 9-year-old and 7-year-old children:

그런 목적이 제일 크지. 그래도 내 아이는 영어권에서 영어를 공부시켜서 좀 더 넓은 세계로... 애들이 지금 이렇게 접해보는 게 애들한테 굉장히 클 것 같 아.... 일단 내가 목표로 하는 것은 좀 더 넓은 마인드를 가지게 하는 거지. 좀 더 많은 나라를 접해보고 또 거기서 살아보고 이런 애들하고 한국에서 한국 사 람들하고 복잡복잡하게 사는 사람하고는 분명히 뭔가 사고하는 게 틀린 게 있 을 거라는 생각을 하고 있지.

That's my biggest goal [of coming to Singapore]. At least to have my children study English in an English-speaking country so that they can go into a wider world. I think this exposure now will have a great influence on the children. . . . My goal for now is for them to have a broader mind, to experience many different countries and to live there. I think their way of thinking will certainly be different from someone who has only lived in Korea mingling with Koreans. [Juni's mother, interviewed by Bae Sohee, August 2010]

In her explanation of why she chose to have their children study in Singapore at such an early age, Juni's mother foregrounds her hope of how the English acquired there will help them "go into a wider world"—which, she further elaborates, entails developing "a broader mind" and a sense of cosmopolitan comfort that comes from having lived in different cultures and countries across the world. In her formulation, English does not so much equip the children with specific skills or competencies, but inculcates in them a sensibility that allows them to be at home in the open world of possibilities. In essence, it is about overcoming one's cultural and social provenance, distinguishing oneself from "someone who has only lived in Korea mingling with Koreans." In other words, through the quote above, Juni's mother projects her hope that English will allow her children to transcend the constraints of Korean society, as their acquired comfort in being in the world opens up new ways of being and new ways of realizing their selves.

The examples above show how parents' desire for their children's global future is mediated by the ideology of language as pure potential. The ideology links the parents' cosmopolitan striving with English by presenting the language as enabling the children to transcend their social constraints. English, imagined as a transparent global medium for communication, is not burdened with the baggage of one's provenance, thus allowing one to experience, interact with, and engage with the world in situ, and to translate oneself in a lossless way into that world. Thus, English makes it possible for the parents to dream of their children going into the world to realize their deep inherent potential. The parents above do not present English language skills as an achievement to be pursued in itself. Instead, English is important only insofar as it allows entrance to a wider world of possibilities, where their children can become whatever they want, and where they can find their true selves. Indeed, such imagination of English is the foundation for the very existence of such a world of possibilities. Without English as a language of pure potential, parents' hopes of their children becoming free transnational subjects are thwarted at their roots, for then the children will be left without the means to transcend borders by experiencing the world firsthand and articulating themselves in ways that would be appreciated by others.

Our discussion also shows how the ideology of language as pure potential plays a role in reframing the desire of English in Korea with the discourse of human capital development. The desire for the racialized other, the orientation to the English-speaking West, which characterized the way English was desired throughout Korea's modern history, still permeates the way English is valorized in neoliberal South Korea. For example, Jaemin's father specifically speaks of the United States as an ideal space for his son to realize his potential, and while Juni's mother talks about experiencing "many different countries" through English, jogi yuhak families are usually less invested in appreciation of local cultural or linguistic practices outside of Anglo-American ones (for instance, see Kang 2012). However, the ideology of English as a language of pure potential, which is propagated by the material and discursive conditions of Korea's globalization, leads Koreans to see that figure of the racialized, English-speaking Other in a different light. While essentialist ideologies of language, race, and ethnicity of the past led that figure to be viewed as a distant, vague object of longing that was deeply desired but always out of reach, now Koreans imagine themselves as *already bearing the potential of actually becoming that figure*—a potential which in itself serves as valuable capital inherent in themselves. All they have to do is to secure English, the transparent global language detached from the speaker's social mooring, and use it to develop and realize their latent potential to become that cosmopolitan subject. This is how the desire for English came to be an integral part of the neoliberal project of human capital development that overtook Korean society through its drive for globalization.

DESIRE AND THE CRAFTING OF NEW SUBJECTIVITIES

The way in which the desire for English becomes incorporated into the logic of human capital development underlines the fact that desire is not simply a passive response to an objectively existing external need, but a socially constituted force that contributes to the crafting of subjectivities. And this is an important point for thinking about the relationship between English and neoliberalism, for it turns our attention to how the desire for English is rooted in material and historical conditions of the political economy. The desire for English that drove the Korean English fever was not something that naturally emerged as people became exposed to the currents of globalization, but was something that was constructed and brought into being by highly specific conditions that Korea's neoliberal transformation engendered. In that process, specific subjectivities of English were formed, as Koreans were positioned as subjects who desire English for its (supposed) power to realize their potential without impediment in the global stage. Taking this perspective on desire, then, allows us to trace how the material conditions of the lives of Koreans under neoliberalism have led them to align with new subjectivities of English.

For instance, the cosmopolitan desires of early study abroad parents, as we observed in the previous section, highlight how they are shaped both by discursive and political economic conditions and by the specific lived experiences of the parents. On the one hand, they emerged among shifts in the Korean job market under neoliberalism, as well as the discourse of globalization, which urged workers to embrace a globally oriented mindset, compelling the parents to desire opportunities for their children to explore their latent potential in a wider world. On the other hand, the parents' own experiences of striving to maintain their middle-class standing and pass it down to their children amidst the increasingly insecure and precarious conditions of labor led them to dream of an alternative world of possibilities in which their children can realize their full potential unencumbered by the limiting circumstances that the parents themselves had to struggle against. It is through these processes that desire for English emerges, providing a ground for the parents to engage with the neoliberal logic of human capital development on an experiential level, and leading them to take up subjectivities of English, in which the language stands for the desires and hopes of becoming an ideal cosmopolitan subject.

This also means that subjectivities of English would emerge in different forms as the specific material conditions of life vary across different groups. Since a project such as early study abroad is contingent upon the availability of social and material resources, it is practically out of reach for many Korean households, and even for those who can afford it, the specific configurations of early study abroad they take would be significantly different from those of the upper middle class. For example, the class standing of jogi yuhak families often conditions where the child will go for early study abroad (the more costly North America vs. more affordable Southeast Asian countries), how long the child can study abroad (short-term sojourn abroad for quick development of English language skills vs. longer stay to achieve a more comprehensive cosmopolitan education), whether both parents need to be working to bear the financial cost of study abroad, the type of school the child can attend (public schools vs private, international schools), and so on (Kim 2010, Kim and Okazaki 2017), each of which are in turn imagined to have an impact on the outcome and efficacy of the child's study abroad. This variation thus has different effects on the lived experiences of parents and children throughout their transnational trajectory. For less affluent parents who struggle to provide for their children's early study abroad, for instance, the desire for their children's English may be tinged with a greater sense of anxiety and desperation, and the cosmopolitan dreams of self-development that English promises for their children would resonate particularly strongly for them, as such dreams are juxtaposed with their own class anxieties and their own daily struggles.

Park and Abelmann's (2004) account of one working class mother is informative in this regard. Hun's mother had been a worker in an electronics factory for over ten years, and at the time of Park's fieldwork was seeking employment in the private after-school market; her husband, who had also been a factory worker, was working at a relative's butcher shop. Compared to other women with comparable class standing, however, Hun's mother was more active in her investment of her two children's English language education. She had her children participate in English worksheet programs (where students work on academic worksheets, with visits from a teacher to grade them), while very few of her class cohorts did the same. Park and Abelmann state that the educational efforts of Hun's mother is partly explained by her past experiences of working closely with college-educated labor activists; her familiarity with people higher on the class hierarchy than herself instilled in her a stronger sense of cosmopolitan striving for her children. Despite such effort, she was still aware that the investment she is making in her children's English language learning will only have minimal effect in comparison to the investments of more wealthy parents, including actual study abroad. Nonetheless, she displayed and maintained a highly notable desire for English; Park and Abelmann report that "sometimes she dreams that her children might someday live abroad in a 'bigger world'—'even if they have to live abroad as beggars'" (2004:654). Her statement shows that her cosmopolitan striving through English is not only about class aspirations; she clearly recognizes the limitations in her ability to help her children transcend their classed position, and recognizes going abroad in itself does not necessarily mean class mobility. Yet, her statement shows that it is precisely her painful awareness of her own class immobility that makes it particularly desirable to pursue English, which made her limited investments in her children's English language learning meaningful to her. In this sense, the case of Hun's mother is a powerful example of classed inflections of the desire for English.

But still, the case of Hun's mother, along with other examples that we considered, underlines the point that the desire for English in Korean society was not a transparent reflection of the pragmatic utility of the language or the objective power it wields in the world, but rather, a process by which subjectivities of English are formed via the mediation of discursive, material, and political economic conditions. The varying modes of desire for English that people display depending on their class, gender, social networks, and other material conditions show how it was the specific sociopolitical realities of life, instead of inherent underlying value of English itself, that gave rise to such desire. In fact, it was through those conditions that the affective value of English came to be established in Korean society. Korea's transformation toward globalization, in which English served as a prominent sign indexing the possibilities of realizing one's deep underlying potential, led Koreans to position themselves as subjects who orient to the global through the English language, even though what the global entails in terms of concrete life experiences varied significantly according to one's social standing. And by such positioning, Koreans came to align themselves with the logic of human capital development—by embracing the idea of endless economic potential that we all hold, by valorizing endless self-development as a way of excavating that valued capital, and by recognizing English as a language that can make it happen. Inflections of desire across Korean society, thus, point to how a desire for English contributed to the Korean English fever by crafting new subjectivities.

CONCLUSIONS

This chapter started out this book's discussion of how subjectivity mediates the relationship between English and neoliberalism by considering the aspect of desire. By looking at how Koreans' desire for English is rooted in the colonial and postcolonial conditions of Korea's modernization, but deeply reshaped by the social transformations that took place in the context of the country's globalization, the chapter discussed how this reframing of desire was mediated by the ideology of language as pure potential, which allowed desire for English to be mobilized for the neoliberal logic of human capital development. The discussion here helps us see how the pursuit of English in the context of neoliberalism is not simply driven by individuals' zeal about the supposed economic benefits the language can bring, but more fundamentally shaped by subjectivity as a social, political, and material condition; the dreams, hopes, and longings that lead Koreans toward English are shaped by socially grounded beliefs, political economic interests, and relational structures such as class, pointing us to the historical and material basis and political consequences of subjectivity. Remembering this socially constituted nature of desire is important for our purposes, for it provides a ground for investigating how English, not only as a specific language but as a loaded sign, comes to serve as a powerful key for neoliberal subjectification. As English in Korea's neoliberal transformation presents human capital development as a highly natural logic, a desire for English also becomes inseparable from embracement of neoliberal projects of self-development. Tracing this ideological and semiotic process, thus, enables us to see how the idea of English as a language of pure potential, taken for granted in the context of Korea's globalization, cannot be a neutral belief, but one that is deeply rooted in political relations that serve as the basis for neoliberalism. In the next chapter, we push this insight further, but looking at another aspect of subjectivity that drove the pursuit of English in the Korean English fever: the implication of morality that was attributed to the act of English language learning.

CHAPTER 5

Language Learning as Technology of the Self

The Moral Grounding of English

ENGLISH AND INEQUALITY IN NEOLIBERALISM

One of the greatest criticisms against the neoliberal promotion of English worldwide is that it exacerbates socioeconomic inequalities. English as a global language, of course, has always played an important part in the reproduction of inequalities. For instance, in the context of British imperialism, the power of colonial elites and inequalities in local intergroup relations were often sustained through control over access to English (Brutt-Griffler 2002). In many postcolonial societies, differential exposure to English in the education system based on socioeconomic conditions becomes an important foundation for the reproduction of class structure (Ramanathan 2005, Tupas 2019). However, under neoliberalism, as competence in English comes to be seen increasingly as a commodifiable skill and is given greater importance in gatekeeping for education and employment, English is more than ever perceived to be the language of socioeconomic inequality, for the economic capital that the upper class can investment in English language learning now has greater potential for maintaining and widening the gap between them and the rest of society.

This is particularly the case in South Korea. Political scientist Nam Taehyun (2012) sardonically claims that Korea has become an "English class society" (*yeongeo gyegeup sahoe*)—that is, a society in which one's class position is determined by one's competence in English. The widespread emphasis on English across society, he argues, gives the wealthy upper class an unfair advantage, as they are able to use their economic power to access the most valued opportunities for English language learning, while the inability of the lower class

In Pursuit of English. Joseph Sung-Yul Park, Oxford University Press. © Oxford University Press 2021.
DOI: 10.1093/oso/9780190855734.003.0005

to afford such opportunities greatly diminishes their hope of social mobility through education and employment. Nam is certainly not alone in making such arguments, as it is a widely shared perception among Koreans that English is a source of growing social inequality. As economist Kim Heesam notes, "if competence in English is determined by one's family background such as parents' wealth and education or the English language learning infrastructure of one's place of residence, and if competence in English serves as a gatekeeping criterion for critical moments of life such as school admission, graduation, employment, and promotion, then this can only strengthen the tendency in which parents' socioeconomic status is passed down to their children through investment in English" (2011:165).

The significant difference in the amount and type of investments made in English language learning between socioeconomic classes illustrates this point saliently. A 2015 report by Statistics Korea, the Korean government's statistics office, shows that households with a monthly income over 70 million Korean won (~61,000 US dollars) spend an average of 139,000 Korean won (~121 US dollars) a month on their children's extracurricular English language learning, compared to households that make less than 1 million Korean won (~880 US dollars), who spend an average of 16,000 Korean won (~14 US dollars), indicating more than an 8 times difference (Statistics Korea 2015). These numbers vastly understate the gap in investment in English language learning between classes, however, as they only show money spent in the private after-school education market. Attending specialized schools, such as foreign language high schools, which provide greater instruction in English and have emerged as the new elite schools that offer a significant advantage in admission into prestigious universities, costs considerably more. Whereas attending ordinary public schools for primary and secondary education would cost around 13.4 million Korean won (~11,700 US dollars) over 12 years, attending the most prestigious specialized schools would cost 140 million Korean won (~122,600 US dollars), making it prohibitive for many students (Nam 2012:161). If we consider the fact that the upper class also pursue early study abroad in English-speaking countries such as the United States as a strategy for their children's English language learning, the gap in the investment in English becomes even larger.

In a context where opportunities for English language learning that are considered the most efficacious are also sharply differentiated by their cost, and as practices such as early study abroad that require significant financial support are actively embraced and used by the upper class as a strategy for reproduction of class privilege and capital accumulation (Shin 2014, M. Lee 2016, Song 2018), it is not surprising to find contestations about the value of the English acquired through such means. Even though English acquired through sojourn abroad is widely considered to be the only way through which Koreans can acquire authentic "native-like" English, there is also a view that negatively evaluates such competence in English when it is seen as acquired through class-based privilege or eliteness (Choi 2007). It is worth noting that such devaluing is often done on moral grounds. For instance, the study abroad student needs to confront the suspicion of others who may see her as an escapee—a Korean who went on early study abroad solely based on her class privilege because she lacked the discipline or determination to make it in the competitive Korean system (Lo and Choi 2017, Lo and Kim 2015). Also, middle-class parents who accompany their children abroad may make much effort to differentiate themselves from other more affluent transnational Koreans who pursue early study abroad for their children, as a way of countering potential moral charges that they are overzealous parents who have spent exorbitant amounts of money overseas for their children's education without considering the classed and cultural implications of early study abroad (Song 2012, 2018).

Such awareness of and tension surrounding the role of English in reproducing inequalities of class suggests that the neoliberal promotion of English does not simply consist of holding out promises that one can gain material wealth and move up the ladder of socioeconomic class through English. The prevalence of such criticism points to the complexity of the logical structure of the Korean English fever. Even though Koreans invest in English because it is demanded in the labor market, their recognition that the system of English language learning constitutes an uneven playing field means that they do not necessarily subscribe to naive dreams of getting rich through English; but at the same time, their continued investment in English also means the allure of English is not entirely falsified, despite the implications of inequality that English obviously represents. An important question, then, is to understand how the neoliberal logic of the market incorporates such critiques of inequality to rationalize the way English serves as a fulcrum in the reproduction of class interests. If neoliberalism valorizes English as the ultimate key for self-realization in the changing new economy, how does it reconcile this vision with the fact that English widens and solidifies the gap between the English haves and have-nots as defined by socioeconomic class?

In this chapter, I examine the role of subjectivity in this process. In particular, I focus on morality as a key for the rationalization of inequalities inherent in the neoliberal promotion of English. My discussion centers on how, throughout the Korean English fever, such inequalities were dissimulated through a sense of morality that was infused into the act of English language learning. Discourses about English that circulated in Korea in the late 1990s and early 2000s presented privileged learners' investments in English as evidence of a responsible act of self-care and self-development, instead of a site for the reproduction of their privilege. I argue that such reframing of English language learning in terms of moral responsibility was crucial in justifying the growing emphasis on English in Korean society and in responding to its widely recognized implications for inequality. Moral positioning of English-speaking elites has long been an important way through which class-based privilege in postcolonial contexts is rationalized, as charges that local elites use their class status to collude with colonial power through English are countered by claiming the moral uprightness of those elites, for instance, as demonstrated through their distinguished competence, nationalist orientation, or responsible modes of consumption (Jahan and Hamid 2019, Reyes 2017). What I show in this chapter, however, is how such valorization of English-speaking elites take up a new significance in the context of neoliberalism, as the moral construction of such elites also works to contribute to the rationalization of neoliberalism and its promotion of English.

As an illustration of this, this chapter turns to the early period of the Korean English fever, during which the conservative press aggressively promoted the importance of English in globalization. In those years, the conservative Korean newspaper media, whose interests closely aligned with the jaebeol, frequently published reports on Koreans who have managed to become fluent and competent speakers of English. By analyzing how those successful learners, many of whom had privileged class backgrounds, were represented in such reports, I argue that these "success stories" of English language learning constructed those elite learners as moral figures of personhood (Agha 2007), who did not rely on their class privilege for the acquisition of English but invested strenuous and responsible effort in their language learning to transform themselves into good speakers of English. I suggest that this illustrates how, in neoliberalism, learning English is transformed into a *technology of the self* (Foucault 1997) through which we mold ourselves as ethical subjects, obscuring its nature as a strategy for class reproduction that only those with sufficient economic resources may successfully exploit.

MORALITY AND TECHNOLOGIES OF THE SELF

As an aspect of subjectivity, morality—our committed sense of what is "good" or "right"—intersects in an important way with political economy. While dominant neoclassical views of the economy, with its focus on rational maximization of utility and profit, tempt us to consider the economic as a domain free from matters of morality, key theorists of capitalism have continuously emphasized the moral and ethical dimension of political economic configurations. Max Weber's (2001[1930]) classic study of the role of the new Protestant ethic in the emergence of capitalism is a prime example of this. According to Weber, Calvinism's validation of material wealth as a sign of salvation led to a view of capital accumulation not as greed but as virtue, spurring a new work ethic that encouraged entrepreneurship and accumulation of capital. In other words, the rise of capitalism was accompanied and facilitated by a profound moral shift, in which a new conviction and ethical assurance supported individuals' political and economic actions (Browne 2009). Examples like this illustrate how cultivation of a sense of what constitutes good vs. bad contributes to the shaping of economic relations as well as rationalization of those relations.

Indeed, constructing particular economic structures as good, virtuous, and honorable is a powerful way of legitimizing them and obscuring the inequalities they produce. In neoliberalism, where unequal distribution of wealth and opportunities is highly intensified, this is a particularly important issue. Thus, initiatives of neoliberalism are commonly framed in moral terms, in a way that masks the inequalities that ground those initiatives. For instance, in her discussion of how "communication" is foregrounded in the neoliberal workplace as a moral mode of management that cares for employees' self-esteem and empowerment, Cohen (2015) observes that this, "like many prior versions of work reform, is an attempt to reconcile the evident inequalities of the capitalist corporation with egalitarian ideals without challenging fundamental inequities of the larger capitalist system," and for this reason, "as with earlier efforts, it can only ever have limited reach" (p.335). But it is also important to note that such invocation of morality does not merely attempt to cover up unequal implications of neoliberalism, but seeks to rationalize neoliberalism by making it a matter of subjectivity. That is, framing neoliberal transformations in terms of morality is to construct particular kinds of subjects, who, driven by their moral impulses and dispositions, are made to willingly align with the ideals of neoliberalism, rather than questioning and contesting them.

Foucault's notion of technologies of the self (1997) can be useful in tracing this process. In Foucault's view, governmentality lies at the intersection of two types of technologies, which he respectively calls technologies of power (or technology of domination) and technologies of the self. Technologies of domination "determine the conduct of individuals and submit them to certain ends or domination" (p.225). Examples of these may include technologies that are developed to control and discipline the bodies of subjects in prisons and asylums, which were highlighted in Foucault's early work. In contrast, technologies of the self "permit individuals to effect by their own means, or with the help of others, a certain number of operations on their own bodies and souls, thoughts, conduct, and way of being, so as to transform themselves in order to attain a certain state of happiness, purity, wisdom, perfection, or immortality" (p.255). For instance, religious practices of confession of sin lead us to reflect on ourselves, behaviors, and thoughts and to further modify our own practices according to the guiding principles of our faith. The point about governmentality, Foucault argues, is how these two technologies come together—how the way in which "the individuals are driven by others is tied to the way they conduct themselves" (Foucault 1993:203). It was such thinking that led Foucault's later work to shift its focus from truth and power to ethics; insofar as technologies of self presuppose a responsible subject involved in the care of the self, these technologies are also moral technologies.

Neoliberal governmentality foregrounds technologies of the self, for the withdrawal of the state from welfare and increasing flexibility and insecurity of work require subjects to take up more responsibility for themselves. As Lemke (2001:201) argues:

> The strategy of rendering individual subjects 'responsible' (and also collectives, such as families, associations, etc.) entails shifting the responsibility for social risks such as illness, unemployment, poverty, etc., and for life in society into the domain for which the individual is responsible and transforming it into a problem of 'self-care.' The key feature of the neo-liberal rationality is the congruence it endeavours to achieve between a responsible and moral individual and an economic-rational actor. It aspires to construct prudent subjects whose moral quality is based on the fact that they rationally assess the costs and benefits of a certain act as opposed to other alternative acts.

In other words, through technologies of the self, inequalities of neoliberalism are not simply glossed over, but transformed into the responsibility of the individual (or isolated collectives such as families), who now have the moral responsibility to engage in care for the self, so as to not burden society through their dependence on welfare or community support.

As I will show in the rest of this chapter, a similar dimension of morality became prominent in rationalizing the neoliberal promotion of English in Korea. In the context of Korea's English fever, the existence of class-based inequalities of Korean society, which were commonly considered as a cause of unequal access to opportunities for English language learning and differential acquisition of valued skills in English, was not denied. In fact, debates over how to address such inequalities were a central point of contention within the Korean English fever. What we find, instead, is a reframing of the nature of such inequalities. Instead of an indicator of the unjust and unfair implications of the neoliberal valorization of English, such inequalities became a mere backdrop for highlighting the active effort that privileged learners invested in their English language learning, thereby revaluing those privileged learners of English as moral subjects and neoliberalism as a moral system. Imagination of English language learning as a technology of self was crucial to this process, as I demonstrate in the rest of this chapter.

SUCCESS STORIES OF ENGLISH LANGUAGE LEARNING IN THE CONSERVATIVE PRESS

One of the actors that played a central role in the promotion of English in the early stages of the Korean English fever was the conservative press, especially the three major newspaper companies, *Chosun Ilbo*, *Joongang Ilbo*, and

Donga Ilbo, collectively referred to as *Cho-Joong-Dong*. The conservative press maintains a strong alliance with the capitalist class and dominant political parties, together forming the conservative ruling bloc that has long held a monopoly of political and economic power for most of Korea's recent history. Though conservatism in Korea is a complicated notion (Kang Jung-In 2005), the conservative press is "conservative" in the sense that it strongly defends the status quo of Korean society through its anti-socialist, pro-US, and pro-jaebeol stances. The conservative press is not simply a mouthpiece of the political right, however. Though their influence is now declining due to the growth of alternative news platforms based on digital and social media as well as the expansion of the liberal political base, Cho-Joong-Dong collectively occupied over 75% share of the newspaper market in Korea during the first decade of the 21st century (An 2006). They continue to exert an enormous influence on the general populace, functioning as a dominant mobilizer of public opinion and a monopolistic capitalist power in itself (Kang 2005).

Such political influence of the conservative media was crucial in transforming the public view of English in Korean society. The conservative press actively propagated the neoliberal discourse of globalization promoted by the government and jaebeol groups, of which the imagination of English as a global language was an integral part (Shin 2018a). In 1998, Chosun Ilbo initiated a public language policy debate on whether English should be made an official language of Korea so as to allow the country to participate more actively in the global stage. The debate generated much controversy, and led to widespread perception of the importance of English as a necessary language of globalization (Park 2009). In 2000, Chosun also launched a campaign called *Yeongeoga gyeonjaenglyeokida* ('English is competitiveness'), which emphasized the importance of English for Korea's survival in the modern world. Through this campaign, it was repeatedly argued that Korea must invest heavily in improving its citizens' English language skills, claiming that in areas such as diplomacy and international business, Korea was facing great losses due to inadequate competence in English and lack of English-friendly infrastructure. These examples show how the conservative press supplied its readership with a barrage of articles that constantly emphasized the importance of English for national and individual competitiveness. And given the widespread influence of the conservative press in Korean society, it is not surprising that such promotion of English contributed significantly to the heightening of the English fever. It was only after the mid-2000s, when English became fully integrated into the structure of neoliberalism and when it achieved a truly hegemonic position in Korean society, that the flow of such articles started to let down (though the media continued to serve as a channel for the circulation of discourses that linked English with global talent that Korea's economy requires; see Shin 2018a and Shin 2018b for detailed discussion).

One important genre of articles that the conservative press published during this early period of the English fever was what I will call *success stories of English language learning*. These are reports about Koreans who have managed to become a fluent and competent speaker of English, written either from the perspective of the journalist or as a self-report from the successful learner, typically consisting of some demonstration of the person's admirable competence in English (often evidenced by the learner's cosmopolitanism and frequent interaction with native speakers of English) followed by an account of how the person has come to be so successful in acquiring the language. Such success stories often implicitly encouraged people to take those successful learners as models for their acquisition efforts. In the case of first-person success stories, for instance, a successful learner-author would often claim to share his or her secret "methods that work" so that the reader could also be as successful in mastering English.

That the success stories as a genre played a central role in the conservative press's efforts to promote the importance of English can be seen from the fact that those stories appeared with a much higher concentration during the early years of the English fever. The 2000 *Chosun* campaign mentioned above, for instance, made heavy use of this genre. Through a weekly column titled *Yeongeoui dalin* ('masters of English'), which accompanied other articles that constituted the 9-month campaign, 23 different successful learners were featured, contrasting their competence with the lamentable incompetence of other Koreans. In contrast, similar stories were virtually absent from the press that represented the "progressive media," such as *Hangyoreh* or *Kyunghyang Sinmun*, which often took a critical stance toward the growing English fever as well as Korea's neoliberalization. This evidences how the success stories were not simply neutral reports on newsworthy individuals but reflected the political role that the conservative press played in Korea's neoliberal transformation.

The discourse of English circulated by the conservative press, then, played an important role in establishing the link between English and neoliberalism, by advocating the interests of powerful actors in Korean society that were deeply invested in the country's neoliberal transformation. The conservative press gave an explicit voice to the state's concern with enhancing Korea's economic competitiveness through its emphasis on English as a key for the country's economic survival in the global economy. They also supported the interests of the jaebeol by arguing for the need of workers with good competence in English who can serve on the front lines of their expansion into the global market. This allowed the conservative press to maintain their alignment with powerful actors of Korean society, strengthening their position of influence and, in some cases, also to directly benefit from their investment in the English language teaching market. Chosun Ilbo, for instance, partnered in 2001 with Seoul National University to develop a standardized test for English proficiency called TEPS (Test of English Proficiency developed by Seoul National University), thereby acquiring a stake in the booming English testing industry through its subsidiary EduCS.

The prominence of success stories of English language learning as a genre, however, shows that the role of the conservative press in the neoliberal promotion of English does not stop there. Because the success stories were not abstract arguments about the importance of English, but foregrounded real individuals as exemplars of successful English language learning, they had the effect of tying broader arguments about the importance of English in the neoliberal economy to a specific image of an ideal English language learner. In other words, they served as a site for connecting English with a specific figure of personhood (Agha 2007). In this case, the figure of the successful learner of English was an elite English learner who was also a moral figure—a person who did not rely on his or her pre-given privilege but made an honest and strenuous effort to acquire good competence in English. Through such mediatized characters (Agha 2011, Androutsopoulos 2016), Koreans came to imagine and understand their relationship with English in more concrete, subjective terms, and this served as one channel through which English language learning became infused with moral significance. It was this dimension of morality which allowed the success stories to function as tales of neoliberal personhood that rationalized class-based inequalities of English language learning. Through these stories, the conservative press was therefore able to do much more than promote the pragmatic utility of English—it was able to perpetuate the perception that investment in English language learning is a moral way of being in a neoliberal world.

THE SUCCESSFUL LEARNER OF ENGLISH AS A MORAL FIGURE

To demonstrate how the success stories reframed class-based inequalities of English language learning in terms of morality, let us turn to a brief analysis based on a collection of success stories of English language learning that appeared in Korean newspapers and news magazines, a total of 60 articles that were published during the early phase of the Korean English fever (1999–2007), gathered through continuous monitoring of major newspapers and magazines as well as regular searches using the online news database KINDS (http://www.kinds.or.kr). The first thing that is noticeable here is that the stories do not deny the indexical connection between class and English. In fact, they actively construct the figure of the successful learner as a social elite through multiple emblems that index social status.

For instance, the success stories often locate the successful learner within a socioeconomic matrix in terms of their occupation or educational background, highlighting how the learner is highly educated or holds a prestigious social position. The most common occupations of the successful learners represented in the data are academics (e.g., professors at Yeonsei University and Korea University, both among the most prestigious institutions in Korea), top-level managers of major corporations (e.g., CEOs of companies such as LG and Korean Air), professionals in journalism and broadcasting, especially those working for global news media companies (e.g., reporters for Korean branches of CNN and Bloomberg), and high-ranking government officials and diplomats (e.g., deputy prime minister and minister of science and technology). The only major occupation group represented in the data that does not fit this mold is that of language teachers; in the data, successful learners belonging to this group are typically famous and popular 'star' instructors at private language institutes.

The success stories also provide detailed information on the successful learner's social background, such as the connections the learner may have with other influential people, as a way of foregrounding their social status. More importantly, such elite connections are frequently offered as an explanation of one's good competence in English. For instance, in the following extract, Hur Chulboo, a professor at Myongji University, recounts his connections with numerous elite members of Korean society, who are also described as *chuljunghan yeongeoui dalin* ('exceptional masters of English'). In this case, the influential social positions that these speakers later achieved is used as evidence of their "qualification and competence to represent Korea" and also indirectly of the quality of their competence in English—which in turn attributes equivalent competence to the author as well, due to the fact that he was a co-participant in the event with these successful learners.

서울의 10개 대학에서 30명이 선발된 영어독서·토론모임에 참가, 한국 최초의 대학생 대표로 미국에서 개최된 학생대회에 참석했다. 당시 학생대표 30명 중에는 아웅산에서 서거한 대통령 경제특보 김재익씨, 전 과기부장관 이태섭씨, 전 중앙대 경영대학장 송용섭 교수, 덕성여대 인문대학장 최은경 교수 등이 있었다. 그곳에 모인 서울 10개 대학 대표들은 모두 출중한 영어의 달인이었고 국제회의에서 한국을 대표하기에 충분한 자격과 영어구사능력을 갖추고 있었다.

I participated in an English reading and discussion group that consisted of 30 students selected from 10 universities in Seoul, and later participated in a student conference in the U.S. as one of the first Korean student representatives. Among those 30 student representatives were Kim Jae-Ik, the economic advisor to the president who was killed in the Rangoon bombing;[1] Li Tae-Seop, ex-Minister of Science and Technology; Song Yong-Seop, ex-dean of Joongang University School of Management; and Choi Eun-Kyeong, Deokseong Women's University's Dean of Humanities. All representatives from the 10 universities were exceptional masters of English, and had the qualification and competence to represent Korea in the international meeting. [Sindonga, June 2001]

In other cases, the learner's family background is highlighted as an index of elite status. For instance, in the following example, which comes from a report on a high school student whose good competence is demonstrated through her perfect score in TOEIC (in a time when such high scores were rare; see Chapter 8), the fact that her parents are scholars is highlighted as an "interesting fact," thereby underlining her class membership.

재미있는 것은, 김양의 부친인 동아대 김성언교수가 한문학자라는 사실. [...] 알고보니 김양의 모친인 김상희씨(부산대 강사)가 불어학을 전공한 학자였다.

One interesting fact is that Miss Kim's father, Professor Kim Seong-Eon at Donga University, is a scholar of Chinese Literature. . . . It turns out that Miss Kim's mother Kim Sang-Hui (lecturer at Pusan University) is a scholar who majored in French linguistics. [Sindonga, June 1999]

The social status of successful learners is also indexed through their experiences abroad. As noted above, since living or studying overseas (in English-speaking countries) requires better access to material resources and opportunities, having such an experience functions as an index of higher social status, as well as cosmopolitanism. In the following example, the overseas experience of the successful learner, who is a reporter for Bloomberg, indexes her class background, as the opportunities that led her to travel frequently since her youth implies a more privileged middle-class upbringing.

사업차 해외출장이 잦은 아버지를 따라 대여섯살부터 외국 여행할 기회가 많았고, 푸른 눈의 또래 아이들과 이야기를 나누고 싶은 마음에 영어에 관심을 갖게 됐다. 워낙 호기심이 많아서인지 영어를 자꾸 배워나가는 게 즐거웠고, 방학이나 휴가 때마다 여행을 다니며 외국인 친구들을 사귀기 시작하면서 영어가 생활의 일부가 됐다.

Because her father often traveled overseas for business, she had many opportunities to go abroad since she was five or six-years old. Her desire to communicate with the blue-eyed children that she met sparked her interest in English.

---

1. In this 1983 incident, top-level cabinet members and advisors accompanying the then-president Chun Doo Hwan in an official visit to Myanmar were killed in an assassination attempt against the president.

Because of her curiosity, she enjoyed learning English. She would travel overseas whenever she had a vacation or break, and as she made more foreign friends, English started to become a part of her life. [Chosun Ilbo, May 12, 2000]

Such emphasis on the featured learner's social status, then, might seem to suggest that the success stories simply reify the dominant indexical association between English and social class that exists in Korean society. However, the success stories also modulate this indexical connection to present a more complex picture of the relationship between the class position and English language competence of the successful learner.

First, despite the widespread discourse that promotes English as a language that promises better economic opportunities for those without privilege, the success stories virtually never present the successful learner as an example of upward class mobility. That is, there is no case in the data in which a Korean learner of English is described to have moved from a lower to higher social class through her newly gained competence in English. Though the possibility of class mobility through English is not explicitly denied, none of the stories in the data explain the featured learner's social positioning as attained through English; instead, either the successful learner is presented as inherently belonging to a privileged class (by virtue of their family background, for instance, as in the two previous examples above), or the previous class positioning of the learner is simply not mentioned at all. This observation is perhaps unsurprising, if we take a critical perspective toward the supposed promise of English (see also Chapter 8); that one can achieve upward class mobility just by acquiring good competence in English is patently false, since who can have access to good opportunities for learning English and who gets to be seen as a competent speaker of English is already inflected by one's class standing, as already discussed. However, there is reason to believe that the lack of examples of upward class mobility through English in the data is not simply due to the lack of such cases in the real world, but due to the specific way in which the success stories construct the relationship between class and successful acquisition of good English, which takes us to the second observation.

This second point is that, while it is a common belief in Korean society that good competence in English is more likely to be found among the upper class, the success stories often deny this. Even though the successful learners are represented as privileged elites, the potential role of such privilege in the learners' acquisition of English is frequently erased in the data, and it is denied that there is a causal relationship between the privileges of successful learners and their competence in English. For instance, in the success stories, it is often explicitly argued that most elites in Korean society actually possess only weak competence in English, reflecting the dominant ideology of self-deprecation that views all Koreans as bad speakers of English (Park 2009; see also Chapter 3). Thus, in effect, while the elite status of the successful learner is noted, it is denied that such status may be the source of her English, as it is not acknowledged as a sufficient condition for good competence. An example of this can be seen in an article on political scientist and university professor Moon Chung-In. Here, the article presents the featured learner's competence in English as exceptional by drawing upon the commonly circulated image of Koreans as incompetent speakers of English, suggesting that even US-educated scholars typically struggle to speak English and suffer from great anxiety:

많은 미국박사들이 기초회화를 하거나 전문서적을 읽는 데에는 별 어려움이 없다. 그러나 우리말 하듯 자유자재로 미국학자들과 토론하고, 때로는 치열하게 논쟁까지 벌이며, 우리말로 쓰듯 '고뇌 없이' 영어논문을 쓸 수 있는 이는 그리 많지 않다. 남부끄러워 내놓고 말은 못 하지만, 우리나라 학자들 중에는 국제회의에 참석해서 '그놈의 영어 때문에' 꿀먹은 벙어리처럼 앉아만 있다가, 혹은 아주 '불만족스러운' 코멘트 한 마디로 만족하고 돌아온 경험이 있는 이가 적지 않고, 개중에는 "영어 한번 속시원히 잘해보는 게 소원"이라고 토로하는 이도 많다. 연세대 문정인 교수는 그런 점에서 특이한 존재다.

Many scholars with doctoral degrees from the US have no difficulty in basic conversation or reading specialist books. However, there are not many people who can engage in discussions with American scholars, debating with them fiercely, or who can write articles in English 'without anguish' as they do in Korean. Though they are ashamed to admit it, many scholars who attend international conferences cannot speak a word because of 'darned English' or have to be satisfied with making a single 'unsatisfactory' comment and return. There are also many who confess that being able to speak English fluently is their greatest wish. Professor Moon Chung-In of Yonsei University is exceptional in this regard. [Sindonga, June 1999]

Similarly, while we have seen above that many stories highlight the successful learner's experience abroad, they are also careful not to present it as the reason for her of his good competence. Thus, if the successful learner does not actually have any experience abroad, this is frequently highlighted in the texts through adjectives such as *sunsu guknaesan* ("pure home-grown") or *suntojong* ("pure local"), which underline that the learner's acquisition of English took place domestically. In fact, the stories often explicitly argue that living and studying overseas is not necessary for one to attain good competence in English. They even claim that, even if one has experience living overseas, that experience must be accompanied by serious effort for learning English in order to lead to success. This can be seen from the following example about Son Jiae, a reporter for CNN, which explicitly states that "language skills easily 'evaporate' [i.e. are easily lost] when not continuously sharpened, even if one has learned it as a child," and uses this as the basis for attributing the featured learner's success to her tenacious effort to further develop her competence in English, rather than her privileged background that allowed her to live abroad at early age.

남보기에는 쉽게 척척 잘도 하는 것 같아도, "하루 종일 공부해야 겨우 체면만 유지한다"는 말이 엄살이 아니다. "부모님 따라 미국에서 초등학교 2학년부터 6학년까지 살았어요. 덕분에 영어와 일찍 친해지기는 했죠." 그러나 어렸을 때 말을 배웠다 해도 그냥 놔두면 금방 '날아가 버리는' 게 언어 감각이다. 그래서 "부모 덕에 얻은 영어 실력을 잃어버리지 않으려고 영어에 '목숨을 걸고' 공부 했다"고 말한다. 중학교 들어가선 영어 웅변대회를 찾아다니며 참가했고, 고등 학교 대학교 때는 영자 신문사에서 일했다.

She is not exaggerating when she says, "I study all day and I'm barely able to save face," even though it looks like she speaks English effortlessly. "I lived with my parents in the US from second to sixth grade in elementary school. So I became familiar with English early on." But language skills easily "evaporate" when not continuously sharpened, even if one has learned it as a child. For this reason, she says, she studied English "as if her life depended on it", so that she would not lose the competence in English that she gained thanks to her parents. In middle school, she actively sought out English speech contests to participate in, and in high school and college she worked for the school English newspaper. [Chosun Ilbo, January 1, 2000]

Even though many good language learners would indeed demonstrate serious effort in learning the target language, examples like this are remarkable because they stand in explicit contrast to the popular discourses of English, in which most Koreans typically assume that classed privileges—such as experience of living overseas at an early age—function as crucial preconditions for good competence in English, as noted above.

If it is consistently denied that the successful learner's class-based privilege serves as the source of her good competence, then, how do the success stories account for the learner's successful English language learning? The data show that the stories frequently attribute good competence in English to the moral character of the featured learner as demonstrated through her intense effort for learning English. We have already seen in the previous example how Son is depicted as displaying strong initiative and will in making calculated investments of time and effort in language learning, "as if her life depended on it"—instead of relying on the English language skills she gained as a child and simply living off of it. Indeed, the featured learner's nearly superhuman efforts in studying English is a common element of the stories, as they frequently emphasize the intensity of their English language learning as highly exceptional and as something that cannot be easily mimicked by ordinary people. For instance, descriptions such as the following are common:

"사춘기 내내 영어랑 사랑에 빠져 지냈습니다. 영어 웅변 대회 출전, 교내 영어 회화반 활동은 기본이었고 대학시절엔 헤르메스(hermes)라는 영어 통역 서클도 만들었습니다." 해외 유학은커녕 연수도 가본 적 없지만, 아침에 일어날 때부터 잠잘 때까지 한국말을 단 한마디도 안한 적도 많았다. 한마디로 영어에 미쳤던 시절이었다.

"When I was a teenager, I was in love with English. Not only did I participate in English speech contests and join English conversation classes at school, but I also organized an English interpretation club called Hermes in college." Even though he never studied in a foreign country or spent time overseas for English study, there were many days during which he never spoke a word of Korean from the time he woke up until he went to bed. In short, he was crazy about English those days. [Chosun Ilbo, January 3, 2000]

In this example, the learner (a manager at a major corporation) is represented as demonstrating exceptional self-management in maintaining an intense regimen of activities to enhance his English language skills. In addition to the initiative he took in participating in a range of activities at school, the claim that he "never spoke a word of Korean from the time he woke up until he went to bed" (while living in Korea with its predominant monolingualism in Korean, no less) presents him as a character with great determination and will.

That the depiction of such effort is not merely a factual report of the learner's investment in English but an active discursive construction can be seen from the success stories' frequent use of evaluative vocabulary (Labov 1972a). Extraordinariness of the learners' effort is often highlighted through lexical expressions that indicate that an action is carried out to the extreme. The following sentences, taken from various stories, illustrate two of these expressions, *daldal* 'thouroughly' and *tongjjaelo* 'wholly/in its entirety.'

daldal

영화 한편 6번씩 보며 주요대사 <u>달달</u> 외웠죠.
I watched each movie 6 times and memorized the important lines <u>thoroughly</u>. [Chosun Ilbo, January 21, 2000]

상황에 알맞은 유머를 구사하기 위해 영어 문장들을 <u>달달</u> 외우곤 했다.
In order to use humorous expressions in appropriate situations, he would memorize English sentences <u>thoroughly</u>. [Chosun Ilbo, February 25, 2000]

그는 평소 영어 포켓북을 하나 들고 다니며 틈이 날 때마다 <u>달달</u> 외운다.
He carries around a pocket book of English expressions and <u>thoroughly</u> memorizes them whenever he has time. [Wolgan Joongang, March 31, 2007]

tongjjaelo

> 미국인들의 "새로운 생활현장 영어"를 <u>통째로</u> 암기하고 반드시 사용하는 습관
> 을 가지고 있다.
> He has the habit of <u>wholly</u> memorizing and using "recent everyday expressions"
> that Americans use. [Chosun Ilbo, February 10, 2000]

> 문장 <u>통째로</u> 외우기, 한 문장 500회 읽기 등의 집요한 노력으로 국내 각종 영어
> 경시대회를 휩쓸었다.
> Through his tenacious effort such as memorizing <u>whole</u> sentences and reading
> a sentence 500 times, he swept prizes at numerous English contests in Korea.
> [Jugan Chosun, October 5, 2000]

> 문장을 <u>통째로</u> 외우니 영어 공부의 길이 훤히 열렸어요.
> Memorizing sentences <u>wholly</u> opened the door to studying English for me.
> [Joongang Ilbo, March 22, 2006]

The addition of adverbs *daldal* and *tongjjaelo* shifts the focus of an otherwise neutral sentence to the intensity of the learner's effort. As we can see in the examples here, both adverbs typically combine with the verb *oeuda* 'memorize,' thereby emphasizing sheer repetition and completeness of the learner's mnemonic project. Ironically, in popular discourses of English in Korea, rote memorization is commonly criticized as one of the vices of Korea's traditional curriculum of English language teaching and a prime reason why Koreans can't speak English well. In the success stories, however, the featured learners' investment in rote memorization is not presented as an ineffective and inefficient mode of language learning, but as a demonstration of the learner's indomitable will to master English. Evaluative vocabulary in the above examples contributes to this reframing, highlighting the extraordinary nature of the successful learners' effort, thereby constructing them as deserving subjects whose good competence is the reward for their persistent commitment to English language learning.

The figure of personhood attributed to the successful learner of English in the success stories, then, has a prominent moral quality. In the success stories, the successful learner is a character who is associated with a privileged background, as indexed through family provenance, educational qualifications, or social networks. But this figure is also shown not to rely on that privilege to acquire good English, instead owing her good competence purely to her own extraordinary effort. The moral nature of this figure is therefore manifest on two levels. First, the successful learner does not profiteer on her privilege, and thus is free from the charges that the upper class has an unwarranted advantage due to their access to valued opportunities for English language learning. Second, the successful learner engages in careful, rigorous, and responsible management of her own English language learning, thereby deserving both her good competence in English and her privileged social position. Through this framing, the successful learners' elite status and their good competence in English are both transformed into indices of their superior moral caliber. That is, good competence in English is no longer an index of the featured learner's privileged status, but a reflection of a deeper characteristic of what makes these learners elites—their constitution as ethical and responsible subjects.

This illustrates how the aspect of morality becomes an important means of rationalizing the implications of inequality that are saliently associated with the neoliberal promotion of English. By acknowledging the privileged status of successful learners, the stories do not deny the material conditions of unequal access to opportunities for English language learning. Instead, they divert the attention of the readers to the inner, moral qualities of the successful learner as an individual, so that structural conditions of inequality take a backseat to the extraordinary effort that the learner has demonstrated regardless of her privilege. If the successful learner is driven by strict moral principles, then there is no need to resent the privilege she has; her privileged social status merely serves as another index of her praiseworthy character, instead of a reminder of the unfair mechanism of gatekeeping that English entails. In short, as successful learners are reified as moral figures, the neoliberal promotion of English is bleached of its unjust implications. It is in this way that morality plays a key role in resolving the contradiction between the neoliberal celebration of English as the ultimate language for unbounded self-realization and widespread criticism of stratified access to English.

ENGLISH LANGUAGE LEARNING AS TECHNOLOGY OF SELF

The discussion above shows how the dimension of morality can work to obscure the inequalities underlying the neoliberal promotion of English. By representing elite learners of English as moral figures, success stories in the conservative press deny the effects of class-based inequalities that condition the acquisition of English, thereby justifying any advantage those learners may gain through the English they acquired with the help of their privilege. The important point about the success stories, however, is not just that they present elite learners of English in a positive light, but that they reframe the significance of English language learning itself. By depicting the successful learners' effort for learning English as responsible management of oneself, the success stories define English language learning as a moral activity of self-care, and it is through this reframing that subjectivity comes to play a truly powerful role in rationalizing the inequalities of English in neoliberalism.

The emphasis that the success stories place on the elite learner's intense effort and initiative as well as their refusal to rely on their privilege conveys a message that English language learning is not just about acquisition of a skill that is valued in the job market. It is more about attitude, an embodied perspective on life, a way of being—for what defines the successful learners as praiseworthy is not their English language competence per se (which in itself could be attained through one's privileged access to valuable opportunities for learning English), but the way they do not take that competence for granted and continuously manage their time, their bodies, and their practices to further enhance their English language skills. In this way, English language learning is highlighted as a technology of the self, through which the successful learners exercise care of themselves to responsibly manage the value of their human capital, as indexed by their English language skills. The fierce commitment to continuous self-development they demonstrate as language learners makes them ideal stewards of their own human capital, and by presenting those learners as elites with desirable social characteristics, the success stories valorize English language learning as a moral responsibility of neoliberal subjects.

The success stories' denial of the link between classed privilege and successful acquisition of English obviously does not lead their readers to completely forget that link, as criticism toward the inequalities exacerbated by the neoliberal promotion of English continues to be raised, as we saw at the beginning of this chapter. The stories' reframing of English language learning into a technology of the self, however, potentially leads readers to reconceptualize the act of learning English, in part due to the way it aligns with the prevailing image of the ideal subject promoted under neoliberalism. Neoliberalism places increasing demand on workers to engage in continuous self-development and self-improvement, and frames this as a moral imperative; they have the ethical responsibility to take part in conscientious care of the valuable human capital that they each embody, and to not let that go to waste by falling back upon discourses that appeal to welfare or equality. The figure of personhood attributed to the successful learners closely overlaps with this ideal image of the neoliberal subject, but grounds that figure within the concrete activity of English language learning. In other words, the success stories present intense and endless investment in English language learning as the ultimate technology of the self that neoliberal subjects must pursue, regardless of one's own class position or one's stance toward the inequalities of English.

Indeed, in neoliberal Korea, English is no longer seen as one of many strategies that a person may choose (or not) to enhance one's value in the educational or job market, but an absolute requirement; having strong competence in another language, say, Chinese, does not exempt one from the responsibility to engage in continuous investment in English. In their discussion of how contemporary Korean university students embody the image of ideal neoliberal subjecthood, Abelmann, Park, and Kim (2009) state that "the present college generation is deeply committed to a cosmopolitan ideal in which people are able to circulate in a wide and increasingly global arena. At the heart of this personal development project is English mastery and many students described English as a necessary 'base'" (p.230). By identifying English as a *beiseu* ('base'), the students are not simply referring to the fact that English becomes unavoidable because of the prevalent use of English as an assessment method in the white-collar job market; they are pointing out how studying English now serves as the most fundamental index that demonstrates one's alignment with the neoliberal desire for self-realization in the global world (as discussed in Chapter 4). In this context, lacking competence in English or neglecting to continuously improve one's skills in English comes to stand for a lax moral attitude.

The true power of the success stories, then, must be found in the way they reframe English language learning as a moral project of self-development. While mediatization of successful elite learners of English may not be the only channel through which such reconceptualizations of English come into being, it nonetheless clearly highlights how the dimension of morality plays a role in this process. By mediatizing the successful learners as moral figures, the conservative press and their success stories of English language learning reinscribed learning English as a fundamental responsibility for anyone who wishes to stay relevant in the changing global economy, urging Koreans to invest in English as an ethical way of being in the neoliberal world. Framing English language learning as a moral project makes questioning and contesting inequalities of English difficult—for regardless of whether one has privileged access to English or not, the moral responsibility to demonstrate one's alignment with the ideal image of the neoliberal subject now rests solely on one's own shoulders. Circulated throughout Korean society by highly influential media institutions with a great stake in establishing the neoliberal order, success stories of English in the conservative press thereby played an important role in justifying the neoliberal promotion of English during the early stages of the English fever.

CONCLUSIONS

In this chapter, I explored how the dimension of morality can play a key role in the neoliberal promotion of English. The reframing of English language learning as a moral technology of the self provides an important way through which English comes to strengthen and expand its grip on people's lives in neoliberalism. If the desire for English as a transparent medium for self-realization guides subjects toward English with the promise of becoming new selves in the global world (as discussed in Chapter 4), it still does not impress upon them the necessity of learning English as a duty and responsibility, leaving room for questioning the hegemonic position attributed to English in the changing economy. But imbuing English with a sense of moral obligation holds subjects accountable for their active investments in English language learning, extending the relevance of English to everyone and demanding that they take initiative in acquiring the language. This of course means neither that everyone actually becomes a willing investor in English language learning nor that everyone can afford to do so. But the moral framing of English means that they will be evaluated against this normative responsibility, regardless of each person's practical need for English or availability of access to opportunities for learning English—as demonstrated by the way English is widely recognized in Korea as a key index for one's preparedness for the job market despite the fact that the language actually becomes pragmatically relevant for only a small segment of workers. The moral grounding of English as a technology of the self, then, becomes a powerful mechanism for guiding subjects toward the neoliberal mandate of endless self-development, as English language learning comes to be seen as the ultimate evidence for responsible care of one's own human capital. Another consequence of this moral framing is that this ethical burden instills in subjects a sense of anxiety about how well one is living up to that ideal image of the neoliberal subject. In the next chapter, we turn to a discussion of this point.

CHAPTER 6

The Biopolitics of Language Learning

Youth, English, and Anxiety

YOUTH AS A VALUABLE RESOURCE

One phenomenon that has been widely discussed in relation to English and neoliberalism is how countries around the world are introducing English into the primary education curriculum as a second/foreign language at an increasingly early age. Numerous states in East Asia (Butler 2015), South Asia (Hamid 2010), Latin America (Sayer 2015), and Europe (Enever 2018) have actively adopted policy that places greater emphasis on the English language learning of young children, either by newly establishing English as a subject of instruction for primary school students, or by lowering the age at which English is first introduced to them. Driven by global institutions of neoliberalism such as the Organization for Economic Cooperation and Development (OECD), the World Bank (WB), and the International Monetary Fund (IMF), and rationalized based on parental demand (Enever 2018), such initiatives are often explicitly framed as national projects of human capital development. The earlier and longer exposure to English that results from these policies is expected to boost the English language competence of the young students, better preparing them for the transnational workplace and the globalized economy. In turn, the greater value of the human capital represented by increased English language competence of the country's youths is meant to contribute to stronger economic growth of the nation.

These policies offer an interesting vantage point on language and neoliberalism, because they are based on very specific assumptions about youth bodies and English language learning—"that younger children are better at learning [English]/find it easier . . . and that a longer period of learning leads to higher proficiency by the end of schooling" (Enever and Moon 2009:6). That is, these

In Pursuit of English. Joseph Sung-Yul Park, Oxford University Press. © Oxford University Press 2021.
DOI: 10.1093/oso/9780190855734.003.0006

policies view young children as possessing the fluid capacity for quickly and easily mastering a language (or languages), something that adult bodies can only emulate with much difficulty, which makes the period of youth a crucial moment for promoting the English language proficiency of citizens. This is why, even though the English language learning of adults is also emphasized in virtually all national contexts where primary English education is strategically promoted, it rarely reaches the level of interest and systematic intervention that we see in the promotion of English in primary education. This is not simply due to the fact that the already available institutional system of national education provides an easy field through which English language education can expand. Discussions on primary English education often intensely focus on how it can be made more efficacious, with issues such as when is the best time for introducing English into the primary curriculum actively debated (Enever, Moon, and Raman 2009, Spolsky and Moon 2012). This points to the significance that such discussions attribute to the notion of youth: more than a mere demographic age bracket, it represents an important window of opportunity that needs to be carefully and effectively exploited for maximum effect in English language learning.

In this sense, such national education projects are essentially attempts at harnessing youth as a period of bio-cognitive development. The trend of earlier introduction of English language education treats the still-developing, malleable bodies of children as an ideal yet time-sensitive site for intervening in the process of language acquisition. In other words, within neoliberal policies of primary English language education, the bodies of the young come to be conceptualized as a resource that should be managed carefully and strategically, an opportunity that must not be wasted, in order to secure and cultivate the value of human capital that they embody. In this chapter, I suggest that the significance given to young bodies in neoliberal projects of English language learning is not incidental, as it illustrates how neoliberalism operates not simply through control of economic resources, institutions, and policies, but more fundamentally by intervention into our bodies as living beings—thus it works as a mode of *biopolitics*, or a process by which life itself is constituted as an object of politics (Foucault 2008, Lemke 2011a, 2011b). Indeed, it is crucial to consider the intersection of language and neoliberalism in terms of biopolitics, because all knowledge and usage of language is embodied (Bucholtz and Hall 2016), and therefore presupposes life as its principal domain. Neoliberal efforts to commodify and profit from language necessarily posit language users as subjects with bodies, and intervenes in their actions, thoughts, feelings, and experiences as living beings.

The Korean English fever is an apt context for considering this point, due to the particularly intense way in which the biological life stage of youth has been imagined as a site for intervention. As briefly introduced in Chapter 3, and to be outlined in more detail later in this chapter, national curricula that introduced English at an increasingly earlier age was only one symptom of Korea's pursuit of English, which also saw the emergence of a slew of technologies, products, and strategies that were designed to exploit the malleability of youth. This chapter focuses on this trend, commonly referred to as "early English education" (*yeongeo jogi gyoyuk*), to consider how looking at English language learning in terms of biopolitics enables us to analyze the general mechanisms through which neoliberalism extends its control into our deepest sense of being, our bodies and minds. Indeed, this chapter argues, this intimate intervention into our bodies and selves concerns not only youth but all subjects under neoliberalism.

One thing that the Korean case informs us is how subjectivity becomes an important aspect that mediates the neoliberal biopolitics of English. While the early English education boom in Korea is a prominent example of active and intensive management of youth's capacity for language, it is also a stark illustration of the dimensions of affect that drive such biopolitical interventions. As I will discuss in this chapter, in Korean early English education, interventions into bodies of youth take on a particularly intensive zeal precisely because they are seen as a limited resource that can be quickly wasted and lost, which triggers a heightened sense of anxiety on the part of those who are charged with managing youth as a resource—parents, states, and ultimately, youths themselves, who are guided to internalize the view of their own selves as human capital that needs to be developed as much as possible before they reach adulthood. Am I making the most of this limited window for English language learning? What if I remain unsuccessful when the window closes? Did I make the right kind of investments in language learning? What could I have done better? This chapter suggests that such anxieties are not mere epiphenomena of intensified competition associated with neoliberalism, but simultaneously an inherent consequence of viewing our bodied selves as capital and a mechanism through which neoliberalism extends its control over our whole living being as a target of management. In this sense, the chapter argues, the anxieties that characterize Korean early English education point to a more general mechanism through which subjectivity becomes a crucial foundation for a biopolitics of English, accounting for how neoliberalism pressures all subjects, and not just youths, to become managers and entrepreneurs of their entire selves, including their bodies and souls.

LANGUAGE LEARNING AS BIOPOLITICS

Biopolitics can be understood as the process by which life emerges as an object of politics (Lemke 2011a:165). As a challenge to the view of biological life as a naturally distinct sphere from that of politics, biopolitics as a concept highlights the instability of the supposed boundary between life and politics, clarifying how they exist in a mutually constituting fashion. Biological life is not so much an entity ontologically prior to politics that simply gets picked up as a target of political action; rather, political strategies constitute its subjects as living beings, actively defining them as populations with demographic, reproductive, and epidemiological characteristics. By the same token, political process is shaped by such life processes, because life so defined in turn conditions how the political subject is understood (Lemke 2011b:4). Such linkage between life and politics is evident through many aspects of modern history. On the one hand, the marks left on contemporary society by racism, sexism, eugenics, concentration camps, xenophobia, and genocide show how the constitution of biological others is fundamental to the exercise of political power (Agamben 1998, Mbembe 2003). On the other hand, modern scientific technologies that place biological bodies under increasing scrutiny and control, such as psychology, biometrics, genomics, and stem cell research, constantly challenge the ontological stability of life, as bodies become reimagined as technologically manipulable, recombinant resources that can be managed for the interest of capital (Lemke 2011b).

The significance of biopolitics for neoliberalism is made clear through Foucault's work, which has been crucial for the development of the concept. Foucault associates biopolitics with the development of liberal political economy, viewing liberalism as a new mode of government in which self-control and self-direction, as opposed to regulation and discipline by a sovereignty, is emphasized. This can be read from his definition of biopolitics: "the attempt, starting from the eighteenth century, to rationalize the problems posed to governmental practice by phenomena characteristic of a set of living beings forming a population" (2008:317). As Foucault notes, the advancement of scientific and statistically oriented methods of studying human populations in the 18th century—the range of technologies that "focused on the species body, the body imbued with the mechanics of life and serving as the basis of the biological processes: propagation, births and mortality, the level of health, life expectancy and longevity, with all the conditions that can cause these to vary" (1978:139)—led to the consideration of populations as self-governing entities with their own natural order. And in this context, the goal of government came to be seen as understanding this nature of the population, leading to a "self-limitation of governmental reason" (Foucault 2008:13)—that is, a scaling back of disciplinary intervention by state power, and greater emphasis on subjects' own self-management that contributes to the ideal working of the self-regulating market.

Foucault's insights about the biological foundations of capitalist political economy have become particularly relevant today. In the context of neoliberalism, biopolitical interventions into living bodies have only intensified due to the more extensive degree of control that capital seeks to exert over workers, as well as the availability of new technologies that allow for deeper intervention into our constitution as living beings. Such interventions now have a more direct implication for subjectivity, as they often mean a more explicit and heightened focus on affect as the center of biopolitical management, identifying feelings and emotions as the key center that needs to be grasped for control of subjects. For instance, Adams, Murphy, and Clarke (2009) note how the growth of biomedical technologies that are designed to address future uncertainties in health, such as probabilistic management of pathologies, vaccination, cancer preparedness, and risk assessment based on genetic information, work to instill *anticipation* as a dominant affective orientation under neoliberalism. That is, by making us view and treat our own bodies as if they are financial capital that must be managed based on careful, speculative forecasts of the future, such technologies lead us to take up "an excited forward looking subjective condition characterized as much by nervous anxiety as a continual refreshing of yearning, of 'needing to know'" (p.247).

In other cases, management of our own affects and emotions as part of our bodily makeup becomes the primary focus. For instance, recent popularity of what Wilce and Fenigsen (2016) call "emotion pedagogies," which instruct individuals to recognize, identify, and confront their own feelings through techniques such as meditation, mindfulness training, reflective sharing, and mediated self-expression, etc., illustrates efforts to normalize a subjective orientation to the self as a living, feeling being that can be channeled into productive capitalist social relations. By confronting, categorizing, and talking about one's emotions, workers learn how to defuse emotions that are harmful to, and to cultivate ones that are conducive to, their active engagement with entrepreneurship. These trends highlight the doubly important role that affect occupies in biopolitical interventions in neoliberalism. Not only are affects, emotions, and feelings, as experiences of embodied, living subjects, an aspect of the body that becomes a target of control, they also serve as a crucial resource that facilitates such process of biopolitical intervention itself, for aligning the subjectivities of workers with ideals of neoliberalism ensures that they remain self-motivated and self-driven in aligning their bodies with the interests of capital. For instance, anxieties about one's future is not only an emotion that must be managed so that it does not interfere with the worker's productivity, but also one that must be carefully channeled so that it will motivate the worker to seek a steady program of self-development lest she lose her relevance to the workplace.

Our discussion above provides us with a basis for considering language learning from the perspective of biopolitics. While current research on language in neoliberalism focuses on critiquing how language comes to be understood as a compartmentalized, commodifiable skill under the forces of commodification, there has not been much serious discussion of an important aspect of language that is obscured by such neoliberal vision—the fact that language is deeply embodied (Bucholtz and Hall 2016). Neoliberal ideology that promotes language learning as development of a technical skill treats the process of language learning as disembodied; it is akin to acquisition of abstract knowledge, picking up of a decontextualized tool that will in turn allow for transparent communication of meaning, completely independent from the material realities of the tool's user, as we discussed in Chapter 4. But language learning, in reality, is intensely embodied all the way through. First, acquisition of a language always involves the body of a learner-speaker, which perceives, experiences, and adopts instantiations of the new language, and in turn undergoes cognitive and social transformation as it engages with new modes of communicative practices. To acquire a language, thus, is to acquire a way of using our bodies—in Bourdieu's (1991) terms, acquisition of a new bodily hexis. Second, following from the first, acquisition of language takes place under physiological constraints, which are in turn shaped by temporalities of bodies. Children's and adults' language acquisition take place in highly different ways, reflecting the relative difference in their cognitive development as well as their social and material positioning in society. Language learning takes time, a temporality that is constrained by conditions of the body: a certain amount of cognitive processing and exposure is required for mastery of linguistic structures, competence once acquired is subject to further growth or loss over time, and so forth. Indeed, to refer to Bourdieu again, it is such temporalities that allow language to serve as symbolic capital, as one's comfort in valued styles of speaking functions as an index of the time and resources one was able to invest in acquiring those ways of speaking. Third, the experience of language learning is a highly subjective one, again mediated by our bodily makeup. Language acquisition rarely takes place in an affective vacuum, and the pleasure, anxiety, insecurity, excitement, frustration, boredom, or satisfaction that we associate with learning a particular language does not simply influence how we perceive and value the language but locates that experience within our bodies that make us feeling, living subjects (Kramsch 2009).

It is unsurprising, then, that language learning would also be a site of biopolitical intervention in neoliberalism. That is, embodiedness of language learning makes our bodies a highly useful node through which capital attempts to shape us into neoliberal subjects. Thus, even as discourses of language as a transparent medium of communication are actively circulated to obscure the embodiedness of language, we see neoliberal projects of national or individual development that precisely exploit that embodiedness—such as projects for boosting competence in English with selective investment in particular kinds of bodies, notably those of youths. There is nothing contradictory about this. As we discussed in Chapters 4 and 5, denying the bodily, materially, and socially embedded nature of English language learning is essential for inculcating a desire for English and rationalizing the inequalities that neoliberal promotion of English intensifies, and therefore for furthering the logic of human capital development. But targeted biopolitical intervention into bodies that are most conducive to effective acquisition of English is *in itself* an instantiation and exercise of that logic; that is, it constitutes an act of careful management of valuable resources embodied in individuals—identifying which bodies will be most amenable to a promising return on investment, weighing the best strategy for such investment, and monitoring their development to ensure a maximization of profit to be gained from them. In this sense, overlooking the embodiedness of language learning and how it is taken up in neoliberal projects of human capital development results in a distorted picture of the relationship between language and neoliberalism. In fact, we may even say it risks aligning with the neoliberal ideology of language as a transparent medium of communication, for it fails to account for the fact that it is precisely such embodiedness of language learning that makes biopolitical intervention possible, thereby further contributing to the imagination of language as a decontextualized skill.

This chapter, then, focuses on subjectivity as a key for critical analysis of the biopolitics of English language learning under neoliberalism. As we will see, what the biopolitics of English as manifest in Korea's early English education boom aimed to achieve was not simply control over youths per se, but inculcation of a self-managing subjectivity, characterized by an anxious anticipation of future returns on investments in English language learning (Zimmerman and Muth 2020). Such anxieties—which may range from a general feeling of uncertainty or vulnerability to psychosomatically specific experiences of unease and nervousness—work as the deepest level of intervention into our bodies and souls, because it has a particularly powerful effect of leading us to see ourselves as living resources that must not be wasted and should be managed with utmost care. In this sense, early English education in Korea had a much wider impact in Korea beyond the English language learning of young children. Tracing how Korean projects of early English education centered around such sense of anxiety, the rest of this chapter will use this insight to consider how the perspective of biopolitics becomes crucial for understanding the way subjectivity mediates the relationship between English and neoliberalism.

EARLY ENGLISH EDUCATION AND ANXIETIES OF THE FUTURE

As introduced in Chapter 3, the early English education boom in South Korea was one of the key manifestations of the country's English fever. The label "early" in this case implies English language learning of primary school-aged children or younger, referencing the fact that, before 1997, English was introduced as a subject in the national curriculum only at middle school, at age thirteen. Given that English language learning of young children has now become a virtual norm in Korean society, "early English education" might be seen as an outdated term. Yet, the term is still useful for our purposes, as it highlights how the trend of early English education is not simply a downward extension of English language learning along the axis of age, but represents a break, a qualitatively new way in which English language learning was conceptualized, and how bodies of youth were at the center of that reconceptualization.

Korean early English education involved a wide range of phenomena. The most important was the national policy that moved the age at which English was introduced into the national curriculum to third grade in primary school (age nine) in 1997, under the sixth revision to the national curriculum. This move was the government's loud and clear statement of the importance of English to be placed in the Korean education system and economy, and this led parents of young children to scramble toward seeking means to prepare their children for this change. A huge market for private English education catering to such children emerged, ranging from English language media products for young children to English language kindergartens, which parents took up with great eagerness. Also emerging in this context was the phenomenon of early study abroad, or jogi yuhak, in which pre-university students went abroad to study for a limited term, often with the goal of mastering English through their sojourn in an English-speaking country. While jogi yuhak was not limited to primary school-aged children and generally referred to any pre-university study abroad, it was typically imagined by parents as a high-end strategy for the development of their children's English language learning, and in this sense occupied a natural and important place within Korea's early English education.

Despite these specific modes, the Korean early English education boom can be understood as part of the global trend in which many countries in Asia, Africa, Latin America, and Europe increasingly invest in the teaching of English as a second/foreign language to young children to spur national development and to foster individual economic opportunities (Enever 2018, Enever, Moon, and Raman 2009). As Sayer (2015) notes, such state-led programs focusing on young children are almost always promoted on the basis of a neoliberal logic that English is necessary for the country's globalization and for better job prospects for individual students, but are also motivated by a particular assumption about youth and language acquisition that is usually less explicitly acknowledged:

> The language learning rationale of PELT [primary English language teaching] programs is quite simple and based largely on folk theories of second language acquisition: the younger children start and the greater exposure to the target language, the greater ultimate attainment will be. . . . it is generally accepted, again usually from first-hand experience, that young children are "language sponges," therefore it makes perfect good sense to take advantage of this natural

propensity by introducing foreign language learning at as young an age as possible. (Sayer 2015:47)

Such programs focusing on children as the target for English language teaching can be critiqued on many fronts. For instance, it is questionable whether such programs really fulfill the promise of prosperity and open doors for all in terms of economic opportunities (Matear 2008, Sayer 2018; see also Chapters 5 and 8). Such projects also ignore the material conditions on the ground in which lack of proper infrastructure and resources (such as training of teachers) makes it impossible for them to deliver outcomes they promise (Hamid 2010, Spowage 2018). From a biopolitical perspective, however, it is also important to critique the ideological assumption such programs make regarding youths. Indeed, it is how youths come to be reconceptualized through these educational programs that mark them as different from regimes of English language teaching that preceded them in many contexts. For instance, in countries where access to English has traditionally been strongly constrained by social class (Matear 2008, López-Gopar and Sughrua 2014), English language skills indexed economic opportunities but were not framed as a national resource that must be inculcated across all strata of the citizenry. In such contexts of elite bilingual education, instruction might still start early as a way of developing a class-based bodily hexis (Bourdieu 1991), leading to reproduction of class privilege for the young English language learner. But in such cases the child's successful language learning would be naturalized as evidence of her classed provenance, rather than a reflection of a general potential for language that all children equally share. In neoliberal projects of early English education, in contrast, the ease with which children acquire language becomes highlighted as a general quality of *all* young bodies that should be mobilized for national economic growth, akin to a natural resource that can, with appropriate development, planning, and management, bring wealth to the country.

It is important to note that youth, as mobilized in such national projects of English language learning, is not so much a biological category as an ideologically constituted position. That is, this focus on youth represents a specific way of imagining youth so that their bodily qualities are appropriated for constructing particular subjectivities. To be more precise, youth in such projects are imagined in terms of a *future orientation*; bodies of youth are understood in relation to the implications they carry for inculcating an anticipation for the future (Adams, Murphy, and Clarke 2009). This can be seen from how these national projects highlight the multiple senses of temporality that the growing, still-developing bodies of youth index. Apart from the unfixed malleability and open potential associated with young bodies, youth also stands for a future world in which the young people of today will live as adults. In addition, youth is understood as a temporally limited resource, as future adulthood looms on the horizon, still distant but approaching with a distinct sense of inevitability. Such temporalities of youth bodies thus jointly serve as a reminder for parents, teachers, citizens, and youth themselves to anticipate the future and orient their lives in the present according to that anticipation, thereby leading them toward a neoliberal subjectivity centered on a nervous drive toward self-management.

Such future orientation was apparent in the official Korean policy documents introducing the revised national curriculum. The sixth revision to the national curricula explained the move to introduce English as a primary school subject in the following brief foreword (Ministry of Education 1995):

영어는 국제적으로 가장 널리 쓰이고 있는 언어로서, 시대적 변화에 대응하고, 질 높은 문화와 삶을 누리기 위해서는 영어를 알아야 한다. 국민 학교 학생은 성장 과정으로 보아 언어를 인식하고 습득하는 데 가장 좋은 시기에 있다. 국민 학교 과정에 영어 교과가 도입된 것은 바로 이 때문이다.

English is the most widely used language internationally. To adapt to the change of the times and to enjoy a high standard of culture and life, knowing English is essential. Given their developmental stage, primary school students are in the best period for recognizing and acquiring language. This is the reason why English language is introduced as a subject in the primary curriculum.

Here, the decision to introduce English into the primary curriculum is justified on the basis of two converging factors: the fact that primary school age is the "best period" for language acquisition, and that English is now a necessary global language for "enjoying a high standard of culture and life." We can note that the status of English as a necessary global language is presented in terms of a changing future. Even though the text represents this global status of English in the grammatical present, the necessity of acquiring English is associated with adapting to "the change of the times," a process of ongoing transformation in which the state of things in the present cannot be taken for granted. It is such orientation to the "changing times" or the coming future that requires we adopt new strategies, which involves mobilizing youth bodies for securing this important global resource of English.

This future orientation is even more explicitly spelled out in more recent articulations of Korea's education policy. The 2011 revision to the national English language curriculum states (Ministry of Education, Science, and Technology 2011):

빠르게 변화하는 지식 정보화 사회에서는 개인 생활에서부터 정치, 경제, 사회, 문화 전반에 이르기까지 여러 분야의 다양한 지식과 정보를 이해할 뿐만 아니라, 지식을 생산하고 전달하는 능력까지 요구되고 있다. . . . 미래를 살아가야 할 학생들에게 영어로 의사소통할 수 있는 능력은 학교에서 길러야 하는 핵심

적인 능력 중의 하나이다. 즉, 세계화와 지식 정보화 시대에 선도적 역할을 수
행하기 위해서는 영어를 이해하고 구사하는 능력은 필수적이라고 할 수 있다.

> The rapidly changing knowledge and information society demands not only the
> ability to understand knowledge and information from diverse domains ranging
> from personal life to politics, economy, society, and culture, but also the ability
> to produce and convey knowledge. [...] For students who will live in the future,
> the ability to communicate in English is one of the key competences that schools
> must develop. That is, to play a leading role in the age of globalization and the
> age of knowledge and information, the ability to understand and use English is
> essential.

This statement, produced in the context of a much more neoliberally advanced
Korea, openly draws upon the rhetoric of neoliberalism. The future is defined
as a "rapidly changing knowledge and information society," where greater demand is placed on workers to flexibly adapt to evolving needs of capital based
on compartmentalized soft skills, including communicative skills in English.
The task of education, then, is to prepare "students who will live in the future"
as such flexible workers, based on a constant speculation of what kind of skills
will be required of them in the future.

Examples like these show that, in national projects of English language
teaching, the linguistic malleability of youth is important to the extent that
it can be appropriated as a resource for preparing for the future. While the
malleability of youth bodies has also been a target of discipline in traditional
modes of national education, such modes of education aimed to mold students
into citizens with a timeless, national essence, with ideal qualities such as diligence, cooperation, loyalty, and integrity, etc., assumed to be shared across
generations past, present, and future. In this sense, the malleability of youth
under older modes of national education was not incorporated into any sense
of a future orientation; the future world in which today's students will live was
presumed to be not so different from that of the present. In contrast, there is
an explicit future orientation in national educational projects in the context
of neoliberalism: it is assumed that the future will be radically different from
the present, essentially unknown except for the fact that it will be a world of
rapid and continuous change, making it necessary to constantly speculate on
what the future will be like and to prepare oneself accordingly in the present
(Park 2018). This is where the malleability of youth becomes of particular importance. The adaptability and flexibility of youth is precisely what makes a
future-oriented education possible; instead of presuming a fixed, normative
course of development that youths of all generations will follow, this new
mode of education constantly reassesses its goals and modes of achieving
them based on a speculation of the future, relying on the capacity of youth
to flexibly redirect itself according to such shifting targets. Youth's malleable

capacity for language acquisition, in particular, becomes an especially valuable resource within this new mode of education, as the acquisition of English as a transparent tool for communication (see Chapter 4) is expected to be a foundational basis for such flexible adaptation to the future.

But such future orientation also leads to great anxiety, as anticipation of the future as an affective condition requires subjects to constantly be on the lookout to shifting goals and to nervously reassess and reevaluate their standing in their educational development. The limited temporality of youth—the fact that the malleability of young bodies has an expiration date—adds to this anxiety. That is, there is a limited window of opportunity in which a young student can acquire the relevant skills in a flexible manner, before fossilized inflexibility of adulthood sets in. Again, the linguistic malleability of youth is the most powerful iconic representation of this temporal limitation, as the ability to acquire language with ease is typically considered forever gone once one reaches adulthood. This makes the management of youth's language acquisition a site of particularly intense anxiety. Youth's capacity for language acquisition is not only one of the most valuable resources, but also one that is most sensitive to time, and for this reason, speculative investment in language acquisition must be done with extreme attention to and nervous obsession over future trends and shifting goals.

Anxiety over management of youth as a resource was indeed a key driving force for the explosive growth of the private English education market catering to young children. English language learning was the most prominent element of Korea's heated private afterschool education market (sometimes called the "shadow education" market: Y. Kim 2016), which also covers all school subjects as well as extracurricular activities such as art, music, and sports. I have already discussed in Chapter 3 how this shadow education market boomed in the context of Korea's neoliberalization, particularly in the aftermath of the Asian financial crisis. This shows that the growth of this market is not simply a reflection of a general educational zeal of Korean parents (as motivated by a Confucian culture, for example), but an outcome of parents' anxiety about their children's future. That is, it was driven by their fear that their children might fall behind in competition with others in school, and in the longer term, in society—in other words, their anticipation of the future, in which they try to forecast what the future world will be like for their children and to mold the children to be best prepared for that speculated future. That English language learning occupied a prominent position within this shadow education market, then, should not come as a surprise, for as we noted above, bodies of youth have particular significance when it comes to language learning, requiring even greater and more intensive management, with bigger risk of loss and mismanagement.

Of course, being capitalist enterprises themselves, service providers in the private English language education market actively appropriate such anxiety of middle-class parents to attract greater profit, which works to further intensify that anxiety. For instance, many high-end private English language institutes, or English *hakwons*, are known to use placement tests for their programs to instill in parents fears that their children's English might not be good enough for the school they are aiming for, etc., and that they must purchase the *hakwon*'s service so that the children can catch up with others. This practice, known as "anxiety marketing" (*bulan maketing*; Bae and Park 2020), not only exploits parental anxieties unabashedly, but also explicitly reinforces the idea that youth is a limited resource that must be subject to careful management and future planning, leading parents even further into the affective condition of anticipation. This reproduction of anxiety is not always done in such a blatant manner, however. In fact, inculcation of parental anxieties in the private English education market is often accomplished in conjunction with an appeal to parents' desire for their children's better English. Again, the future orientation that shapes imagination of youth bodies is what makes this linkage between anxiety and desire compelling for the parents. An advertisement for a prestigious (and costly) English language kindergarten discussed in Bae and Park (2020) can be used to illustrate this. The advertisement, which appears in the school's web page, shows an image of a well-dressed and confidently posed smiling young girl, along with a text that states:

이 아이는 25년 후, 영어로 글을 쓰는 베스트셀러 작가가 됩니다.
미래 우리 아이에게 필요한 것은 스스로 생각하고 표현하는 영어.
SLP 만의 영어, 인성 교육으로 아이의 꿈까지 키워주세요.
영어로 키우자 우리 아이 꿈, SLP.

25 years later, this child becomes a best-selling author who writes in English.
What your child needs in the future is an ability in English to think independently and express herself freely.
Through SLP's unique program that develops both English and character, nurture your child's dream as well.
Nurture your child's dream through English—SLP.

The advertisement directly speaks to the parental desire for their children's English that drives the Korean English fever (as discussed in Chapter 4), presenting the girl as a future successful cosmopolitan elite, who has used her good competence in English to achieve material success and recognition on the global stage ("a best-selling author who writes in English"). But by reminding the parent that this success lies in the future ("what your child needs in the future is . . ."), it also instills an anticipatory subjectivity in the parent. To ensure the child's future success indeed becomes a reality (which is presented as "your child's dream," after all), parents must anticipate "what [their] child [will] need in the future" and provide it to her today—that is, they have the responsibility to "nurture [their] child's dream" in the present through anticipation of the future. And such anticipation entails fear and anxiety, for failing to correctly anticipate the future means the child's dream being ruined: a particularly painful outcome given the child's great potential for success that the advertisement projects.

This example illustrates how parental anxieties about their children's English language learning heavily depended on the temporalities of youth bodies. The ideological conception of youth, which in this case focuses on their bodies both as a malleable resource that facilitates a flexible becoming of the child's future self and as a limited resource whose potency will evaporate in time, results in nervous anxiety on the part of the parents, leading them into an anticipation of the future in which they constantly reassess what is needed for the children's success in later life. The anxieties that drive the Korean projects of early English education, in this sense, is a site of biopolitics. But it is important to note that it is not only youth that emerges as the object of biopolitical control here. Even as such projects lead to a close and intensive management of bodies of youth, they also exert control over the *parents* (or whoever is positioned as the manager of youth bodies) as living, embodied beings, for the anxiety they experience also drives them to adopt a subjectivity that constantly orients to the future in endless speculation of how best to ensure the child's success.

ANXIETIES OF EARLY STUDY ABROAD: FEARS OF BEING LOST IN TIME

Anxieties that derive from the biopolitical nature of early English education can be noticed even more saliently in the context of early study abroad, or jogi yuhak. This transnational education project of youth, in which acquisition of good English language skills serves as an important goal, is interesting for our purposes. Arguably, jogi yuhak is the most advanced mode of investment in English language learning within Korea's early English education boom, both in terms of the amount of resources that need to be mobilized and the supposed efficacy in bringing about the child's acquisition of good English. Yet, engagement in jogi yuhak neither guarantees a release from the anxieties of early English education that we have discussed above nor offers a sense of satisfaction that one has done everything possible to prepare for the future appropriately. On the contrary, jogi yuhak is frequently a process fraught with even greater anxieties, fears of the future, and constant concerns over whether the choice one has made earlier was the best choice for going forward (Bae 2014b). Looking closely at the subjective experiences of jogi yuhak, then, becomes a useful way of understanding how the anxieties of early English education is not something that can be quelled by deeper investment in English language learning or something that will go away when the child reaches a certain level of success in her English language learning—instead, it is an inherent effect of neoliberal governmentality that the biopolitics of English language learning is meant to produce.

A large part of the reason why feelings of anxiety permeate jogi yuhak has to do with the fact that it is a project highly dependent on managing the temporalities of youth bodies, even more so than the range of other language learning strategies represented by Korean early English education. First of all, it is based upon transnational movement of the body of the young student into an entirely new sociolinguistic environment, which not only requires significant financial resources, but also subjects that body to a fraught process of resettlement and adjustment. Also, jogi yuhak is a short-term migration strategy that involves flexible movement between multiple destinations, all within the limited time period of youth, and for this reason, one of the most prominent concerns for jogi yuhak families is strategizing when is the best time to go abroad, when is the best time to return to Korea or to move on to another destination, etc., so that the child's capacity for language acquisition can be utilized maximally (Bae 2014b, Gao and Park 2015, Kang 2018, Park and Lo 2012). Such decisions need to take into consideration the relative value of the linguistic capital the child may acquire at varying destinations and how that will contribute to further movement along her jogi yuhak itinerary, particularly in terms of smoothly progressing between the different educational systems of each destination country. These characteristics of jogi yuhak, then, lead to the subjective condition of anticipation, in which families must constantly orient to the future to calculate and calibrate their current strategies for maximally facilitating the capacity for language acquisition inherent in the child's body.

Jogi yuhak to Singapore, which became particularly prominent during the latter half of the first decade of the 21st century, illustrates well the operation of such anxiety. Singapore emerged as a jogi yuhak destination as the early study abroad boom became more mainstream and as parents increasingly sought alternative destinations that are less costly and more accessible than the United States or Canada. Several factors, such as Singapore's relative proximity to Korea, its reputation as a safe, modern city-state, its education system that highlights discipline and competition, and the country's multilingualism, in which both English and Mandarin are widely used, led to an increase of Korean students coming to study in Singapore from around 2003, which was also when the Singapore government started to actively promote the country as a study abroad destination (Park and Bae 2009, 2015). But the majority of the families who came to Singapore for early study abroad considered it as a stepping stone, a site where the child stays only for a short term to develop valuable linguistic skills and educational credentials before moving on to other sites—for instance, back to Korea, and then to more prestigious destinations such as the United States. The trajectory of jogi yuhak that involves Singapore as one of the sites, then, is more complex than one which focuses only on one destination, say, the United States, as a family in Singapore needs to ponder many more possibilities and scenarios of future movement and properly strategize their choice among them to make the most out of the child's period of youth.

The ethnographic work that Bae Sohee conducted with several jogi yuhak families between 2008 and 2012 illustrates how the above conditions of early study abroad in Singapore highlight and magnify the anxieties that are inherent in Korean early English education. One example is the family of Minsu, a nine-year-old boy who had been studying in Singapore for two years by the time Bae started her fieldwork in 2010 (Bae 2014a, 2014b). In a typical arrangement for jogi yuhak, Minsu was staying in Singapore with her mother and two younger siblings, while his father remained in Korea to work for a multinational corporation and support the family financially. But Minsu's family already had significant transnational experience before their current sojourn in Singapore. Minsu was in fact born in Canada when his father worked there for a year due to his job, and the family also had lived in Singapore in 2005 due to the father's previous work attachment as well. This was in fact not unusual among the Korean families coming to Singapore for their children's education; many (though not all) of them had at least some previous experience of living abroad and chose Singapore as part of a progressive movement along a transnational educational trajectory that spans the child's period of growth.

Such families paid much attention to the timing for each step of their early study abroad journey. For instance, Minsu's parents originally had been considering starting his study in Singapore from third grade of primary school, but they changed that plan and came to Singapore earlier so that he could start his primary education there from first grade. The main reason for this was to optimize his acquisition of Mandarin. While Minsu's parents believed that his previous experience of living abroad gave him a good basis for his English language skills, they thought the additional acquisition of Mandarin would be beneficial for their present stay in Singapore. Shifting their move to Singapore forward and enrolling him in a government school, where all students are required to take one of Singapore's "mother tongues" (Mandarin, Malay, and Tamil), was thus a strategy for maximizing the use of Minsu's linguistic malleability for bilingual acquisition. Minsu's parents were in fact quite satisfied with the outcome of this strategy, as after three years in Singapore, Minsu developed both proficient competence in English and good literacy skills in Mandarin. Despite this, however, Minsu's parents felt much anxiety as they considered the future trajectory of Minsu's transnational education, and constantly worried about when would be the ideal time for him to move on to the next stop of his itinerary. In her interview with Bae conducted in 2012, Minsu's mother stated:

요즘은 한국으로 곧 돌아가야겠다는 생각이 들어. 민수가 학교에서 모범생 소리 들으면서 상위권을 유지하고 있고 또 영어도 잘 하지만 어쨌든 3학년 영어 밖에 안 되잖아. 어쩌면 지금 배운 영어 가지고는 어른 수준의 영어를 할 수 없을 것 같다는 생각이 들어. 지금 민수 영어로는 어른이 됐을 때 다른 영어 사용자하고 경쟁이 안 될 것 같아. [...] 그래서 한국으로 일단 갔다가 몇 년 후에, 민수가 고등학교나 대학교 갈 때, 다시 미국이나 영국 같은 나라로 가는 게 나을 듯도 해. 아직 너무 어리잖아. 지금 싱가포르에서 해 놓은 게 나중에 좋은 대학이나 좋은 직장을 가는데 도움이 될지 안 될지도 잘 모르겠어 [...] 아직도 갈 길이 멀다.

Nowadays I think we need to go back to Korea soon. Minsu is a so-called model student and is among the top in his class, and his English is quite good, but it is just the English of a 3rd grader. I realized maybe he would not be able to reach the level of an adult English (native) speaker with the English he has now. So with the English Minsu has acquired, he might not be able to compete with other speakers of English when he becomes an adult. . . . I think it would be better to return to Korea for now, and go to the US or UK a few years later, when Minsu goes to secondary school or university. He is still too young. I'm not even sure the things he has achieved in Singapore so far would be helpful for him to apply for a good university or to get a good job in the future. . . . Still a long way to go.

This example shows how, despite Minsu's admirable achievements in Singapore, his mother is still forced to consider the value of the linguistic skills he acquired in terms of how it will aid him in competition in the future educational market. Though Minsu's time in Singapore has been well spent, the returns from that sojourn will gradually diminish, as Minsu's mother anticipates he will need to compete on a more global stage with other speakers of English, including native speakers. In other words, she believes Minsu will soon be reaching a different stage in his linguistic and academic development where he needs to move to a different environment that can facilitate acquisition of more advanced skills that would properly equip him for such future competition—such as prestigious secondary schools in Korea that provide specialized preparation for elite universities—as opposed to Singaporean government schools, which (the parents considered) were good for acquiring foundational skills in English, Mandarin, and disciplined study habits, but not ideal for attaining a more globally recognizable linguistic and cultural capital (due to, for instance, potential influence of the local variety of English, called Singlish; Kang 2012, Bae 2015). Such anticipation of the future thus leads her to view Minsu's current achievements with a sense of dissatisfaction and anxiety; his English "is just the English of a 3rd grader," and the family must not be complacent with his accomplishments but continuously move forward, nervously considering when will be the ideal time to make the next move.

The anxiety invoked by such forward-looking anticipation of the future may also lead jogi yuhak families to look back upon their past trajectories to reevaluate them in anxious regret. This can be illustrated through a 2008 interview Bae conducted with Junhyeon, a 14-year-old boy who came to Singapore with his mother the previous year and was attending one of the international schools. Junhyeon displayed much awareness of the practical benefits his study abroad would bring him in competition back in Korea. We can see this in the way he explained the benefits of studying English:

영어를 잘 하면 중학교 점수도 잘 맞고, 고등학교도 좋은 데 가고, 외고 같은 것 도 영어를 진짜 잘 하면 토플 잘 하면 들어갈 수 있고 그러면 대학도 좋은 데 가 고 대학에서도 잘 하면 다른 외국 회사에서도 뽑아주고... 요즘 영어 잘 하면 모 든 게 다 편해지죠.

If you speak English well you could get good grades in middle school, and go to a good high school. You can go to a special purpose high school if you speak English really well and have good TOEFL scores. Then you can go to a good university, and if you do well at the university, a foreign company will hire you. Nowadays if you have good English everything is easy.

Junhyeon's explanation outlines in a logical, sequential fashion the cumulative benefits that he expects English will bring: good skills in English will lead to good grades in middle school, which will open the door to a good high school, and then to a good university, and then to a good job, and so on. According to this logic, English is the pivot for a good future, and his time in Singapore—the remaining one year before his planned return to Korea—is a strategic period for securing that linguistic capital of English. While this response, on the surface, might look like a "model answer" that Junhyeon provided to satisfy an adult researcher inquiring on the importance of English and jogi yuhak, we should also note the specific way he chose to frame this forward-looking vision in terms of affect. Even as Junhyeon claimed that his time in Singapore provided him with strong English language skills that would benefit him back in Korea, he also associated that time with a sense of mild regret or frustration, a feeling that he could have done more to fill his future journey with even more potential—a feeling that can be characterized as *aswium* in Korean. For instance, when asked if he thought it was a wise choice to come to study in Singapore, rather than simply presenting it as a good decision, Junhyeon said:

좀 더 빨리 왔으면 좋았을 걸.. [. . .] 한 일년 전쯤.. [. . .] 이제 돌아가자마자 중3, 고등학생 될 차례인데 고등학교를 생각하다 보니까 너무 시간도 없고...

It would have been better if I came earlier, . . . about a year earlier. . . . When I return I will be third grade in middle school, then high school, and when I think of that, there's too little time.

By referring to the specific milestones in his future academic trajectory ("third grade in middle school, then high school"), he alludes to the competition with other students that he will face in trying to enter prestigious high schools and universities. Whether he indeed will be able to move along his planned course toward a valuable future career will be determined by his performance at these junctures. As that competition will leave him "too little time" to attend to developing fundamental skills such as those in English, this anticipation of the future leads him to look back at his stay in Singapore and wish that he had come a year earlier. In other words, despite his achievements, there is always that something more that he could have done, a little more time that he could have invested, a little more effort that he could have put in, before he moves on to his next stage of life—in terms of his development as a youth, in terms of his academic progression, and in terms of his transnational itinerary.

Such feeling of aswium was not unique to Junhyeon. Many other students that Bae spoke with, who were high achievers during their stay in Singapore, expressed similar sense of regret. One of those youths, Jiyeong, a 10-year-old girl who had been attending a government school for about a year at the time of her interview with Bae in 2008, performed extremely well in the competition-oriented Singaporean education system. She obsessively studied to get good grades and ranking, studying until late at night and ploughing through workbook after workbook in preparation for exams. Moreover, she also displayed a strong spirit of linguistic entrepreneurship (De Costa, Park, and Wee 2016), or an affective and moral commitment to exploiting linguistic resources for enhancing her worth in the world. She was highly enthusiastic about language learning; she professed to have a desire to learn to speak eight languages, such as Mandarin, French, Spanish, German, in addition to English. She also looked up to her cousin, who, in addition to being a high academic achiever, wrote a diary in English and published it as a book, as her ideal model. For pursuing her dreams, Jiyoung found Singapore to be a highly conducive context. She cherished the academic challenge of the intense curriculum of Singaporean schools and its English-medium instruction, and also was excited by the fact that her fellow students at school read many books in English and tried to emulate them. In other words, for Jiyoung, learning English was not just about mastering another school subject or securing a skill she would need for a future job; it was an index of an attitude that aims to continuously enrich oneself by delving into an ever-growing repertoire of cultural activities that expanded her horizons.

But despite her active entrepreneurial spirit—or rather, precisely because of it—Jiyoung found her time of jogi yuhak to be wanting; the year she spent in Singapore was not enough, as there was always more there to desire, more to achieve, and more to accomplish. When Bae asked whether she ever considered giving up her study abroad to return to Korea, Jiyeong said:

가고 싶다는 생각을 한 적은 없고요, 딱 일년만 더 있으면 중국어 마스터할 수 있을텐데. [...] 더 있고 싶은 건 아니고 그냥 더 있을 수 있다면, 더 있다면 더 잘 할 수 있을텐데.

I never thought of going back, (but I thought) if I had one more year I could master Chinese. . . . Not that I want to stay longer, it's just that if I were to stay longer, I feel I could do better.

Again, while this response might be viewed as an expression of modesty from a child interacting with an adult researcher, such display of aswium gains significance when we understand it in the context of Jiyoung's entrepreneurial spirit. Though she articulates her satisfaction with her study abroad by claiming she never thought of giving up, Jiyoung also chooses to highlight the lingering sense of aswium that she feels as she reflects on her stay in Singapore. It was not the case that she had any actual reason to regret not working harder or needed more time ("not that I want to stay longer"); it was Jiyeong's forward-looking entrepreneurial spirit for developing her multilingual skills that pushed her to continuously imagine what more she could have done to make the most out of the time she had in Singapore. With just a little bit more time, with a little bit more effort, how much could she have done, how much could she have achieved and grown—and with these questions reverberating in her mind, Jiyoung had no time for being proud and satisfied. Jiyoung's case, then, is a perfect illustration of Kang Yoonhee's observation that jogi yuhak students see themselves in a "state of constant becoming" and as "a work in progress" (2015, 2018).

The persistent feelings of anxiety, regret, and nervousness that both jogi yuhak parents and children experience point to how the future orientation inherent in early study abroad invokes anticipation as an affective condition. They also indicate the extent to which such anticipation leads to an internalization of the logic of human capital development that valorizes continuous self-management and self-development. Through jogi yuhak, careful and continuous management of the resource of youth takes on a moral significance, as investment in youth bodies based on speculation of the future comes to be understood as responsible acts of self-care and preparation for the future. One illustration of this can be found in the following example, in which Junhyeon, the boy we saw above, responds to the researcher who asks him how he feels about other Koreans who cannot speak English well, given that he has now become more confident in his English:

저 같은 시기에 왔었어야 할 거 같아서요. [...] 나이가 어린 사람들은 아직 기회가 있으니까 하면 좋고. [...] 아주 긴 기간이 아니라 짧은 시간 오면 좋을텐데. 중3 이런 사람들이 영어 못하는 걸 보면, 어떻게 보면 안쓰럽죠.

I think they should have come [abroad] at an age like I did. . . . For those who are young, they still have the chance so it would be good if they [studied abroad]. . . . Not for a long period of time, just a short stay abroad will be good. When I see middle school seniors who can't speak English well, well, it's sort of pitiful.

Speaking of more senior jogi yuhak students who are not as successful in acquiring English as he is, Junhyeon attributes their lack of strong competence in English to (what he presents as) a miscalculation they made in the past: they should have made more efficient use of their capacity for language acquisition by going abroad at an earlier age. In this formulation, the lack of careful management of youth as a valuable resource amounts to a reckless abandonment of one's responsibility to make the most out of that resource. Those who waste that opportunity of youth without doing something about their English (such as going on early study abroad) are "pitiful" (*ansseuleopda*)—a term in Korean that indicates sympathy, but possibly also contempt.

The case of jogi yuhak, then, evidences how strong orientation to the temporalities of youth bodies gives rise to an anxiety that leads both parents and students to align with the ideal image of the self promulgated under neoliberalism. Junhyeon and Jiyeong, for instance, present themselves as subjects who have at their disposal a powerful but limited resource (their youth, as well as their time abroad), as subjects who must strategically prioritize their investment in language so that they can maximally benefit from that resource. Our discussion above shows how the anxieties of jogi yuhak play an important mediating role in this process, guiding people to become self-motivated and self-activated in their entrepreneurial aspirations for their future and to desire the English language that enables realization of their full potential in the global market. In other words, participation in youth-based strategies of English language learning also implies taking up a particular subjective position regarding youth: it instills in the students, as well as parents, particular affects that dispose them to value and desire a self-activation and self-development that makes full use of the time of youth, indexed by success in English language learning. And we may argue that it is here where the power of biopolitics of early English education lies— projects of English language learning that seek to capitalize on the malleability of youth necessarily inculcate an anxious outlook toward the future, guiding subjects toward careful management of "their own bodies and souls, thoughts, conduct, and way of being" (Foucault 1997:225), thus functioning as a deeply intimate mode of government.

BEYOND YOUTH

While this chapter focused on the biopolitical management of youth in Korea's early English education boom, it also offers general insights that extend beyond the situation of Korean youths. Even though the great emphasis placed on young children's English language learning is clearly one of the most prominent aspects of neoliberal Korea, this does not mean that alignment with ideals of neoliberalism through English language learning is the burden of youths and their parents alone. Indeed, we may argue that the anticipatory affects that led Koreans to turn to the management of youth bodies with intense zeal also came to serve as a normative condition for all to follow. The salient position that the early English education boom occupied within Korea's English fever conveyed an important message about what constitutes ideal neoliberal subjecthood, and this led not just youth but also adult Koreans to engage in anxious management of their bodies and selves, despite no longer being deemed to have the malleable capacity for language acquisition.

This broader effect of early English education can be seen through what became of the first generation of youths whose bodies and minds were enlisted in the intense national and familial project of English language learning, and whose life conditions came to define that of young adults in contemporary Korean society. This generation, in fact, has been the subject of many studies as well as popular discussion. Born in the mid-1980s, this generation grew up during the Asian financial crisis and thus spent their youth experiencing first-hand the blunt force of the social transformations brought about by Korea's neoliberalization (see Chapter 3). A prominent aspect of this generation's experience is the intense precarity they are subjected to. Woo Suk-hoon and Park Il-kwon's popular book (2007) famously coined the term "the 880,000-won generation," referring to the fact that the great majority of this generation was never able to enjoy the security of stable, regular employment that the generation before them took for granted. Instead, they were made to toil in unstable, irregular jobs that only offered 880,000 Korean won a month (approximately 830 US dollars; Cho 2015), hardly enough to sustain a pleasant life in hyper-consumerist Korean society. Such socioeconomic conditions forced this generation to forgo many mundane goals of life that the previous generations took for granted, such as socializing, romantic relationships, marriage, having children, or purchasing a home—a situation that led them to be characterized as *enpo sedae* "N-po generation," or a generation that has no choice but to give up (*pogi*) numerous (N) ordinary things (see also Chapter 8).

This abject condition of neoliberalism forced this generation into endless competition and self-management as a means of survival. Pressed by anxious parents who feared for their children's future job prospects in the increasingly bleak job market, they were made to internalize the logic of the market and prioritize development of their own human capital, especially in terms of preparation for high-stakes exams and résumé building. Anthropologist Cho Hae-joang (2015) highlights the term *seupek* ("spec") as a keyword for understanding this generation, who, due to the intense competition for stable employment, had to spend their youth solely on accumulating specs—a clipping of "specifications," as in a list of features and characteristics of a consumer electronics product, a term that refers to various enumerable qualifications, credentials, and achievements that can enrich one's résumé and give one an edge in competition with others.

This generation has acute critical awareness of such forced competition. For instance, they gripe about the endless and uncompensated hard work unreasonably demanded of them by their superiors and seniors (who belong to the older generation and thus did not have to experience the same competition themselves) by labeling it as *noolyeok*, the elongated vowel of which adds a meaning of disdainful sarcasm to *nolyeok* "effort" that the discourse of endless self-improvement calls for. They are also deeply upset about how this competition is deeply conditioned by inequalities, as complaints abound about how the *geumsujeo* ("gold spoon," or those of socioeconomic upbringing even better than people born with a silver spoon in their mouths) will always trump the *heulgsujeo* ("dirt spoon," or those with no socioeconomic privilege to back them up; H. Kim 2017, Choi 2021). Such anger, frustration, and cynicism lead some young Koreans to exit the system altogether—for instance, such as the downwardly mobile millennials who give up their pursuit of the neoliberal rules of the game by relocating from metropolitan Seoul to the semi-rural island of Jeju, as described by Jordan (2019). However, others in this generation who cannot afford to make that exit have no other recourse than to push themselves into even deeper subjection to the logic of the market.

We may argue that the biopolitics of early English education, which taught this generation early on to see themselves as bodies with value that must be cultivated and developed with keen affective orientation to the future, provided them with a strong model that guides their lives as adults. Even after reaching adulthood, and thus no longer possessing the valuable malleability that characterized their youth, they are forced to internalize an anticipation of the future to engage in close management of their bodies and selves in the present, thus enduring the bleak socioeconomic conditions of their present. For these young adults, surviving in neoliberal Korea means doing things to one's own body, subjecting themselves to harsh regimes of work and cutting oneself off from life's ordinary pleasures and necessities—toiling for long hours of work with little rest, accepting insecure and low-paying jobs that promise little upward mobility, indefinitely postponing ordinary pleasures of life—not necessarily in hope of a future gratification, but for fear of being cut off from life. As in the case of early English education, what drives them toward management of their embodied selves is not only the specific economic conditions of the job market, but the affective conditions that neoliberal anticipation of the future instills in them. For instance, Cho (2015) discusses how deep anxiety that results from bleak hopes of the future, often characterized as *menbung* (combination of English 'mental' and *bunggoe* 'collapse'), drives many of this generation toward even more intense self-management, as can be seen from a quote she provides from a university student in 2009: "What should I do? I just had to continue working at improving myself. Otherwise, I will become a leftover human being with no value in the market" (Cho 2015:449).

English language learning is not a task that they can leave behind once they have reached adulthood, either. Particularly for those who did not have access to privileged opportunities learning English during their childhood days, young adulthood is a time of heightened anxiety and uncertainty. It is their last opportunity to acquire, improve, and enhance their English language skills before they fully enter the intensely competitive job market, but it is also a period when they are no longer seen as possessing the malleable capacity for language learning that characterizes youth—in other words, they have become "pitiful" beings according to Junhyeon's formulation in the previous section. Such anxieties again drive these young adults toward projects of English language learning, with many investing in boosting their TOEIC scores or interview skills in English (see also Chapter 8). But the material conditions of adulthood, in which they can no longer take parental support for granted and in which they have little time left for improving their English language skills, lead them to even greater anxiety, creating an intensifying feedback loop that results in nervous restlessness. Such anxiety is salient, for instance, in the experiences of those who choose to go abroad on short-term language study (*eohak yeonsu*) or working holiday (Chun and Han 2015, Jang 2015, 2017, Yoon 2014) to seek better success in the job market. Despite their hopes of improving their English through this overseas tour, guilt about living overseas with parents' support, frustration over limited opportunities for practicing English, fatigue and burnout from constantly focusing on enhancing their market value often lead them to even greater stress and anxiety (Jang 2017). They struggle with "perennial doubts about whether they made the 'right' or 'best' choices for maximizing the value of their sojourn, assessing and reassessing everything from mundane household decisions to the quality of social interactions and friendships" (Chun and Han 2015:570). Such affects are carried over throughout their adulthood, as they endure the harsh conditions of employment in the neoliberal job market.

The precarious situation of young adults in contemporary Korea, then, shows how the biopolitical management of youth bodies underlying the early English education boom points to a more general process by which English language learning gets incorporated into neoliberalism. The neoliberal conceptualization of people as embodied human capital with various cognitive and physiological capacities, including those for language learning, is not simply an ideology that is promulgated by educational policies or conditions of the job market, but one that is mediated by subjectivity. In particular, it is mediated by feelings of anxiety that guide individuals to constantly anticipate future conditions of the market and to seek to manage their own bodies and selves in light of such anticipation. Even as Korean youth, their parents, and young adults remain frustrated, disillusioned, and critical of the neoliberal order that dominates the education and job market, such anxieties lead them to take for granted the subjection their bodies and minds must endure, and to focus on their selves as human capital that must constantly be mined and developed. For youths, the malleability and flexibility of their bodies make them particularly important resources that must be managed for future profit. But even for adults, whose bodies rapidly diminish in value as their capacity for language learning become ossified, it is precisely anxieties about their bodies being stuck in flow of time that cause them to turn with greater urgency toward neoliberal projects of self-development. In this way, the logic of human capital development not only extends its reach across generations, but also deep into their bodies and souls.

CONCLUSIONS

This chapter adopted the perspective of biopolitics to clarify the role of subjectivity in Korea's early English education boom. It argued that national projects that invest in children's English language learning cannot be understood apart from the framing of youth bodies as valuable human capital, and that this process both gives rise to and is sustained by the anxieties of the future that it triggers. In this sense, the Korean case has deep implications for understanding similar projects of youth-centered English language learning elsewhere. Our discussion above suggests that the significance of such projects lies not simply in the way in which the English language is promoted as an economic resource for which national efforts and policy must be mobilized; rather, it serves as a way through which neoliberalism extends its control over our bodies and deeper sense of self. This point extends the discussion of this book so far in an important way, by demonstrating how the desire for English and the moral significance attributed to the act of English language learning, as discussed in Chapters 4 and 5, find a more concrete way of rooting themselves within the bodies and minds of subjects. The perspective of biopolitics highlights how understanding subjects as bodied entities is crucial for understanding this process. Even though neoliberal language ideologies represent English as an isolable, decontextualized skill (as we discussed in Chapter 4), neoliberalism as a political economic process also focuses on how language is deeply embodied and zooms in onto our bodies as a site for transforming us into human capital. By tracing the convergence between such competing ideologies—the view of language as a commodifiable skill on the one hand, and the view of youth as a resource to be managed for profit on the other hand—and by investigating how feelings of anxieties characterize the tension between these ideologies, we are able to develop a more holistic picture of the role of subjectivity in the neoliberal promotion of English. In the next chapter, we turn to another set of competing ideologies that have complex implications for the neoliberal promotion of English—ideologies that conceptualize the relationship between language and identity in either essentialist or flexible terms—investigating that tension in terms of the linguistic insecurity Koreans experience as non-native speakers of English.

CHAPTER 7

Deferring to the Other

English and Linguistic Insecurity

COMMODIFICATION AND COMPETING IDEOLOGIES OF LANGUAGE

Current research on commodification of language has focused on how the ties between language and identity are becoming malleable and detachable. Under the conditions of neoliberalism, in which language is increasingly appropriated as a resource for economic profit, language and identity are seen less in essentialist terms, as speakers are expected to adopt languages and styles in flexible ways to meet the demand of capital, as if ways of speaking can be picked up or left behind regardless of one's more stable identities. However, the same body of research also notes that such new ideologies of language coexist with older modernist ideologies, which rearticulate languages as bounded entities inherently tied with static identities of social groups (e.g., Duchêne and Heller 2012, Park 2013b). While this coexistence of older and newer ideologies derives from the specific material conditions of late capitalist production, it also reflects another important aspect of work in the new economy—the tensions and insecurities that workers experience in the context of neoliberalism.

For instance, the large body of research on call centers shows how commodifying language and communication places conflicting pressures on workers (Heller 2003, Cameron 2005, Mirchandani 2012, Rajan-Rankin 2016). While such workers are pressed to use their language in a way that performs sincerity and genuineness—either by adopting styles that simulate friendliness and rapport, or by using particular languages that allow them to enact authentic personae for customers from different linguacultures—they

In Pursuit of English. Joseph Sung-Yul Park, Oxford University Press. © Oxford University Press 2021.
DOI: 10.1093/oso/9780190855734.003.0007

are also instructed to disassociate themselves from the stylized role they are performing and to process customers quickly and efficiently and abide by productivity targets. Such contradictions lead call center workers to much confusion, stress, and resentment, for instance in situations when they are unable to defend themselves against angry and abusive customers due to the guidelines that demand they maintain the dual facade of sincerity and impersonality (Cameron 2005, Hochschild 2003). Conflicting ideologies of language, then, become an important site for understanding how work in the new economy has significant implications for the feelings and affects of workers by pulling them toward different directions. And such tensions become crucial elements that define our subjective experiences of neoliberalism (Walkerdine 2006, Sennet 2006).

In this chapter, I suggest that the insecurities that derive from such contradictions are more than a mere consequence of neoliberalism, but can serve as an important basis for its rationalization, especially when the way in which language is commodified draws upon hierarchical regimes of language tied to unequal social and historical relations. Neoliberalism is indeed a site of much tension and contradiction, because even as it seeks to dismantle older, modernist ideologies of belonging and identity, it also perpetuates and relies on those ideologies to construct regimes of value that determine the order of the market. The resulting insecurities that we experience under the contradictory conditions of neoliberalism in turn shape us into specific kinds of subjects, as it guides us into particular feelings, emotions, and positionalities. Understood in this way, the contradictory ideologies that constitute commodification of language is not a slippage in which older ideologies lag as new ideologies step in, but an essential aspect of neoliberalism's ideological architecture that produces effects of subjectification.

In particular, this chapter focuses on how ideologies that attribute authority and hegemony to the racialized figure of the native speaker of English contribute to the valorization of English as a global language that all neoliberal subjects must pursue. While we have considered in Chapter 4 how English in neoliberalism is promoted as a language of pure potential that allows its users to transcend ethnolinguistic boundaries for full realization of their selves, it is also undeniable that ideologies of nativeness that have their roots in colonial and racial inequalities continue to condition who may benefit from speaking and using English. For instance, practices of English language learning and teaching around the world are still embedded within unequal relations of race and ethnicity (Holliday 2005, Hsu 2015, Kumaravadivelu 2016, Motha 2014, Shin 2006, Tupas 2019), and this shows that the essentialist ideologies of ethnonational identification that gave rise to the notion of nativeness remain active in these global times (Bonfiglio 2013). In other words, English in neoliberalism continues to be a site of *coloniality*—how colonialism remains a condition relevant to life far beyond the immediate realms of direct colonial administration and control (Maldonado-Torres 2007, Mignolo and Walsh 2018, Quijano 2000).

This chapter suggests that such colonial ideologies of nativeness do not simply survive in neoliberalism, but contribute to neoliberal subjectivities of English through the tensions they generate with newer ideologies that view English in terms of its commodified value. More than a contradiction, these ideologies jointly drive those users of English who are considered non-native speakers toward internalizing the neoliberal hegemony of English grounded upon inequalities of race, ethnicity, and national identity as well as those of class. As I will argue, this is what makes English particularly powerful as a language of neoliberalism. In Chapter 1, we considered how, even though English is often identified as a language that best represents the ideals of neoliberalism, neoliberalism in itself does not privilege English, as it is open to the commodification of any linguistic resource that can contribute to the maximization of profit. The question was thus, how can we account for the apparent hegemony with which English comes to be promoted in the process of neoliberalization in many parts of the world? While previous chapters highlighted the specific discursive and ideological processes that attribute special significance to English in neoliberal subjecthood, this chapter's discussion points out that the historical condition of English as a language of colonialism plays an important role in this process. The colonial notion of nativeness, for instance, by triggering a sense of insecurity in English language users who are not traditionally seen as native speakers, leads them to rationalize the various inequalities implicated in the neoliberal valorization of English and to internalize a subjectivity that takes responsibility for their own self-development.

For this purpose, this chapter considers the notion of linguistic insecurity as another dimension of the subjectivities that link English and neoliberalism. Linguistic insecurity, which figured prominently in William Labov's (1966) early variationist sociolinguistic work, highlights the patterns in which hierarchical relations between speech varieties become manifest in speakers' linguistic behavior. But here I reframe the notion in a way that gives greater emphasis to the dimension of subjectivity, so that it may be used as a tool for illuminating the dilemmas of the non-native English language user caught in the tension between shifting ideologies of language and identity. By focusing on transnational Koreans working as mid-level managers for multinational corporations abroad, and by analyzing their linguistic insecurity in terms of tensions between persistent ideologies of nativeness and emerging ideologies of linguistic self-development, this chapter shows how this reframed notion of linguistic insecurity can offer a useful perspective for understanding the way in which conditions of coloniality may intersect with the neoliberal valorization of English.

REFRAMING LINGUISTIC INSECURITY

While the previous chapter focused on the sense of anxiety that neoliberal subjects experience as they are driven toward projects of constant self-development and human capital management, this chapter centers on feelings of insecurity that derive from the relative difference in the values attributed to different language varieties and speaker identities. In order to differentiate between the two, I specify the latter as *linguistic insecurity*, even though the particular feelings and emotions discussed in this chapter may also be characterized in terms of anxiety as well. In Chapter 3, we have seen how Koreans' affective relationship to English is often characterized in terms of *junuk*—a feeling of debilitating unease, nervousness, inadequacy, timidity, and apprehension that one experiences in front of a superior figure (Park 2012, 2015). Rooted in Korea's dependent relationship on the United States, feelings of junuk lead Koreans to view themselves as illegitimate speakers of the all-important language of English, and thus can be understood as a characteristic example of linguistic insecurity. But more generally, instances of linguistic insecurity may be found across many contexts where there are competing language ideologies that lead language users to see their own linguistic practices as illegitimate.

This chapter's approach that considers linguistic insecurity in terms of tensions that arise due to competing ideologies of language derives from Labov's (1966) early work on sociolinguistic variation, in which he defines linguistic insecurity as "the subject's recognition of an exterior standard of correctness" that does not match with the speaker's (self-reported or actual) language use (Labov 2001:277). In his work on sociolinguistic stratification in New York City, Labov developed several methods for identifying and studying linguistic insecurity. For instance, in what Labov called the Index of Linguistic Insecurity procedure, a researcher shows the subject a pair of forms, and asks subjects to choose which form is correct, and which form they actually use; the frequency of mismatch between the two is in turn taken to be a measure of the subject's linguistic insecurity. What Labov captures through the idea of linguistic insecurity is, then, conflicting language ideologies—for example, the speaker's belief in the legitimacy of the standard variety vs. the authenticity of the vernacular—which have negative consequences for the speaker's own positioning (i.e., legitimacy is attributed to the variety not associated with the speaker, resulting in a self-illegitimization of the speaker).

For Labov, linguistic insecurity was an interesting and useful phenomenon because the speaker's recognition of an external standard was seen as having implications for the speaker's language use. For instance, Labov (1972b) linked lower middle-class New York speakers' hypercorrect speech behavior with their high degree of linguistic insecurity. But Labov's conception of linguistic insecurity may be seen as limited in the sense that it was mostly conceptualized as a surface manifestation of an underlying hierarchical relationship between language varieties. Despite his choice of the term 'linguistic insecurity,' Labov did not seriously delve into an analysis of speakers' subjectivity itself, for his primary interest was to explain patterns of sociolinguistic variation. Repurposing linguistic insecurity with a focus on the subjective experiences of insecurity that arise due to competing language ideologies can thus be beneficial in expanding Labov's insights. On the one hand, it is in line with this book's approach that views subjectivity as a discursively and socially constituted phenomenon instead of an internal psychological state of self-contained individuals. On the other hand, it also allows us to situate that constitution of subjects within specific ideologies that represent material conditions of social life where multiple interests and power relations intersect.

On a methodological level, Labov's focus on conflicting ideologies offers us a vantage point for investigating experiences of linguistic insecurity in concrete analytic terms. That is, focusing on how speakers mediate the tensions generated by conflicting ideologies through the way they deploy those ideologies in metapragmatic discourse, we can gain access to specific moments where experiences of insecurity are intersubjectively negotiated and participants in interaction present themselves as particular kinds of subjects. In Labov's case, the key analytic point was to identify tensions in the way speakers reify the legitimacy of the standard variety through their explicit metalinguistic statements, yet structure their practices based on ideologies that attribute authenticity to the vernacular. Similarly, we may strategically observe how multiple language ideologies are manifest within a given speakers' metapragmatic discourse to investigate the underlying tensions among them and how they may be linked with the speakers' sense of being. This will not only serve as evidence of linguistic insecurity, but also offer us a way of grounding its analysis on specific discursive practices.

For this chapter's purpose of tracing how coloniality may contribute to the neoliberal valorization of English via linguistic insecurity, then, the key is identifying the notion of nativeness not as a reflection of a quality that an individual speaker of English has or not, but as a historically, socially, and discursively constructed positioning of the speaker, and thus as a language ideology that reifies colonial relations and subjectivities (Aneja 2016, Bonfiglio 2013, Henry 2010, Shin 2006). While the insecurities or anxieties that second-language learners of English experience have been discussed extensively in the applied linguistics literature, such work frequently failed to consider anxiety as a discursively and socially constituted phenomenon (De Costa 2015), and tended to view linguistic insecurity as a simple reflection of the language learner's lack of competence in the language that will naturally be overcome as the learner proceeds toward greater proficiency. As a result, this perspective has overlooked how the notion of nativeness is an ideological construct that forms a part of the broader co-naturalization of language and race (Flores and Rosa 2015, Lo 2020, Rosa and Flores 2017).

It is also important to note that, while any language can have speakers who use it "natively," our understanding of nativeness as a historically constituted relation makes it relevant to seek effects of nativeness in cases where the colonizer exerts their power over the colonized through linguistic authority. For example, the subjective experiences of a Korean non-native speaker of English will never be the simple mirror image of the subjective experiences of a white American non-native speaker of Korean, because the historical relation between white Americans and the Korean language is drastically different from the relation that Koreans have with English. For this reason, nativeness is ultimately about historical contingencies of colonialism, rather than a neutral category for classifying speakers of a given language.

The notion of linguistic insecurity, conceptualized in terms of conflicting ideologies, can serve as an important way of situating non-native speakers' feelings of nervousness and apprehension within historical conditions of power. More specifically, for the purposes of this book, it also allows us to consider linguistic insecurity as a site for investigating how ideologies of neoliberalism build upon and incorporate ideologies of coloniality, as it provides a way for operationalizing insecurity in terms of specific ideologies that can in turn be traced back to historical and material conditions of social life. As I will argue in this chapter, this is an indispensable juncture for understanding the significance of English within neoliberalism. If English occupies a special position in the neoliberal social order, it is not simply because of forced imposition by some institutional power or because of any objective economic value it supposedly represents, but because of the enduring relations of coloniality deeply ingrained in the logic of capitalist exploitation, which neoliberalism drives to the max—and linguistic insecurity that non-native speakers of English experience in neoliberalism is one important window for grasping this. The rest of this chapter will illustrate this point by turning to one specific group of Koreans for whom linguistic insecurity becomes a major element of understanding their own selves as neoliberal subjects: transnational white-collar workers employed by multinational corporations abroad.

KOREAN MID-LEVEL MANAGERS IN NON-KOREAN MULTINATIONAL CORPORATIONS

This chapter focuses on South Korean nationals working in non-Korean multinational corporations (MNCs) in Singapore. The data that I discuss consist of a series of interviews with 12 mid-level managers employed in various industries, which I conducted between 2010 and 2011 for the purpose of understanding their transnational experience. The participants were all males in their early or mid-40s who were married and living with their families in Singapore. They were working in a wide range of industries including manufacturing, logistics, and finance. The reason that I focus on this particular group of Koreans for a discussion of linguistic insecurity, coloniality, and neoliberalism is because the feelings of anxiety they experienced in terms of their transnational career trajectories were closely linked with the linguistic insecurity they faced as neoliberal subjects. On the one hand, they are a key example of the ideal neoliberal individual that realizes one's self beyond the confines of one's ethnolinguistic provenance through English; on the other hand, through their work in intercultural contexts, they are constantly confronted with essentialist ideologies of language that posit a hierarchical relationship between different speaker identities, including those of native- vs. non-native speakerhood. Before we move into an analysis of how the Korean managers mediated their linguistic insecurity by negotiating these ideologies in their discourse, an ethnographic outline of the specific positionality implicated by their transnational careers is in order.

These managers at non-Korean MNCs in Singapore are illustrative of the changing conditions of Korean migration that emerged during the country's neoliberalization, in which a more flexible mode of outmigration, less constrained by the framework of the nation-state, had becoming prominent (Park and Lo 2012, Park 2014). With Korea's globalization since the 1990s, new forms of outmigration, such as *jogi yuhak*, or early study abroad (see Chapter 6), became prominent. As opposed to long-term migration that characterized Korean outmigration up to the 1980s, these new modes of Korean transnationalism often found people moving from one destination to another, seeking better opportunities for education and work, and cumulatively building up valuable linguistic and cultural capital that will allow them to secure even more beneficial opportunities. In other words, these modes of migration differed from previous patterns of outmigration due to their flexibility, more explicit orientation to class reproduction, and relative independence from discourses of the nation-state that highlighted the ties of overseas Koreans to the homeland (Shin and Choi 2015).

Prior to the 1990s, the most typical mode for Koreans to work abroad in corporate white-collar jobs was to work in foreign branches of Korean MNCs, as *jujaewon* 'resident employees.' Under Korea's export-driven model of the developmental state, *jujaewon* were seen as representing Korea abroad, contributing to their home country's prosperity by striking successful business deals and bringing in dollars. Also, going abroad as a *jujaewon* was often framed not so much as an individual project of career development but more as fulfilling one's responsibility to the company—even though it did bring certain economic and career rewards as well. In contrast, deciding to work for a non-Korean MNC abroad has strong implications for personal career development and strategic calculation of benefits. For those working in Singapore, in particular, accepting a job in the Southeast Asian city state was generally an upward career move, as the position would typically involve overseeing the work of various country offices in the region, sometimes under lucrative expatriate contracts. Working at the regional headquarters also indicated potential for further movement and promotion to the global headquarters located in the West, or moving to another non-Korean MNC using one's current position as a springboard. Working for a non-Korean MNC is obviously tied less to discourses of the nation-state, and allows (or forces) the employee to think more flexibly about future career paths, unlike under the corporate culture of Korean MNCs, where loyalty to the company may still be expected of employees despite increasingly unstable conditions of employment. In this sense, Korean managers at non-Korean MNCs abroad represented another example of the new mode of strategic migration that characterized Korea's shifting transnationalism.

Insofar as the Korean managers were salient examples of the new Korean transnationalism, they could also be seen as ideal neoliberal subjects who actively seek to enhance the value of their human capital in the global stage. Indeed, their transnational career trajectories involved taking risks that come with breaking away from familiar and well-established paths for career development, thus aligning well with the entrepreneurial spirit valorized in neoliberalism. Among Korean white-collar workers, employment at one of the major Korean conglomerates, or *jaebeol*s, has long been considered the most stable and rewarding types of jobs. In particular, prior to the Asian financial crisis of 1997, working for a *jaebeol* company offered a high salary, relatively predictable system of promotion, expectation of lifetime employment, and a well-structured benefit system that made up for the lack of state welfare (Song 2009:16–17). But the Korean managers that I spoke to either left work at such Korean corporations or started their careers at non-Korean MNCs to seek alternative paths from their white-collar peers, eventually choosing to work in Singapore at the regional office of their companies. And indeed they were successful in their careers. As noted above, by working at the regional offices in Singapore, they occupied a relatively high managerial position within their companies, supervising work done in the country offices of the corporation across the Asia Pacific region, and they were well remunerated for their work. In other words, their entrepreneurial choice to work transnationally through non-Korean MNCs paid off well, and in this way, they could be seen as successful models of Korea's new transnationalism who managed to make it in the world through strategic choices that took them beyond the borders of Korea.

However, the transnational career trajectories of the managers also showed clear limitations. Despite their successful careers, the managers that I spoke with generally considered the position of mid-level manager as the highest they will be able to go up the ladder within the non-Korean MNC. Even though the Korean managers could potentially be promoted to higher management positions in the branch office or even the headquarters of the MNC, in reality this was rare. In fact, none of the managers I studied were aware of any Korean who has moved into the ranks of higher management in the MNC they were working for. Most of the companies where the managers were working had their headquarters in Europe and the United States, and their top managerial positions were almost exclusively occupied with white men. In other words, even as the Korean managers' transnational careers could be seen on the surface as an exemplary realization of a globally oriented neoliberal selfhood, and thus as an ideal tale of new Korean transnationalism, they also illustrated the gap between this neoliberal ideal and material realities of transnational work. The space of transnationalism, as reflected in the managers' experience, did not represent a boundless land of opportunity where one's potential could be realized without limit, but still consisted of multiple constraints and restrictions against spatial and social mobility that the managers sought to pursue by choosing to work overseas.

This meant that the Korean managers experienced their transnational career trajectory in terms of a sense of anxiety. Much like the *jogi yuhak* families in Chapter 6, who were pushed by the logic of human capital development to constantly invest in the bodies of youth, yet also struggled with the uncertainty of the future, the mid-level managers working in Singapore also actively engaged in self-development to craft their career trajectory, yet faced uncertain future possibilities as they encountered limited pathways for further upward mobility. In the data, the managers' frustrations and nervousness about their career trajectories were also closely tied to the linguistic insecurity they expressed through their metapragmatic discourse. That is, they often made sense of their reasonably successful but limited careers by referring to aspects of language and communication, particularly their English language competence, which they characterized as good enough to warrant a position in the transnational workplace, but not sufficient for higher managerial positions in the global corporate world. In the following section, we turn to a discussion of how such expressions of linguistic insecurity can be analyzed in terms of language ideologies, and what this tells us about the role of essentialist ideologies of nativeness in the link between coloniality and neoliberal subjectivity.

LINGUISTIC INSECURITY IN THE KOREAN MANAGERS' DISCOURSE

As noted above, the Korean mid-level managers' accounts of their transnational career trajectory were often mediated by metalinguistic talk, particularly in relation to English. Such metalinguistic talk, in turn, was permeated significantly with aspects of emotion and affect. The data show subjective tension underlying the managers' discourse, pointing to much linguistic insecurity. On the one hand, the managers displayed much confidence and sense of achievement about their competence in English, but on the other hand, maintained much anxiety about the legitimacy of their English as many Koreans typically do.

When asked whether they faced any problems communicating in English in their workplaces, the Korean managers commonly responded in a matter-of-fact way that they had no difficulty using English throughout their routine work at the office. This is perhaps unsurprising, since for all of the managers I interviewed, work at the regional office in Singapore was predominantly in English (even though this is not always the case for work in MNCs in other contexts: see Kubota 2013), and because of this, being selected to work at the Singapore regional office strongly presupposed reasonable communicative skills in English. Nonetheless, this claim of competence was significant as it represents a clear departure from the widespread ideology in Korea in which Koreans tend to see themselves as incompetent speakers of English (see Chapter 3). Indeed, the managers often used such claims to justify their presence at the regional office and their transnational careers. In this way, they were much like the Korean graduate students studying in the United States who Lee Jin Choi (2016) worked with, who felt that their situationally appropriate competence in English was legitimate despite their non-nativeness, and used that legitimacy to present themselves as "good" and responsible bilinguals and transnational Koreans.

For instance, the following is how one manager named Jang, who was working at a global logistics company, responded when I asked him whether he struggled with using English at work:

장: 그렇게 불편하면은 나와서 생활하는 자체가 굉장히 고역이죠. 나올 가능성도 적기도 적을 거고, 예. 예. 아무래도 한국 비즈니스, 한국이랑 관련된 비지니스가 있는 사람들은 이렇게 나올 수 있는 가능성이 있겠구나. 저 같은 경우는 한국이랑 상관이 없기 때문에, 제가 뭐 한국 사람이어가지고 여기 나온 건 아니거든요. 예, 그러니까,

박: 한국 쪽이랑 전혀 일을 안 하시는군요.

장: 아니, 한국도 관련은 돼 있는데, 별로 그러니까 한국에 관련돼 있는 거 있으면 야 이거 네가 해봐라 하고 던져주고 하는데, 워낙 비중이 그렇게 크지가 않으니까. 예. 예. 그냥 그건 보너스지 그게 메인 잡은 절대 될 수 없거든요. 저는. 그러니까 예, 커뮤니케이션에 문제가 좀 있다고 느꼈으면 저를 뽑지를 안 했겠죠. 오란 얘기를 안 했겠죠.

Jang: If I had such difficulties, living here abroad would be unbearable. And it's not likely I could have come here in the first place, yes. Yes. Well, if someone does work on Korea, work related to Korea, then there could be a chance that they might be able to come. In my case, my work is unrelated to Korea, and I'm not here because I'm a Korean. Yes, so,

Park: So you don't do any work related to Korea.

Jang: Well, I do work related to Korea, but it's more like, if there's something related to Korea, they pass it to me saying, hey, why don't you deal with this. But that's not a significant part of my job. Yes, yes. That's more like additional stuff, never my main job. So yes, if they thought there was a problem with my communicative ability, they wouldn't have hired me. They wouldn't have told me to come.

Here, Jang states quite bluntly—and rightly—that if there was a problem with his competence in English, he simply wouldn't have got his current job. The straightforward manner with which he makes this statement ("If I had such difficulties . . . it's not likely I could have come here in the first place"; "If they thought there was a problem with my communicative ability, they wouldn't have hired me.") points to a sense of confidence regarding this claim. Also noticeable is how Jang's claim of competence is tied to a sense of achievement. He emphasizes "I'm not here because I'm Korean," distinguishing himself from other Koreans with limited competence in English who, even if they were given the opportunity to work in the same company, would be restricted to working on issues related to Korea (which one could deal with just using Korean). Moreover, when I ask whether he does any work related to Korea at all, he quickly admits that he does, but makes great effort to emphasize that it is neither "a significant part" of his job nor his "main job," thereby underlining that his competence in English allows him to be responsible for work that other Koreans would not be able to carry out.

Similar claims of confidence and achievement are also apparent in the following example from Seong, a marketing manager at a manufacturing firm:

외국 사람들하고 이야기하고 그리고 제가 싱가폴까지 와서 별로 뭐 적응 하는 것도 크게 랭귀지 측면에서 크게, 물론 힘들 때도 많지만 그래도 스트레스 받을 만큼 힘들다고 느낀 적 없거든요. 그거야 이제 첫 직장에서 트레이닝을 잘 받아 가지고 [...] 그런 거고, 그거 아니고는 힘들죠. 솔직히 저 같은 경우에는 좀 운이 좋은 케이스고, 대부분이 특히 외국계회사에서 한국에 일한다고 하지마는, 그 유럽은 또 애들이 워낙 영어를 잘하니까 그건 모르겠습니다만, 일단은 그래도 영어로서는 토익영어랑 실상에서 쓰는 영어랑 좀 많이 비즈니스 영어랑 차이 가 많이 나니까, 아마 진짜 외국계에서 일하고 싶지마는 겁이 나서 못 가는 사 람도 많을 거예요.

I don't think I have much difficulty in communicating in English, in speaking with foreigners or adjusting to work in Singapore. Of course sometimes it can be difficult, but I never felt stressed about it. That's because I was trained well in my first job . . . but for others, it would be difficult. In my case, I've been lucky, and even for most Koreans working at a foreign company in Korea, and the case in Europe may be different because they speak English well, but in terms of English, TOEIC English is quite different from English as it is actually used, from business English, so there would be a lot of people who want to work at foreign companies but are afraid to go abroad.

Seong, who first worked at the Korean branch office of the company and was later transferred to the regional office in Singapore, states that he didn't experience difficulty in communicating in English, attributing his competence to the work environment of his first job (elsewhere in the interview, he explained that there was a particularly strong emphasis on using English for daily communication in the office that he worked, even more so compared to other foreign firms in Korea). Though he avoids directly presenting his competence as his own achievement by attributing it to "luck" ("I've been lucky"), he nonetheless makes a strong implied claim of competence in English by differentiating his own English from that of other Koreans, characterizing the latter as "TOEIC English"—that is, English acquired only for the purpose of getting a high score on TOEIC, the standardized English test that is frequently used in Korea as an indicator of the English language competence of white-collar job applicants (see Chapter 3, and also Chapter 8, for further discussion). TOEIC English is further contrasted with "English as it is actually used" or "business English," with the implication that it has little practical utility, particularly in a business context, and that this must serve as a great source of insecurity for those who hope to work abroad ("there would be a lot of people who want to work at foreign companies but are afraid to go abroad"). The image of TOEIC English, then, provides a ground against which Seong claims a position as a competent speaker of English; while Koreans back in Korea lack appropriate communicative skills in English and feel nervous about their incompetence, he is confident about his competence to carry out his work through the language of English, which justifies him occupying his position in the regional office in Singapore.

Such confident claims of competence in English, however, became much more qualified when the managers talked about using English not in the context of routine work, but in internal meetings with other managers and superiors at the regional office, where higher-order issues such as long-term business strategies and visions were debated, and where discussion of abstract ideas and fast-paced contributions to the exchange became necessary. The managers felt that, as non-native speakers of English, it was very difficult for them to actively participate in such discussions. And since it was strongly believed that performance in such meetings had important implications for further recognition and promotion, the managers frequently mentioned their inability to quickly engage in such debates as one major reason why they could not move up to the ranks of higher management. Understandably, such metapragmatic accounts of their limited competence in English were also strongly infused with affect, this time with much frustration and nervousness, reflecting the feelings of insecurity the managers experienced in the meeting.

In the following example, for instance, Noh, a manager at a US-based manufacturing company, explains his discomfort with high-speed exchanges in internal meetings and how it makes him feel inadequate:

사실 지금도 백퍼센트를 알아 들을 수는 없는 거고 놓치죠 뭐. [...] 듣는 부분이야 상대편이 얘기하는 사람이 나를 신경쓰지 않을 때는 뭐 그냥 알아들었든 못 알아들었든 상관없이 회의가 흘러가니까 그나마 괜찮은데, 인제 내가 뭔가 얘기를 해야 할 때는 근데 이제 천천히 얘기를 해라 천천히 얘기를 해라 하지마는 상당히 뭐 우리나라 회의에서, 가령 삼성전자에서 회의를 하는데, 전 사람들이 흥분을 해가지고 막 회의를 하고 있는데, 갑자기 동남아시아나 뭐 어떤 외국인이 하나 끼어들어가지고 떠벅떠벅 한국말로 어, 뭐, 그, 그게 아닌, 뭐 이런 식으로 얘기할 때 그 회의 분위기가 상당히 쫙악 하듯이, 여기서도 뭔가 얘기를 했을 때 그 스피드라는 부분을 같이 못 따라가게 되면은 약간 좀 분위기가 어색해져요.

Actually I still cannot understand one hundred percent and I miss things. . . . When I'm listening and when others are not paying attention to me it's still okay, because the meeting will go on whether I understood or not. But when I'm required to say something, even though they say "take your time, take your time," well it's like when they're having a meeting at Samsung Electronics in Korea and everyone is excited and then a Southeast Asian or some foreigner jumps in and speaks in halting Korean, "um, that, it's not . . ." and the whole atmosphere just dies down. Here too, if I can't catch up with the speed then things get a bit awkward.

Here, Noh conveys the feelings of junuk he experiences in the internal meetings by depicting a hypothetical meeting taking place at a Korean MNC and by invoking the figure of a "Southeast Asian," which represents Koreans' racialized subordination of non-white foreigners living and working in Korea. In Noh's imagined scenario, this racialized figure is presented as speaking Korean with a slower rate of speech and low fluency, blocking the heated flow of the meeting. By likening his performance in English to a racialized Other's incompetent performance in Korean, and projecting his subjective evaluations of the incompetent speaker of Korean onto the effect his performance has on the internal meetings ("the whole atmosphere just dies down . . . things get a bit awkward"), Noh articulates the anxieties and frustrations he feels about speaking English. The encouragement of other participants in the meeting telling him "take your time, take your time" only makes it worse, since the condescension further solidifies his feelings of inferiority. It is through such accounts of internal meetings that the Korean managers make sense of why they fail to get promoted beyond their current position.

The managers' subjective experiences of using English in the transnational workplace of the MNC, then, can be characterized by a set of contradictory feelings—feelings of confidence and pride of achievement, on the one hand; and feelings of inadequacy and frustration, on the other. But it is important to not simply see these feelings as contrasting psychological responses to two different situations that demand different levels of competence (e.g., confidence when carrying out routine tasks, inferiority when participating in internal meetings). Rather, it is important to understand the managers' whole range of affective responses to English holistically and consider what the subjective tension represented by these range of emotions means for the managers' self-positioning as subjects. For this purpose, the notion of linguistic insecurity, conceptualized in terms of competing language ideologies, becomes useful. By analyzing the language ideologies that underlie the subjective tensions and how they are deployed in discourse, we can not only better discern the nature of the managers' subjective experiences but also trace more precisely the implications such tensions have for the managers' subjective positioning.

Based on this perspective, two competing ideologies of language can be identified from the managers' metapragmatic discourse. On the one hand, the Korean managers posited a flexible ideological link between language and identity. Dissociating themselves from the image of the incompetent Korean speaker of English, the managers confidently claimed competence in English, presenting their English language skills as an individual achievement that make them deserving of the job they currently occupy—as we saw in the examples from Jang and Seong. It is this ideology that allows the managers to view themselves as owing their competence to nothing but themselves. Indeed, such ideological conception of language and identity is what underlies the neoliberal valorization of English as a language of self-development. The flexible ideological link between language and identity offers hope that Koreans, as anybody else from any ethnolinguistic background, would be fully capable of mastering the global language of English provided that they make the necessary effort. If one's achievements in English are not constrained by one's ethnolinguistic provenance, whatever accomplishment one makes in developing English language skills is their own to claim, while those who fail to secure such skills have only themselves to blame.

On the other hand, the managers also relied on a more traditional language ideology that posits an essentialist link between language and identity. The managers' metapragmatic discourse was frequently dependent on the ethnonationally defined identity category of nativeness, which was in turn linked to hierarchically valued competencies in English. Legitimate and valuable competence in English was still seen as belonging to native speakers of English identified in terms of race and nationality, while Koreans as non-native speakers of English were seen as lacking good competence in English due to their inherent characteristic as Koreans. Noh's example clearly evidences that such identity categories are not simply presented as different, but hierarchically ordered. The fact that Noh invokes a figure that is perceived in highly racialized terms in Korea to characterize how other participants in the meeting may see his struggle is telling in this regard. The negative stereotype of the "Southeast Asian" in Korea—imagined to be dark-skinned, poor, incompetent, and inferior to Koreans—is used to index the deep sense of inferiority Noh experiences in the meetings, particularly in relation to other participants, who are not only competent in English but also beneficent and understanding, telling him to take his time rather than being outwardly annoyed by him. In other words, Koreans' incompetence in English is not presented as a neutral difference, but conceived as a sign of their underlying inferiority to native speakers, a source of embarrassment and shame. In this sense, this essentialist ideology of nativeness was also an ideology of coloniality, through which colonial relations of inequality were reproduced through the co-constitution of language and race.

What is also important to note, however, is how these two ideologies work together. Even though they may be seen as competing, and even contradictory ideologies—one positing a flexible link between language and identity, the other positing an essentialist one—they are deployed together in the data as the managers made sense of their transnational career trajectory in their metapragmatic discourse. For instance, Jang's and Seong's examples show that, even as they claim good competence in English as an individual achievement, they do so against the backdrop of other Koreans. The managers' good competence is notable precisely because it is an achievement that they have made despite them being Korean, who are supposed to lack good competence in English due to their inherent Koreanness. Also, in Noh's example, it is not simply the inherent incompetence in English that supposedly comes with being Korean that frustrates him; it is the fact that he is held back by his ethnolinguistic identity *despite* the expectation that he should be appropriating language as a commodifiable skill to move his career forward. In other words, regardless of whether the managers seem to be displaying affects of confidence or frustration at a given moment, they are constantly navigating a tension between competing ideologies, which points to a more fundamental sense of linguistic insecurity. Even when the managers present themselves as competent speakers of English who acquired good competence through careful management of their human capital, the colonial ideology that devalues that competence on grounds of their non-nativeness is lurking in the background, generating a latent insecurity that colors the managers' understanding of their own position in the global workplace.

Our discussion so far suggests how analyzing the subjective experiences of the Korean managers in terms of linguistic insecurity may provide us with a glimpse of how the colonial language ideology of nativeness can contribute to the neoliberal ideology which views language as a commodifiable resource that can be flexibly acquired regardless of one's social provenance. While the Korean managers' transnational career trajectory is largely shaped and driven by the neoliberal ideology of flexible commodification, the way the managers account for that experience does not just draw upon that ideology alone. The managers find it necessary to invoke and refer to the ideology of nativeness both as a way of articulating the insecurities they experience and as a way of making sense of the practical constraints of their career paths. Even though the two ideologies are opposite in the way they posit the relationship between language and identity, the managers do not treat the ideologies as contradictory in themselves, but bring them together in their discourse to account for the subjective experiences and the material conditions of work in transnational space. And while this process can potentially create room for the managers to highlight the contradiction between the two ideologies, it may also work to rationalize those contradictions and the inequalities that they sustain. For instance, the ideology of nativeness may be invoked to further reify the ideology of flexible commodification, enhancing the value of English acquired by people such as Jang and Seong, while devaluing and illegitimizing the English of other Koreans. Likewise, it may be used to justify why Noh and many Koreans will never be seen as good candidates for higher managerial positions compared to white, native speakers of English. In this way, the juxtaposition of language ideologies as manifest through linguistic insecurity can help us trace how colonial ideologies of language may be fused with neoliberal ideologies to extend its subjective effects into contexts of neoliberalism. In the next section, we consider this point further by turning to an extended example that can illustrate this process in greater detail.

COLONIALITY AND THE NEOLIBERAL VALORIZATION OF ENGLISH

The specific example that I consider here is a narrative produced by Shin, a manager who works for a MNC headquartered in Switzerland. In his interview with me, Shin explained how he had recently become one of the candidates for promotion to a higher position. While he had been quite optimistic about the outcome, the position was eventually given to another candidate, who was an Indian national. When he asked his supervisor (a white, British national working at the headquarters) why he didn't get the job, the supervisor answered that it was because of his English—Shin's line manager (a white, German national) had complained that his English was difficult to understand. This made Shin very upset, and as a result, Shin gave up the line of promotion that he was aiming for, and started to pursue a different line within the company, seeking out other potential supervisors who would support him. A few years later, he eventually left the company to move to another MNC with a branch office in Singapore. The narrative discussed here mainly consists of him accounting for what he said to his supervisor upon hearing the news of his failed promotion. I focus on Shin's narrative here because it offers a closer look at how, as the managers deploy the competing ideologies strategically to make sense of their emotions and experiences, those ideologies also come to be reproduced and rearticulated via such metadiscursive talk, leading the managers into recalibrating their positioning as neoliberal subjects. The narrative segment is shown below.[1]

1	Shin:	제가 이렇게 얘기하고 싶었어요.	This is what I wanted to say.
2		너 나랑 옛날에 한국에- 한국에서 내가, 근무할 때, 니가 내, 여기, 취업 <X해 주는데X> 내 펑션 보스였어.	"Back in Korea- when I was working in Korea, you were my function boss who helped me get this job."
3		우리 매=일 이메일로 얘기했고, 그리고 전화로 매일 얘기했어.	"We spoke through email everyday and spoke over the phone everyday."
4		너 그때 나한테 영어 못 알아들어서 이야기- 이해 못 했다고 얘기한 적 한번도 없어.	"Back then, you never said you couldn't understand me because of my English."
5		그때 영어가 <X내가 더 시원X>찮았을 거야.	"My English must have been worse back then."
6		너 그때 영어 때문에 못 알아듣는다고 얘기한 적 없어.	"But you never said you couldn't understand me because of my English."
7		심지어, 니 옆에 있는 친구는 나한테 엑셀런트 커뮤니케이터라는 말까지 썼어.	"The guy next to you even called me an excellent communicator."
8		이거 뭐가 문제 있지 않냐.	"Don't you think there's a problem here?"
9	Park:	그러니까 뭐래요?	So what did he say?
10	Shin:	제가 얘기 못 했어요.	I couldn't tell him.
11	Park:	@@	@@
12	Shin:	너무 너무 화가 나갖고,	Because I was so angry,
13	Park:	얘기는 못하셨고,	So you couldn't tell him.
14	Shin:	거기서 너무너무 화가 나갖고,	I was so angry there,
15		제가 이렇게 얘기했어요.	so I said this:
16		니가 얘기하는 수준은,	"The level that you are talking about,"
17		내가 이렇게 말했다고	This is what I said.

1. Transcription symbols used: <X X>: uncertain hearing; =: lengthening; @: laughter; - : cut-off intonation.

18	내가 지금까지 기본적으로 딴 대화 문제기 없는데, 일을 내가, 진짜 어려우면 어떻게 딜리버리를 했겠어요.	So far I basically didn't have any communication problems, and my work, if I really had difficulty, how could I have delivered the results?
19	네이티브 수- 준의 영어를 요구하는 거구나.	((I realized)) he's asking for native-level English.
20	내가 솔직하게- 난 못 해. 이랬어요.	I told him honestly, "I can't do it."
21	이거를 안 하겠다는 얘기가 아니라, 할 수가 없는 거예요 이거는.	It's not that I won't do it, but that I simply can't do it.
22	길가에 가다가 딱 부딪혔을 때, 너는 아우치 하고 나는 아야 이렇게 얘기한다고.	"When we bump into something while walking along the street, you say *ouch* and I say *aya*."
23	말이 틀려.	"Totally different words."
24	반응이 틀린 거야.	"The response itself is different."
25	감이, 감이 다른 걸 가지고 얘기를 한다고 그러면, 나 할 수 없는- 할 수 없는 얘기를 하는 거야.	"If you're talking about such matters of empathy, then you're asking for something that I cannot do."
26	제가 그렇게 얘기했어요 제 보스한테.	That's what I told my boss.

A significant aspect of the narrative is its organizational structure, in which Shin presents and contrasts two versions of his reaction to the supervisor: what he wanted to say to his supervisor (lines 2–8) and what he actually said (lines 16–25). What is interesting about these two versions is how they are put in a contrastive relationship not only through their designation as "imagined" and "real" responses, but also through the affective and formal differential that is generated between the two. Such difference between the two versions align with the two language ideologies, thereby contributing to Shin's negotiation between competing ideologies of language and identity.

From lines 1 to 8, Shin tells me about his reaction to the supervisor's comment that his English was a problem by stating "what he wanted to say" to his boss (line 1). As Shin conveys to me this imagined version of his complaint, his tone of voice rises higher, and pace of speech becomes faster, as if the memory of the incident brings back the anger. But it is also important to note that Shin later represents this first version as a rational response that he was unable to deliver due to being upset ("I couldn't tell him . . . because I was so angry": lines 10 and 12). This supposed rationality of this response is also reflected in the focus of the argument he makes, which points out the logical problems with the supervisor's comment—that it was Shin's supervisor who helped him get the job in Singapore in the first place (line 2), and he had ample opportunities to evaluate his English (lines 3–4); that Shin's competence in English had never been an issue, and that if it were, it was certainly the supervisor's responsibility to point it out earlier (lines 5–6); that some of the supervisor's colleagues even praised Shin for his communicative effectiveness (line 7). By laying out these points, step by step, this version makes a clear, rational argument of why Shin cannot be seen as lacking good English and why he cannot be denied promotion on such grounds.

This first version also centers heavily around the ideology of language as an acquirable and commodifiable skill. Shin presents his competence in English as his own achievement as an individual, something that he has accumulated over time, as we can infer from Shin's statement "my English must have been worse back then" (line 5), and thus implied to be an outcome of his own efforts. Shin's Koreanness is not treated here as a hindrance to working in the global workplace—it may have been a problem for him in the past when he was confined to the space of Korea and presumably had a weaker command of English (line 5), but now he has acquired and demonstrated good competence in English, to the extent of being called an "excellent communicator" (line 7). Shin's voice in the first version thus unabashedly demands recognition of his competence on the grounds of the linguistic skills he demonstrates.

Not realizing that what Shin was telling me was not an actual complaint he made to the supervisor, however, I ask in line 9 how the supervisor responded. Shin restates that that was not actually what he had told the supervisor, and for the rest of the transcript, goes on to report on what he actually said. In lines 14 and 15, he reiterates that this second version was driven by anger. Indeed, while this version of his complaint still has its own logic, in structural terms it is much less coherent. Unlike the first version, which consists of a smooth, continuous direct quotation, the second version is a mixture of direction quotations reporting what Shin said to his supervisor (lines 16, 20, 22–25), reports of his inner thoughts as he was speaking to the supervisor (line 19), and rationalizations of his argument that are directed to me (lines 18, 21). It also includes at least one restart where Shin cuts off a direct quotation in production (line 16) and starts over with a new quotative frame (line 17), which itself lacks a direct quotation immediately following.

The emotional quality of the second version is also reflected in its content. We can note that a strong sense of frustration is conveyed through the way Shin frames this response. Unlike the first version, which tries to argue its way toward a solution, the second version is much more confrontational, and declares the conversation to have reached a dead end, highlighting the frustration Shin feels over this situation. Central to this formulation is Shin's interpretation of the supervisor's comment as demanding a native-speaker-level English (line 19). Here, Shin distinguishes his English from "native-level" English, characterizing this difference as an insurmountable one. "I can't do it," he says in line 20, and then immediately elaborates that it is not really a matter of his choice or will, giving up any further negotiation with his supervisor; it is simply impossible for him to speak the English that his supervisor is expecting of him (line 21). He further presents the difference between his English and the English the supervisor expects as highly natural (i.e., rooted in essentialized speaker identities) by using a metaphor of unconditioned response—when a native speaker is hurt, he or she will automatically say *ouch*, but Shin, being Korean, will say *aya* (the Korean interjection for pain; line 22). This difference in "words" (*mal*: line 23) is not a superficial difference, according to Shin, because it ultimately points to different kinds of "responses" (*baneung*: line 24) or different modes of "empathy" (*gam*: line 25); that is, it is a matter of visceral reaction that cannot be subjected to conscious and effortful manipulation. In this way, Shin formulates the distance between his own competence and the native-like English he is expected to perform as a fundamental and absolute cultural difference.

In other words, the second version is permeated by the colonial ideology of nativeness, as competence in English is conceptualized as rooted deeply in an essentialist sense of cultural being defined in terms of native speakerhood. The supervisor's reference to Shin's supposed lack of competence in English is thus treated not as a criticism that is open for negotiation, but as a fatal blow to Shin's claim of competence that does not leave any room for further discussion, as it points to Shin's immutable identity of being Korean. Such difference is not simply treated as a general difference, but a hierarchical one, in which the native speaker has the power to judge what is legitimate English, while the non-native speaker is left only with the option to acquiesce to the former's assessment. Shin's opinion that he has developed sufficiently good communicative skills in English for the higher position does not matter; the native-speaker supervisor's perception that his English is not good enough is sufficient basis for rejecting Shin's claim.

The narrative above provides an interesting display of linguistic insecurity precisely because of the fact that Shin presents the two ideologies as distinct. In contrast to the earlier examples, where the competing ideologies have a more overlapping presence, here Shin uses the two ideologies to construct two different versions of the argument he presented to his supervisor. In this sense, it can be argued that Shin tries to highlight the contradictory relationship between the two ideologies. The narrative's structure, in which the two different responses are presented as standing for clearly contrasting stances, affects, and positions, is used to highlight the conflict between the two ideologies—while one ideology presents competence in English as an acquirable skill, the other treats it as constrained by nativeness as a cultural essence; while one ideology suggests that linguistic skills should be seen as an individual's achievement, the other denies recognition of the individual's competence as long as the individual's provenance does not point to that of a native speaker. Since it is ultimately the latter version that prevails, Shin's narrative may therefore be seen as a critique of the neoliberal ideology of English language as a commodifiable skill; the promise that anyone may benefit from developing good competence in English regardless of their ethnolinguistic provenance is shown to be false, as such promise can always be nullified if one is not born as a native speaker of English. In this sense, the narrative can be seen as a sophisticated discourse in which Shin problematizes the way English language skills are evaluated in the context of the non-Korean MNC and in which he articulates his linguistic insecurity as an employee caught between two contradictory ideologies.

But at the same time, we may also note that despite such critical undertones, the narrative also reproduces those two ideologies. On the one hand, the ideology of nativeness is presented as uncontestable, thereby naturalizing the colonial relationship of a native vs. non-native speaker. The hierarchy of legitimacy and authority that is associated with the native vs. non-native distinction is considered to be one that cannot be contested or subverted through the non-native speaker's active acquisition of English language skills. Through this, unequal relations of race, ethnicity and nationality, which are constituted by the history of colonialism and indexed by the notion of nativeness, are reproduced; the privilege of Shin's supervisor as a white native speaker of English remains intact, while Shin himself defers to his authority by admitting his position as the illegitimate non-native speaker. In fact, it is worth remembering that, in the narrative, it was Shin himself, rather than his supervisor, who invoked the category of nativeness in the process of making sense of his situation. This evidences the deep coloniality of the ideology of nativeness; the strong naturalness accorded to the notion of nativeness means that those branded as non-native speakers are led to internalize and take it for granted, thereby colluding in their own illegitimization.

On the other hand, even as the ideology of English as a commodifiable skill is problematized, this does not mean the entrepreneurial spirit of self-development that the ideology stands for is now rejected. Though Shin identifies achieving native-like competence as something that he "cannot do," this is not so much a dismissal of the mandate to invest in English language learning as a project of self-development, as it is an acknowledgment of the fact that he will never amass the authority to declare that he has done enough to develop his English language skills required for the higher management position. Indeed, Shin did not abandon his efforts in seeking further career opportunities through careful management of his human capital; a few years later, he was recruited by a US-based MNC to work at its Singapore office, and continued to extend his career trajectory in transnational space. The juxtaposition of the two ideologies in Shin's narrative, then, does not lead to a rejection of the neoliberal ideology of English as commodifiable skill. Rather, it simply reiterates the endless nature of the project of self-development, except that constant self-development is now grounded upon a more essentialist basis—the inherent lack of authority of the non-native speaker who must forever depend on the native-speaking Other for that approving nod that will never come.

Returning to our concern about coloniality in this chapter, then, we can say that the ideology of nativeness further reinforces the neoliberal valorization of English by recalibrating the subjectivities of non-native speakers who engage in English language learning as a project of self-development. The Korean mid-level managers discussed in this chapter are not agentive neoliberal subjects who can decide what skills and competencies to pursue, to what extent, for how long, and whether they have "done enough"—they are constantly dependent on the approval of the native speaker as the superior racial Other, which leads them deeper into linguistic insecurity, caught between the mandate to pursue English for the realization of their potential beyond their ethnolinguistic provenance on the one hand, and the constant subordination to the authority of the native speaker on the other. It is in this way that coloniality plays an indispensable role in the neoliberal valorization of English— by burdening the souls of non-native speakers with linguistic insecurity, to keep them from wondering if they haven't already done enough to deserve the fruits that that English as a language of neoliberal self-development promises.

CONCLUSIONS

This chapter conceptualized linguistic insecurity in terms of competing language ideologies, using that notion to explore how conditions of coloniality may contribute to the neoliberal valorization of English. Taking the case of Korean mid-level managers working abroad in non-Korean MNCs, it looked at how the linguistic insecurity they experienced in the course of their transnational work could be understood in terms of a tension between the neoliberal ideology of English as a commodifiable skill and the colonial ideology of nativeness. This tension, in turn, led to a neoliberal subjectivity in which deference to the authority of the native speaker as racial Other drove the managers into greater internalization of the logic of endless self-development through English. While the case of these transnational workers cannot necessarily be generalized across different contexts both in and beyond Korea, the strong influence that the ideology of nativeness exerted over the managers' articulation of their neoliberal subjectivity shows that colonial ideologies not only survive in times of neoliberalism, but are actively recruited in the reproduction and naturalization of neoliberal ideologies. The colonial ideology of nativeness, which keeps perfect English constantly out of reach of non-native speakers, makes English the ideal language of neoliberalism, for it iconically represents endless projects of self-development and self-improvement that good neoliberal subjects are expected to pursue. In this way, as the figure of the native speaker of English continues to wield its hegemony over non-native speakers of English around the world, the linguistic insecurity the figure generates leads non-native speakers of English to submit not only to the native speaker's authority, but also to the logic of neoliberalism.

CHAPTER 8

Becoming Precarious Subjects

The Unfulfilled Promise of English

PRECARITY AS SUBJECTIVE CONDITION

The previous chapters provided a detailed exploration of the neoliberal valorization of English in Korea, considering how various aspects of subjectivity
mediate that process. Language ideologies that present English as a transparent medium of communication that can realize the true potential of one's
latent human capital across ethnolinguistic borders inculcates a desire for
English; framing English language learning as a responsible moral project of
self-management obscures the class-based inequalities inherent in the promotion of English to naturalize its neoliberal underpinnings; English language
learning as a neoliberal project triggers anxieties about the future by presenting the embodied nature of our capacity for language acquisition as a limited
resource, thereby extending its control over our bodies and minds as living
beings; finally, the coloniality of English as manifest in ideologies of nativeness guide Korean learners of English to internalize the image of English as
a language of endless self-development, as linguistic insecurity leads them to
defer to the authority of the native speaker. These processes of subjectivity,
as we discussed in the chapters of this book, evidence how the promotion of
English in neoliberalism is not simply about the supposed economic value of
the language, but more fundamentally about shaping us as neoliberal subjects who willingly and constantly engage in the management of our selves as
human capital.

As we near the book's conclusion, it is useful to pause for a moment and
consider the consequences of all this. Part of this book's underlying premise
has been that it is important to study the neoliberal promotion of English

In Pursuit of English. Joseph Sung-Yul Park, Oxford University Press. © Oxford University Press 2021.
DOI: 10.1093/oso/9780190855734.003.0008

not just because it is about the changing status of English, but because it has broader social implications in justifying, extending, and reproducing the neoliberal social order. While we have seen glimpses of social consequences of the neoliberal valorization of English throughout the chapters so far, in this penultimate chapter we will take a broader perspective to situate those consequences in the context of Korea's neoliberalization, and consider how subjectivities of English may contribute to one of the defining features of contemporary Korean society and of neoliberalism in general—the condition of rampant precarity.

Precarity refers to the state of insecurity, instability, and unpredictability that characterizes work under neoliberalism, in which workers, instead of employers or the state, are expected to be responsible for the risks and burdens of labor (Kalleberg and Vallas 2008). Flexibilization of work, which constituted one key pillar of neoliberal transformations around the world, expanded the scope of short-term, contract-based, non-standard work, and led to a weakening of job security; at the same time, attacks on labor unions and retreat of state welfare greatly reduced the social protection that workers could rely on. Though specific manifestations of precarity vary significantly across national and regional economies, precarious work has become a prominent phenomenon worldwide, to the extent that some observers identify it as an indication of a new shift in class structure, with those in precarious labor constituting an emerging precariat (Standing 2011). But others note that precarity is historically a much more fundamental element of capitalism, in which keeping workers under conditions of precarity—where they serve as an "industrial reserve army" in Marx's sense, driving down the cost of labor—serves as a practical basis for capital's exploitation of workers (Jonna and Foster 2016).

Of particular relevance for our discussion here is how precarity is not simply a political economic condition, but also a subjective one. Scholars have turned to the phenomenon of precarity to understand not only economic relations of labor but also "states of anxiety, desperation, unbelonging, and risk experienced by temporary and irregularly employed workers" (Millar 2014:34). Such a state of precarity can push people toward greater weariness, depression, anger, and isolation, leading to perhaps one of the most damaging outcomes of neoliberal capitalism—undermining of collective values that constitute the very foundations of human dignity (Bourdieu 1998). Berardi (2009:192) thus identifies precarity as capital's appropriation and exploitation of our souls:

> The neoliberal values presented in the 1980s and the 1990s as vectors of independence and self-entrepreneurship, revealed themselves to be manifestations of a new form of slavery producing insecurity and most of all a psychological catastrophe. . . . Industrial factories used the body, forcing it to leave the soul

outside of the assembly line, so that the worker looked like a soulless body. The immaterial factory asks instead to place our very souls at its disposal: intelligence, sensibility, creativity and language.

This chapter considers how such conditions of precarity can be related to the neoliberal valorization of English. While pervasiveness of precarity under neoliberalism in itself is a product of material conditions of labor aligned with shifting interests of capital, what this chapter addresses is how the subjectivities of English as we have observed through this book may groom workers to become precarious subjects, modulating their hopes and expectations about life and work to be in tune with the insecure and uncertain conditions of labor. An important consequence of the neoliberal valorization of English that this chapter suggests, thus, is a naturalization and internalization of a precarious life—a molding of subjects who take precarity for granted and make it their own responsibility to endure such weary realities. For this we will look at how the elusive promise of English—the idea that English promises a successful, happy, desirable future—and the constant delaying of its gratification functioned as an iconic model for neoliberal subjectivity in Korea's neoliberal transformation where conditions of precarity were greatly exacerbated.

PROMISE OF ENGLISH IN A STATE OF PRECARITY

As outlined in Chapter 3, precarization of work and life has been a major characteristic of Korea's neoliberalization. Amidst the country's move toward neoliberal globalization, new labor laws introduced in 1996 removed many restrictions on mass layoffs and use of contingent labor, and in the aftermath of the Asian financial crisis of 1997, opportunities for full-time employment with secure contracts were drastically reduced. As a result, labor in 21st-century Korea came to be dominated by various forms of insecure work that offer low pay and provide little or no benefits, welfare, union representation, or stability of employment. This is typically represented by two broad categories of work: low-income self-employment, which often attracts layoffed middle-aged men and women who are forced to start a business in an overcrowded, low value-added service sector facing great risk of bankruptcy; and what is called irregular employment (*bijeongyujik*), encompassing a wide range of insecure employment such as short-term contract work, open contract work with limited possibility of promotion, dispatch work in which the worker is employed indirectly through an agency, and platform labor that offers little job security (Y. Lee 2015b). In 2018, 25.1% of the Korean population was working in self-employment (Kim 2019) and 40.6% in irregular work (Kim 2018), which demonstrates the alarming extent to which precarious labor pervades contemporary Korean society.

The Korean situation highlights how precarity is not just about insecure arrangements of employment, but also about the state of life. The expansion of precarious work has had a major impact on the fabric of Korean society. Poor and exploitative conditions of labor offered by insecure work expose workers to greater risk of overwork, health problems, work-related accidents, and even death. On December 10, 2018, Kim Yonggyun, a 24-year-old worker at Taean Power Station, was killed during his nightshift, when his body was sucked into a coal conveyor belt that decapitated him. He was a subcontracted irregular worker who was deployed with minimal safety training and safety equipment, doing a job meant for two people by himself, thereby deprived of a co-worker who could have saved his life by stopping the conveyor belt when he fell onto it. But he was not the first worker who faced such fate. According to the Korean Confederation of Trade Unions, 40 workers were killed in similar power plants across Korea between 2012 and 2016, 37 of whom were subcontracted workers like Kim (Jeong 2018). South Korea has one of the highest rates of workplace fatalities among OECD countries, and such deaths disproportionately consume irregular workers (G. Shin 2014). Precarious work in Korea thus not only devalues labor, but devalues life. It sends a clear message that human life is expendable—its extinguishment not an event worth stopping the conveyor belt of profit making.

Even young Koreans who manage to survive without facing such tragic demise as Kim do not get to live life to its full extent, as precarious life for them means that they need to give up many basic things in life to survive in the labor market that does not offer any stability, and moreover, pushes everyone into intense competition with everyone else for a way out of this state of insecurity. As discussed in Chapter 6, *enpo sedae* 'N-po generation' is a neologism that the younger generation uses to sarcastically refer to themselves, capturing how they are giving up (*pogi*) an increasing number (N) of things—romantic relations, marriage, having children, getting a decent job, owning a home, friendship, health, and eventually, hope—as precarious life in Korea simply does not leave them with the time, money, or energy to pursue any of these. Precarity takes its toll on Koreans as it leaves them high-strung on day-to-day survival, forgoing basic pleasures of life that become unaffordable and unimaginable. In this sense, precarity in neoliberal Korea also means taking on a particular subjectivity—one that takes a constant deferral on life itself. It reconceptualizes life as a series of accumulation of quantifiable skills that contribute to the value of one's human capital, and considers as wasted time and effort anything that does not add to that goal. It means relinquishing the right to declare, "I have worked hard enough for the day; now it is time to take off my worker's boots and relax with my loved ones, not worry about tomorrow; today I will savor life."

How do Koreans come to accept such a deal? Certainly socioeconomic realities leave them no choice but to invest everything in enhancing the value of one's human capital, or else, be consumed as expendable labor in the factory of death, metaphorical or literal. But how do such imperatives reach into their souls? How do they come to agree to defer life itself? In this chapter, I suggest subjectivities of English that mediate the neoliberal valorization of English facilitate that process. My argument here hinges on what I call "the promise of English"—the idea that acquiring good English language skills will lead to better jobs, better opportunities, and a better future—and how the logic of neoliberalism rationalizes the constant delaying of the fulfillment of that promise by convincing Koreans that they should do more to make that promise come true. English is, after all, one of the most crucial *seupek* ("spec"), or amassable qualifications (see Chapter 6), that young Koreans are expected to pursue in their struggle out of precarity, and for this reason, making Koreans responsible for the unrealized promise of English becomes a powerful way of inculcating subjects who take the same perspective on life as well—one which takes the deferral of life itself for granted.

The promise of English, of course, has been widely discussed and critiqued in previous literature. The belief that, with English, one can get a better job, absorb knowledge and information from sources all over the world, and ultimately, be recognized as a better person, someone who is respected and appreciated as well-rooted and competitive in the global market, is pervasive. Such assumptions often shape the linguistic investment of individuals, motivating them to learn English and improve their skills so that they may access better opportunities in education and in the job market. They influence language policies of states, leading to the choice of English over other languages as medium of instruction or official language. They serve as a discourse of justification for the global spread of English, by promoting English as an emancipatory and liberating language that allows disadvantaged people to escape abject poverty, immigrants to English-speaking countries to find a home, and underdeveloped states to participate in the global economy. However, as the chapters of this book have already shown, English does not exist in some neutral social space, but in regimes of language organized by relations of power and inequality. Thus, the rosy picture of English as a liberating language of social and economic advancement is an overly simplistic and facile assumption. Though certainly many people in many contexts do benefit from learning English, often the reality is that the promise of English remains unfulfilled, as learning English in itself does not necessarily guarantee better employment, national development, or social emancipation (Warriner 2007, 2016, Erling 2017, among others). Rather, it is more likely that such promise will work to obscure the historical, material, and political basis that gave rise to the myth of such promise in the first place. As Alastair Pennycook (2007b:100–101) argues:

Particularly salient today are claims that . . . English holds out promise of social and economic development to all those who learn it (rather than a language tied to very particular class positions and possibilities of development); and that English is a language of equal opportunity (rather than a language that creates barriers as much as it presents possibilities) . . . This thing called English colludes with many of the pernicious processes of globalisation, [and] deludes many learners through the false promises it holds out for social and material gain.

What I focus on in this chapter is not so much the fallacy of this promise itself, however, but how the unfulfilled promise of English is rationalized through a constant resetting of what counts as "good" English that has value in the capitalist market. The discussion follows how the most popular means of assessing candidates' English language competence in the Korean white-collar job market has changed throughout Korea's English fever—in particular, how the popularity of TOEIC (Test of English for International Communication) as a major assessment tool dramatically shifted over the course of a decade—and how such changes reflected a response to the increasingly heavy investments job seekers were making in learning the language. Such recurrent calibration of the linguistic market, I argue, is an important mechanism through which the fulfillment of the promise of English could be constantly deferred while keeping the allure of the promise alive; the job seeker who pursues that promise is led to a greater internalization of the logic of neoliberal capitalism, where the worker is expected to carry the burden of endless self-development. The prominence given to English in Korea's neoliberal transformation meant that such rationalization of the unfulfilled promise of English served as an iconic model for Koreans to make sense of the specter of precarity that was engulfing their lives, preparing them to accept a constant deferral on life itself.

THE RISE AND FALL OF TOEIC

As discussed in Chapter 3, beginning in the mid-1990s, Korean corporations, led by jaebeol groups that were actively invested in global expansion, reformulated their corporate culture by replacing past traditions which relied on hierarchical organizational structure with a new order that promoted employees' continuous self-development and entrepreneurship. In abolishing the seniority-based award system, corporations sought evidence of employees' active and flexible accumulation of soft skills, moving away from systems of assessment that focused on past achievements such as academic qualifications. It was in this context that English language skills became one of the most prominent points of assessment for employment and promotion. But what is important to note is not only the new emphasis placed on English language competence, but also the specific modes and means of evaluating such competence that were adopted in this process, and how they were justified. Indeed, throughout the first decade of the Korean English fever, the dominant modes of assessing workers' English language competence went through significant evolution. Tracing this process provides us with important insights about how such technologies of assessment were intertwined with ideologies of the neoliberal job market that worked to naturalize the promise of English.

Under the older regime of corporate evaluation of employees, testing competence in English was modeled after traditional written tests administered in the national educational system, which stereotypically focused on knowledge of grammatical structure. But by 1995, many companies started to replace those tests with various standardized tests. In particular, TOEIC became the test of choice for many corporations. Developed by the Educational Testing Service of the United States, TOEIC was claimed to be a test of communicative ability in an international business context, and for this reason, was presented as an appropriate instrument for assessing one's ability to use English in the global workplace. It was also presented as contrasting with traditional English tests tied to the national curriculum for English language learning, which was widely believed to be incapable of inculcating actual communicative competence in Koreans, therefore a more practical evaluation of communicative skills relevant to global communication.

This led to a veritable boom in studying for TOEIC. As shown in Chapter 3, preparing for TOEIC quickly became one of the most important tasks for university students, as many universities adopted it as part of their requirements for graduation, arguing that it would make their students more competitive in the job market. This was the context in which the neoliberal transformation of the Korean white-collar workplace was closely tied to the heightened interest in English across many domains of society. In the tumultuous period after the Asian financial crisis of 1997 and the subsequent neoliberal reform of many aspects of Korean society, during which job security became greatly threatened and unemployment and irregular employment skyrocketed, the importance of such tests was greatly intensified. The enormous significance of TOEIC in the Korean job market could be seen from the fact that, according to one report, among the 4 million people taking TOEIC worldwide every year, those taking the test in Korea accounted for more than 1.68 million (Hwang 2005).

But by 2005, another major change in the means for assessing English language skills took place, as TOEIC, which had been hailed as the best indicator of globally relevant English language competence, came to be seen with distrust. After 10 years of highlighting the importance of TOEIC, many companies started to reduce the weighting given to TOEIC in their overall scheme of evaluation, or abandoned using it altogether. Complaints about TOEIC started to abound, and corporations switched their preferred mode of assessment to methods that can directly observe the candidate's oral language skills, such as interviews or group discussions conducted in English. In most companies,

it was not the case that TOEIC was completely eliminated from the evaluation system of candidates' skills; but as a result of the criticism, TOEIC was
demoted from the most significant criterion to merely one item on the long
list of assessment tools that companies consider.

Why did this change take place? Why did TOEIC, one of the most prominent
emblems of the Korean English fever, suddenly turn into a target of criticism?
It was not the case that the emphasis on English language skills in corporate
culture or Korean society in general had waned; on the contrary, English had
become all the more important during the preceding decade. Ironically, it was
the persistence of the English fever and Koreans' large investments in English
that ultimately drove down the value of high TOEIC scores. After a decade's
worth of university graduates investing their time and money in TOEIC, levels of achievement gradually rose over time, to the extent that the standardized test came to lose its discriminatory power. In the words of one personnel
manager at a major corporation, "unlike 5, 6 years ago when there were only
a few candidates with scores of 900 and above, nowadays there are so many
high scorers that TOEIC scores are becoming meaningless" (Kwon and Heo
2005). In a sense, then, it was the very emphasis on TOEIC that ultimately
reduced its value as a key to securing white-collar jobs.

However, this phenomenon should not be seen as a mere case of the test's
reduced capacity for discriminating between applicants. This is because the
rise in overall TOEIC scores was not interpreted as a result of an actual increase in applicants' competence in English—that is, it was flatly denied that
high TOEIC scores had anything to do with candidates' actual English language skills. The general discourse surrounding the move away from TOEIC
was that, despite the abundance of high scores, speakers of good English
were still rare. According to one news report, managers at major corporations
were saying, "getting a perfect score on TOEIC does not mean one can speak
English well," and that "we cannot trust that a candidate with a high score in
TOEIC will have the ability to use English effectively, so we are testing their
skills in speaking and listening" (Kwon and Heo 2005). Another article reports
on Samsung's decision to reject any applicant whose conversational English
skills are insufficient, citing the jaebeol group's representative as saying, "according to an analysis of the scores of the applicants for the past three years,
the scores based on written tests such as TOEIC were generally high, but
there weren't many people who also had the conversational skills that are required for carrying out global business tasks" (Chu 2006). Such publicly circulated statements made clear that the perceived problem was not a general
rise in English language skills that necessitated a new mode of assessment,
but the persistent lack of good competence in English among Koreans despite
improved test scores.

Because of this, the problem was attributed to the testing instrument itself; if a high TOEIC score does not translate into good competence in English,

then it must be the test that is flawed. Again, such criticism could be widely found in the media. It was commonly claimed that the high scores in TOEIC are simply a reflection of the fact that many applicants have learned to beat the system by developing test-taking skills, rather than their competence in English. One article states that "there has been much debate about the credibility of TOEIC . . . there has been criticism that one can raise one's score in a short period of time just by learning how to make the right guess, regardless of one's English language skills" (Kim 2005). Another article (Hwang 2005) claims:

> it is possible to get a high score of 800–900 if one studies for a certain period of time at a cram school which provides specialized training . . . TOEIC leads to the study of "mute English" (*beongeoli yeongeo gongbu*). The speaking skills actually needed by corporations cannot be acquired by preparing for TOEIC, which focuses on listening and reading.

Arguably, there is some truth to such criticism. To anyone with minimal familiarity with language testing, it is obvious that results of written tests such as TOEIC cannot be seen as an ideal indicator of a speaker's communicative competence. The claim that language study in the Korean context often highlights test preparation rather than building communicative skills also reflects some real constraints on English language learning in Korea. Even if we acknowledge this, though, the new discourse on TOEIC was remarkable in its blanket denial that the rise in TOEIC scores could mean a rise in any kind of relevant communicative competence among Korean workers. While a high TOEIC score should not be equated with good competence in English, such an increase in TOEIC scores, particularly one that is so widespread and across-the-board as to necessitate the introduction of new modes of evaluation, certainly is an achievement of some sort. Moreover, it is problematic to assume Korean job seekers would have focused solely on test preparation when studying English. Given the widely promoted importance of English in Korean society over the previous decade, it is not likely that a reasonable white-collar job seeker with an awareness of the scarcity of good jobs would have completely neglected to develop her oral communication skills and chosen to invest all her effort only in getting a high score on TOEIC. We would also expect at least some of the effort put into studying for TOEIC to spill over into improvement of communicative competence. In fact, as noted earlier (Chapter 3), developing communicative competence had been an important task for university students and white-collar job seekers all along: "English conversation" (*yeongeo hoehwa*) had always been a lucrative business in Korea, with many English language schools specializing in conversational English and agencies that broker short-term overseas language study (*eohak yeonsu*) (Shin 2016). How effective such efforts are in helping Koreans develop good communicative competence is, of course, another question. But the point here is this: to argue that the rise in TOEIC scores had nothing to do with candidates' actual communicative skills is at best an unfair statement about Koreans' English language competence.

Complaints about Koreans' lack of good competence in English, indeed, as we have already seen, were a central aspect of Korea's language ideological landscape. The ideology of self-deprecation, discussed in Chapter 3, in which Koreans view themselves as "bad speakers of English" who are unable to speak English well despite many years of investment in learning the language (Park 2009), was clearly at work here. Claims about the inappropriateness of TOEIC and candidates' alleged focus on test-taking skills closely mirrored the popular figure of the Korean who is unable to speak a word upon meeting an English-speaking foreigner, despite having learned English in school and private study for over 10 years—an image that was frequently invoked as a main cause for Korea's weak economic influence in international relations and a major stumbling block to the country's globalization. Complaints about TOEIC also reflected common discourses that attributed Koreans' bad English to the "traditional" methods of English language teaching practiced in the Korean national curriculum, which are often assumed to focus on methods of grammar translation and rote memorization of grammatical rules or obscure lexical items. Here, it was again claimed that Koreans only learn English to pass tests—for instance, the college scholastic ability test for university admission—which leads to communication skills being largely neglected.

In other words, complaints about candidates' lack of English skills that served as the basis for repositioning TOEIC should be seen as part of this broader, situated, and highly particular ideological view of Koreans' English. In fact, it was an almost identical rhetoric of complaint that drove the English fever and brought TOEIC into prominence in the first place a decade earlier. TOEIC was initially hailed as an appropriate measure of communicative competence in English, thus an assessment tool that could lead Koreans to develop spoken skills in English and overcome their limitations as "bad speakers of English." For instance, it was claimed in one media report that "TOEIC, which quantifies one's ability to use English (*yeongeo gusa neunglyeok*), is being highlighted these days because it is appropriate in evaluating practical work aptitude such as conversational skills, compared to other tests" (Kang 1995). Such claims were made against the background of criticism that the education system is not producing Koreans who are able to speak English in a competent way, as illustrated in statements in the media that argued, "instead of grammar and reading comprehension, the society now needs skills in speaking and listening. The greatest goal for university seniors is to open one's mouth and ears to English" (Kim 1995).

This allows us to project a circulating pattern. Building upon broader discourses of English that problematize Koreans' English language competence, corporations initiate a renewed emphasis on the importance of English, setting the bar according to which "good competence in English" will be identified. This leads job seekers to invest in the achievement of that goal, and over time, more and more people start to meet that new criterion of "good English." The image of Koreans as bad speakers of English is then reinvoked, invalidating the achievements of those job seekers who have invested in satisfying the goals identified by the corporations, and the bar is reset to a higher point. This pattern shows that it is truly problematic to assume that meeting the target for good English as proposed by the corporate sorting machine would offer a chance for better jobs and a better financial future. The only ones who are guaranteed to gain in the circular pursuit of the promise of English are the English language teaching industry, which has indeed profited immensely through the Korean English fever (Nam 2012), and the corporations themselves, who get precisely what they wanted in the first place—workers with better English language skills—without having to acknowledge whatever achievements in learning English those workers have made. As the fulfillment of the promise of English is repeatedly deferred, job seekers in the Korean white-collar job market are now pressured into an even more intensified pursuit of English and kept under its great burden. The ironic outcome, then, is that despite TOEIC's reduced significance, job seekers still need to strive hard to get exceptionally high TOEIC scores above 900, in addition to pursuing a growing number of other skills and qualifications (Kim, Choi, and Kim 2018).

More important for our purposes, though, is how the corporate strategy of cyclic upgrading of the criteria for good English produces a joint effect of subjectivity that leads Korean white-collar workers to take this constant deferral for granted. The way in which the ever-evolving regimes of English language testing are rationalized serves as a technology of government, as it posits subjects who actively and continuously immerse themselves into enhancement of their skills in the English language (Shin 2018b). Indeed, as TOEIC's monopolistic significance declined, one rarely encountered complaints from Korean workers that high TOEIC scores were no longer recognized as evidence of good competence in English, or more generally, claims that Korean workers' competence in English has developed sufficiently through decades of heavy investment and hard work. Never was a voice of protest heard against the blatant disregard for the significant rise in TOEIC scores among job candidates or against the constant moving of the bar that left Koreans in an endless struggle with English. Most Koreans accepted that, regardless of their test scores, they are still lacking in good English skills, and continued to place the burden upon themselves to continuously develop better communicative competence in the language. In other words, the idea that the fulfillment of the promise of English may be indefinitely deferred was deeply internalized, inculcating in Koreans a subjectivity that led them to embrace the investments, efforts, and sacrifices they made for developing good English skills as a natural part of life—rather than rejecting them as a heavy burden and imposition that sucks away the time and energy needed to appreciate and nourish other aspects of their lives. The story of the rise and fall of TOEIC in Korea, then, offers insights into how political economic interests underlying the neoliberal promotion of English and subjective orientations to life may intersect. As I will outline in the next section, subjectivities of English may not only work to obscure the interests that underlie the constant upgrading of what counts as good English, but also serve as a model for a subjectivity that takes precarity for granted.

CONSEQUENCES FOR PRECARITY

The logic of deferral manifest in the constant delay of the fulfillment of the promise of English, in fact, is part of a more general mechanism through which capitalism operates. Deferred gratification, for instance, in which groups and individuals are guided to postpone pleasure and consumption in favor of working for some larger reward to be enjoyed later, is a fundamental ideological premise of capitalist accumulation, as noted by many including Max Weber in his work on Protestantism and the rise of capitalism (2001[1930]). Moreover, such continuous revisions in what counts as valued competence in the workplace can be seen as a process through which capital maximizes surplus value by devaluing the qualifications of workers. Such recalibrations operate through an underlying principle of distinction, where the classed structure of society is reproduced through a constant negotiation and struggle over the value of cultural, social, and symbolic capital. Pierre Bourdieu has noted, for instance, how the value of educational capital, in the form of academic qualifications, may be regularly recalibrated as the perceived value of those qualifications leads a wider section of the population to pursue them.

> The overproduction of qualifications, and the consequent devaluation, tend to become a structural constant when theoretically equal chances of obtaining qualifications are offered to all the offspring of the bourgeoisie . . . while the access of other classes to these qualifications also increases (in absolute terms). (Bourdieu 1984:147)

That such recalibration can be a powerful means of maintaining and reproducing structures of social inequality is also highlighted by the work of Krais (1993), who analyzes how the system of gender discrimination was reset with the introduction of women into the workforce. When women moved into the labor market during the 20th century, the system by which jobs were valued was reorganized so that men's labor ended up being valued more. This was done by distinguishing jobs into "skilled" and "unskilled" jobs, and then claiming that the "unskilled" ones were appropriate for women, thus reinscribing the unequal gender dichotomy that existed before women's foray into the job market. In this case, what played a significant role is how the definition of "skill" was ideologically controlled by power: "gender discrimination on the labor market, as is shown above, operates by the social recognition or denial of competences and skills. Recognition of skills . . . is mediated by power relations" (Krais 1993:167–68).

In other words, the structure of social inequality does not dissipate with more people investing in skills, competencies, and qualifications that supposedly lead to economic profit and social mobility. Capital continually refuses to recognize the value of the workers' labor even as it directly benefits from such investments, justifying its devaluing of labor on the basis of supposedly objective criteria, such as new classifications of skills or technologies of assessment deriving from "scientific" and "authoritative" principles. In this sense, the constant upgrading of skills, qualifications, and competencies expected of workers is a reflection of how capital views labor only as an expendable resource for profit making, through which each worker's hopes, efforts, desires, and sacrifices in working to improve themselves are denied any value. While workers around the world have always resisted and struggled against the devaluing of their labor, this strategy of constant deferral can be particularly powerful in undermining such resistance. This is not only because the devaluing of labor in this case is grounded on supposedly objective criteria, but also because the promise of better opportunities through accumulation of skills and qualifications are still left open; despite the dismal conditions of my current job, perhaps—just perhaps—there is some hope that I might have a better tomorrow if I do my best to improve myself today? In this way, the constant upgrading of criteria as a strategy of devaluing labor leaves the worker in a state of perpetual dependency on capital's recognition of her work as valuable, leading to an internalization of the logic of endless human capital development.

We can note that this state of dependency is also a state of precarity. On the one hand, it is unpredictable when and how the skills, qualifications, and competencies a worker has amassed for her job will be reevaluated—and it *will* be reevaluated as an absolute certainty—leaving the worker constantly wondering and worried about the future of her job and her preparedness for it. On the other hand, it leads the worker to take the devaluing of her labor for granted—for this is the implicit message that capital is constantly sending out—driving her toward permanent deferment of life to secure the time, effort, and energy demanded by the constant work of self-development. For this reason, while the constant reevaluation of skills is an inherent aspect of capitalism, it becomes particularly prominent in the context of neoliberalism, as it perfectly aligns with the neoliberal subjectivity in which the worker is guided to embody the project of human capital development. The anxious uncertainty instilled in the worker by the constant upgrading of criteria for valuable skills, then, is a major condition of the neoliberal job market that propagates a sense of precarity.

In the Korean case, we may argue that the shifting criteria for what counts as good English played an especially significant role in naturalizing this sense of precarity. As discussed throughout this book, good competence in English was probably the most prominent sign in Korea's neoliberalization that directly represented the ideal neoliberal subject, yet it was also a sign that was consistently presented as being out of reach for Koreans. Neoliberal valorization of English in the Korean fever, indeed, was framed precisely in terms of a discourse of crisis, in which Koreans' persistent inability to master good English was lamented as a handicap that was holding back Koreans in the new global economy. Also, what is meant by achieving good competence in English is inherently a more nebulous matter than, say, achieving good competence in computer programming or presentation skills, not only due to the nature of language as an unbounded communicative resource whose mastery cannot be measured meaningfully in terms of accomplishment of an arbitrary set of tasks, but also due to the fact that the notion of good English is a social construct entangled with histories of race, class, and colonialism that is political in nature and thus always open to contestation. For this reason, the constant deferral of the promise of English in the Korean job market was more likely to be perceived as natural and uncontroversial—which was indeed the case, as we have seen above.

This means that the recurrent devaluing of Koreans' achievements in English language learning served as an iconic model for neoliberal subjecthood in times of precarity. Just as the Korean English language learner does not question capital's assessment that her English language competence is not up to the level demanded by the global economy and instead invests in more English language learning despite uncertain prospects of return, the Korean worker is expected to not question the conditions of precarity in which time and effort spent in the accumulation of skills is rewarded only with insecure employment, and instead to take it upon herself to carry on in her continuous self-development, deferring a full and secure life to an indefinite future. In this sense, while the Korean English fever was obviously not the source of precarity in Korea, it certainly functioned as an effective arena that primed Koreans toward accepting precarity as normative. What was accomplished by the valorization of English in Korea's neoliberal transformation surrounding the turn of the century was to inculcate in Koreans a mindset that embraces precarity as a way of life. Through their struggles with English, in which they were constantly required to adapt to new modes of assessing English language competence, Korean workers were presented with a model for dealing with increasing precarity that was engulfing them—to accept that the need for self-improvement is a constant in life, that insecurity and instability of work is my responsibility to endure, and for that reason, that it is necessary to forgo the mundane pleasures of life today.

One of the questions this book started out with was why the neoliberal valorization of English should be an important issue for us, when the ills of neoliberalism are often much more violent and tragic, leading to loss of jobs, communities, and even lives—which makes having to learn a foreign language seem relatively benign. The chapters of this book have addressed this question by showing how the Korean English fever was not just about the learning of English but about shaping of subjectivities, thus leading to consequences that reach far beyond the domain of language, such as the conditions of precarity that overwhelm life under neoliberalism. One point to add by way of closing the argument, though, might be that such apparent benignness of language makes it an ideal entry point for the logic of neoliberalism to penetrate our lives. In the heated politics of English in Korea, issues like unequal access to opportunities for English language learning or the implications of the English fever for national identity are fiercely debated (Park 2009); however, when it comes to everyday realities of learning English, the loud argumentative voices of such debate fade away, and mundane and trivial routines of learning English often come to be seen an apolitical site. But the perspective that this book has tried to offer suggests otherwise. It may be precisely such moments—every evening a white-collar worker has to go to an English language class instead of spending time with her children after a long working day, every painstaking consideration of how much one can fork out to enroll in an English language learning program, every disappointment of failed job applications justified on the ground of lacking English language skills, every confusion experienced at the news of another new mode of assessing English language skills that corporations are introducing, and many others—where neoliberalism's devaluation of life seeps into our souls without suspicion. While English itself may not be evil, the way Koreans and other people around the world encounter the language as feeling, experiencing subjects under conditions of neoliberalism serves as a channel through which the logic of neoliberal capitalism seeps into their lives. This is why subjectivities of English can be a critical starting point for contesting the conditions of precarity that neoliberalism brings.

CONCLUSIONS

This chapter provided final reflections on this book's argument that the neoliberal valorization of English in South Korea had consequences beyond just the domain of language, contributing to the country's process of neoliberalization by offering an iconic model for the neoliberal subject who takes life of precarity for granted. The discussion above thus further emphasizes the importance of subjectivity in mediating the relationship between English and neoliberalism. If previous chapters focused on how Korea's pursuit of English in neoliberalism was not a mere pursuit of economic profit but a process of shaping English language learners into neoliberal subjects, this chapter highlighted how those subjectivities of English allowed the neoliberal logic of human capital development to penetrate deep into their souls, via the way experiences of language shape us as social beings. This points out how subjectivities of English and political economic conditions of neoliberalism can exist in a mutually constitutive relationship. As this chapter has argued, while the neoliberal condition of precarity and the fatal consequences it brings derive from the more fundamental characteristic of capitalism that constantly exploits workers for surplus value, the way language, particularly English, is appropriated in neoliberalism can be a powerful basis for naturalizing and rationalizing such bleak and insecure conditions of life. Questioning, critiquing, and contesting the neoliberal hegemony of English, then, becomes a task all the more important for us, as it can lead us to ponder the possibilities of undoing the devaluation of life brought about by conditions of precarity. And this makes subjectivities of English, as a site for the constitution of that hegemony, an unavoidable juncture for that task.

CHAPTER 9
Conclusions

RETHINKING ENGLISH, NEOLIBERALISM, AND SUBJECTIVITY

This chapter closes this book by summarizing the arguments made in the previous chapters and considering their implications. We started out with the question of the relationship between English and neoliberalism. What makes English such a sought-after language in the neoliberal global economy, when neoliberalism does not depend on English in itself and is in fact eager to appropriate any linguistic resource for the maximization of profit? This book tried to answer this question by considering how the neoliberal valorization of English is mediated by the perceptual, moral, and affective constitution of our selves. Foregrounding the nature of neoliberalism not just as an economic doctrine, but as an ideological regime that seeks to constitute us as particular kinds of subjects, it argued that it is the complex subjectivities of English that lead us to imbue the language with special significance—a language that stands for the ideal neoliberal subject. The chapters of this book traced this process using South Korea as an example, discussing how the feelings, affects, desires, hopes, and moral concerns that Koreans hold in relation to English are shaped by the historical, material, and ideological conditions of South Korea's neoliberalization, and how those subjectivities guide them to rationalize, naturalize, and internalize both the hegemonic status of English in neoliberalism and the neoliberal logic of human capital development.

An important benefit of this book's approach was that it allowed us to avoid taking the supposed economic worth of English at face value, but to question it as an ideological construction that is mediated by subjective positions we are guided to occupy. The multiple dimensions of subjectivity explored in previous chapters jointly work to shape Koreans into particular subjects—subjects who see English not simply as an economic resource but as an object of desire, the pursuit of which is a moral imperative that is closely tied with responsibly

In Pursuit of English. Joseph Sung-Yul Park, Oxford University Press. © Oxford University Press 2021.
DOI: 10.1093/oso/9780190855734.003.0009

cultivating the precious human capital residing in their bodies. Being such a subject also implies being in a constant state of anxiety and insecurity, which leads them to embrace and embody the logic of endless competition and self-development under neoliberalism. While much critical work has pointed out the problems of the neoliberal promotion of English, including shrinking domains reserved for local languages and the inequalities this produces, the findings of this book suggest that a more fundamental issue is how subjectivities of English lead us to view the neoliberal subject, who willingly engages in never-ending projects of self-improvement, as the ideal way of living, thereby rationalizing the structures of control inherent in neoliberalism.

This book's focus on subjectivity as a key for understanding the relationship between English and neoliberalism, therefore, offers a broader perspective on both English as a global language and neoliberalism as a political economic regime. It presses us to recognize that neither of them are natural, inevitable trends that define our time—instead, they are ideologically mediated by dimensions of subjectivity that represent specific historical and political interests. It thereby tells us that they are human processes, shaped, experienced, contested, and enacted through human agents who act within and against structural and material conditions of social life. However, the discussion of this book also suggests that they are not orderly processes accountable in terms of linear networks of cause and effect. Rather, the convergence of English, neoliberalism, and subjectivity is a process where the messiness of being a subject in a material world is highlighted. While the neoliberal valorization of English spurs Koreans toward being good subjects of neoliberalism, their experience of this is one of much tension, contradiction, and struggle—desiring English while being frustrated about the possibilities of securing it; morally driven to pursue English but also intensely troubled by its inequalities; nervous about losing the potential for acquiring the language but also confronted by one's illegitimacy as non-native speakers, and so on. This book's focus on subjectivity as a link between English and neoliberalism, then, also opens up room for identifying cracks in the position of hegemony that English and neoliberalism both claim. By outlining the ideologically fraught process by which English as a global language and the logic of neoliberalism mutually constitute each other, our attention to subjectivities of English language users in times of neoliberalism enables us to question that co-constitution.

TOWARD A GLOBAL ACCOUNT OF ENGLISH AND NEOLIBERALISM

This book based its discussion on the Korean context, arguing that the interlocking of widespread neoliberalization, intense English fever, and the strong affective and emotional significance attributed to English in Korean society made the country an ideal site for its investigation. The chapters of this book thus sought to understand the role of subjectivity in mediating English and neoliberalism through the lens of specific subjectivities salient in Korean context. To what extent would the findings of this book be generalizable? The neoliberal promotion of English has been explored in many national contexts now, and a growing number of them have attended to some aspect of subjectivity as a key for their investigation. For instance, neoliberal consolidation of higher education mediated by English in various countries of the Middle East and Southeast Asia has been analyzed in terms of desire for internationalization and economic development (Barnawi 2017, Phan 2017, Phan and Barnawi 2015); anxieties about future selves in the increasingly competition-driven job market have been emphasized to characterize experiences of English language learning in Asian states like Taiwan (Price 2014, Seilhamer 2019); colonial insecurities about English are shown to underlie class-based inequalities in postcolonial countries like the Philippines, where commodification of English language skills serves as a key source for profit (Tupas and Salonga 2016, Tupas 2019); and the notion of shame has been used to capture the tension between neoliberal orientation to English and local community norms in contexts such as Kiribati (Liyanage and Canagarajah 2019) and Qatar (Hillman and Ocampo Eibenschutz 2018). Such a body of work that turns to aspects of subjectivity for their accounts of the neoliberal valorization of English in specific national, regional, or cultural contexts suggests that the findings of this book would have much relevance beyond Korean context.

One caveat worth repeating here is that it was not a goal of this book to offer a systematic comparison between national contexts. In fact, the perspective of subjectivity adopted by this book, which views subjectivity as the socially situated and discursively mediated experience of being a subject, would probably require us to avoid treating aspects of desire, morality, anxiety, and insecurity as "parameters" that enable a structured analysis of correlations between social variables that can in turn explain and even predict national differences and similarities in the way neoliberal valorization of English proceeds. Considering the intersection of English and neoliberalism through the lens of subjectivity requires us to attend to the embodied, emplaced, and embedded nature of language use, and to resist the temptation to disaggregate aspects of subjectivity and social life into variables amenable to easy comparison. What we need instead is a deeper understanding about how individuals and communities under neoliberalism experience being an English language user within their specific contexts, which can only be obtained at the juncture of political economic conditions, socially circulating discourses, and ethnographic textures of life. Some exemplary studies have been pursuing this path through site-specific investigations of subjectivities of English in neoliberalism (for instance, Gao 2019, Seilhamer 2019), and this book's discussion attempted to push such efforts further, through a more explicit and substantial theorization of subjectivity as a link between English and neoliberalism.

Having said that, the uniqueness of the Korean context is also important to reiterate at this point. What most clearly distinguishes the Korean situation from that of other national contexts is probably the intensity of the investments in English across all levels of society—not simply the intensity of the economic investments, but the intensity of affective investments that characterize the country's English fever. Earlier in this book (see Chapter 3) I explained how, while strong (sometimes seemingly excessive) emotional responses to English in Korea might appear to derive from certain underlying traits that are associated with Korean culture, ultimately we need to attend to subjectivity as a materially grounded phenomenon, and situate Koreans' subjective experiences of English within political economic context. The chapters of this book thus outlined in detail how Korean subjectivities of English can only be understood in relation to the specific historical, political, and economic conditions of South Korea—such as the heavily dependent relationship the country had with the United States throughout its modern history, the exorbitant power that jaebeol corporations and conservative media institutions wield over Korean society, and rapidly changing relations of class that complicate notions of socioeconomic mobility and stability amidst the country's rapid economic ascent. But at the same time, the salience of such political economic conditions in shaping subjectivities found in the Korean case provides us with an important lesson for the study of English, neoliberalism, and subjectivity in other national contexts. That is, even though the subjectivities of English and the material conditions that are experienced by Koreans pursuing English may be unique to Korea, the Korean case nonetheless illustrates why subjectivity needs to be situated within political economic context for us to account for the neoliberal valorization of English that is taking place across many contexts of the world. In other words, the generalizability of the Korean case is likely to lie in the way it highlights the important links between subjectivity and political economy, urging studies of the neoliberal promotion of English in other national and cultural contexts to focus on subjectivity as the materially, ideologically, and politically mediated constitution of subjects.

SUBJECTIVITY IN LANGUAGE AND POLITICAL ECONOMY

Our discussion in the previous section also points to how the findings of this book have general implications that allow us to look beyond the case of English, as they show that research on language and political economy has much to gain by attending to aspects of subjectivity that underlie the incorporation of language into conditions of the changing economy. Though the valorization of English as a language of economic opportunity is only one specific instance of how language becomes a salient point of contention in contemporary global capitalism, the way in which it illustrates how such processes can be mediated by complex layers of subjectivities provides important clues for imagining future directions for expanding our research. While the materialist foundations of most research on political economy may lead us to consider the subjective as separate from the material and political, the discussion of this book demonstrates how the two cannot be conceived in terms of distinct realms. The Korean case shows how subjectivities of English are embedded in the embodied, material processes of political economic relations, and how conditions of neoliberalism in themselves constitute shaping of subjectivities. In fact, we may argue that the separation of the material from the subjective is an ideological construct to begin with. That is, by presenting Koreans' feelings, desires, and struggles about English as purely individual matters disconnected from material conditions of everyday life, such dualism of the material and the subjective can work to conceal how systems of exploitation based on the valorization of English as a global language may operate. The focus on subjectivity that this book proposes can thus help us to rethink the relationship between language and political economy by undoing such dichotomies.

Currently, within the field of sociolinguistics, research on commodification of language serves as a prominent framework for exploring language and political economy, and most productive studies in this area work by tracing the specific economic processes by which language gets incorporated into market-based systems of valuation, such as "the ways in which language skills operate as selection criteria, and how they get alternately emphasized and marginalized in relation to the fluctuation of the market" (Heller and Duchêne 2016:153), and how such processes in turn serve specific interests of capital. Attending to subjectivities of language can be an important way of extending the remit of such studies, for it will allow us to uncover how language is not simply one of the aspects of human life that gets incorporated in the commodifying machine of neoliberalism, but an important channel through which neoliberalism extends its control over our minds, bodies, and sense of being (Shin and Park 2016). In this way, the approach to language and political economy that foregrounds subjectivity, as promoted in this book, not only offers a more sophisticated account of the role of language in neoliberalism, but also helps to expand the relevance of sociolinguistic research to the study of neoliberalism. But in order to do this, we need to recognize that subjective experiences of being a language user is fraught with tensions based on material relations, and make them a serious focus for the study of language and political economy. This will also necessarily mean broadening of our ideas of what constitutes language; it requires us to accept that language is not an abstract code for transmitting messages, but socially embedded communicative practice of perceiving, feeling, and experiencing subjects acting in a material world.

Balancing our study of the material conditions of language in neoliberalism with an attention to the subjective also has broader implications for how sociolinguistic research positions itself in relation to the everyday struggles that people experience in the conditions of the global economy. Overlooking dimensions of subjectivity can lead us to lose sight of how we, as subjects who reside in the tension between structure and agency, must constantly operate against social constraints that limit our choices and life courses, but at the same time, are never completely deprived of the possibility of transforming and transcending those constraints. Focusing purely on economic relations that pertain to the promotion of English, for instance, carries the danger of inadvertently aligning with the neoliberal celebration of language as commodity (e.g., by naturalizing the indexical ties between English and economic profit that, in reality, only a minority of people can fully exploit) or falling into cynicism (e.g., by dismissing investments in English language learning as buying into a false and naive belief in the economic value of language). An approach to language and political economy that foregrounds people's subjective experiences can help us overcome such problems. By pointing toward our constitution as subjects entangled in material relations of power, it would instead remind us of the anxieties, desires, and tensions that permeate people's sociolinguistic choices in a neoliberal world, and guide us to seek ways in which sociolinguistic research can help address those struggles.

REFERENCES

Abelmann, Nancy, So Jin Park, and Hyunhee Kim. 2009. "College Rank and Neo-Liberal Subjectivity in South Korea: The Burden of Self-Development." *Inter-Asia Cultural Studies* 10 (2): 229–47. https://doi.org/10.1080/14649370902823371.

Adams, Vincanne, Michelle Murphy, and Adele E. Clarke. 2009. "Anticipation: Technoscience, Life, Affect, Temporality." *Subjectivity* 28 (1): 246–65. https://doi.org/10.1057/sub.2009.18.

Agamben, Giorgio. 1998. *Homo Sacer: Sovereign Power and Bare Life*. Stanford, CA: Stanford University Press.

Agha, Asif. 2005. "Voice, Footing, Enregisterment." *Journal of Linguistic Anthropology* 15 (1): 38–59.

Agha, Asif. 2007. *Language and Social Relations*. Cambridge: Cambridge University Press.

Agha, Asif. 2011. "Large and Small Scale Forms of Personhood." *Language & Communication* 31 (3): 171–80. https://doi.org/10.1016/j.langcom.2011.02.006.

Ahn, Hyejeong. 2013. "English Policy in South Korea: A Role in Attaining Global Competitiveness or a Vehicle of Social Mobility?" *Journal of English as an International Language* 8 (1): 1–20.

Alarcón, Amado, and Josiah McC. Heyman. 2013. "Bilingual Call Centers at the US-Mexico Border: Location and Linguistic Markers of Exploitability." *Language in Society* 42 (1): 1–21. https://doi.org/10.1017/S0047404512000875.

Allan, Kori. 2013. "Skilling the Self: The Communicability of Immigrants as Flexible Labour." In *Language, Migration and Social Inequalities: A Critical Sociolinguistic Perspective on Institutions and Work*, edited by Alexandre Duchêne, Melissa G. Moyer, and Celia Roberts, 56–78. Bristol: Multilingual Matters.

Allison, Anne. 2012. "Ordinary Refugees: Social Precarity and Soul in 21st Century Japan." *Anthropological Quarterly* 85 (2): 345–70. https://doi.org/10.1353/anq.2012.0027.

An, Gyeong-suk. 2006. "Balhaengbusu jeomyuyul jojungdong 75% isang." *Midieo Oneul*, October 19, 2006. http://www.mediatoday.co.kr/news/articleView.html?idxno=50964.

Anagnost, Ann. 2000. "Scenes of Misrecognition: Maternal Citizenship in the Age of Transnational Adoption." *Positions* 8 (2): 389–421.

Androutsopoulos, Jannis. 2016. "Theorizing Media, Mediation and Mediatization." In *Sociolinguistics: Theoretical Debates*, edited by Nikolas Coupland, 282–302. Cambridge: Cambridge University Press.

Aneja, Geeta A. 2016. "Rethinking Nativeness: Toward a Dynamic Paradigm of (Non) Native Speakering." *Critical Inquiry in Language Studies* 13 (4): 351–79. https://doi.org/10.1080/15427587.2016.1185373.

Archibugi, Daniele. 2005. "The Language of Democracy: Vernacular or Esperanto? A Comparison between the Multiculturalist and Cosmopolitan Perspectives." *Political Studies* 53 (3): 537–55.

Bae, So Hee. 2013. "The Pursuit of Multilingualism in Transnational Educational Migration: Strategies of Linguistic Investment among Korean *Jogi Yuhak* Families in Singapore." *Language and Education* 27 (5): 415–31. https://doi.org/10.1080/09500782.2012.709863.

Bae, So Hee. 2014a. "Language Ideology and Linguistic Investment among Korean Educational Migrant Families in Singapore." PhD dissertation, Singapore: National University of Singapore.

Bae, So Hee. 2014b. "Anxiety, Insecurity and Complexity of Transnational Educational Migration among Korean Middle Class Families." *Journal of Asian Pacific Communication* 24 (2): 152–72. https://doi.org/10.1075/japc.24.2.01hee.

Bae, So Hee. 2015. "Complexity of Language Ideologies in Transnational Movement: Korean *Jogi Yuhak* Families' Ambivalent Attitudes towards Local Varieties of English in Singapore." *International Journal of Bilingual Education and Bilingualism* 18 (6): 643–59. https://doi.org/10.1080/13670050.2014.932326.

Bae, So Hee, and Joseph Sung-Yul Park. 2020. "Investing in the Future: Korean Early English Education as Neoliberal Management of Youth." *Multilingua* 39 (3): 277–297. https://doi.org/10.1515/multi-2019-0009.

Bailey, Keiron. 2006. "Marketing the Eikaiwa Wonderland: Ideology, Akogare, and Gender Alterity in English Conversation School Advertising in Japan." *Environment and Planning D: Society and Space* 24 (1): 105–30. https://doi.org/10.1068/d418.

Bakhtin, Mikhail. M. 1986. *Speech Genres and Other Late Essays.* Austin: University of Texas Press.

Barnawi, Osman. 2017. *Neoliberalism and English Language Education Policies in the Arabian Gulf.* New York: Taylor & Francis.

Bauman, Richard, and Charles L. Briggs. 2003. *Voices of Modernity: Language Ideologies and the Politics of Inequality.* Cambridge: Cambridge University Press.

Becker, Gary. 1993. *Human Capital: A Theoretical and Empirical Analysis, with Special Reference to Education* (3rd ed.). Chicago: The University of Chicago Press.

Berardi, Franco. 2009. *The Soul at Work: From Alienation to Autonomy.* Los Angeles: Semiotext(e).

Berardi, Franco. 2013. "Journey to Seoul (2)." July 23, 2013. http://through-eu.s3-website.eu-west-2.amazonaws.com/th-rough.eu/writers/bifo-eng/journey-seoul-2/index.html.

Bernstein, Katie A., Emily A. Hellmich, Noah Katznelson, Jaran Shin, and Kimberly Vinall. 2015. "Critical Perspectives on Neoliberalism in Second/Foreign Language Education: Introduction." *L2 Journal* 7 (3): 3–14.

Besnier, Niko. 1990. "Language and Affect." *Annual Review of Anthropology* 19 (1): 419–51. https://doi.org/10.1146/annurev.an.19.100190.002223.

Biehl, João, Byron Good, and Arthur Kleinman, eds. 2007. *Subjectivity: Ethnographic Investigations.* Berkeley: University of California Press.

Blackman, Lisa, John Cromby, Derek Hook, Dimitris Papadopoulos, and Valerie Walkerdine. 2008. "Creating Subjectivities." *Subjectivity* 22 (1): 1–27. https://doi.org/10.1057/sub.2008.8.

Block, David. 2014. *Social Class in Applied Linguistics.* New York: Routledge.

Block, David, and John Gray. 2016. "'Just Go Away and Do It and You Get Marks': The Degradation of Language Teaching in Neoliberal Times." *Journal of Multilingual and Multicultural Development* 37 (5): 481–94. https://doi.org/10.1080/01434632.2015.1071826.

Block, David, John Gray, and Marnie Holborow. 2012. *Neoliberalism and Applied Linguistics*. London: Routledge.

Blustein, Paul. 2001. *The Chastening: Inside the Crisis That Rocked the Global Financial System and Humbled the IMF*. New York: Public Affairs.

Boas, Taylor C., and Jordan Gans-Morse. 2009. "Neoliberalism: From New Liberal Philosophy to Anti-Liberal Slogan." *Studies in Comparative International Development* 44 (2): 137–61. https://doi.org/10.1007/s12116-009-9040-5.

Bonfiglio, Thomas Paul. 2013. "Inventing the Native Speaker." *Critical Multilingualism Studies* 1 (2): 29–58.

Bourdieu, Pierre. 1984. *Distinction: A Social Critique of the Judgement of Taste*. London: Routledge.

Bourdieu, Pierre. 1991. *Language and Symbolic Power*. Cambridge, MA: Harvard University Press.

Bourdieu, Pierre. 1998. "The Essence of Neoliberalism." *Le Monde Diplomatique (English Edition)*, December. http://mondediplo.com/1998/12/08bourdieu.

Brenner, Neil, Jamie Peck, and Nik Theodore. 2010. "Variegated Neoliberalization: Geographies, Modalities, Pathways." *Global Networks* 10 (2): 182–222.

Brenner, Neil, and Nik Theodore. 2002. "Cities and the Geographies of 'Actually Existing Neoliberalism.'" *Antipode* 34 (3): 349–79. https://doi.org/10.1111/1467-8330.00246.

British Council. 2013. *The English Effect: The Impact of English, What It's Worth to the UK and Why It Matters to the World*. The British Council.

Brown, Megan. 2009. *The Cultural Work of Corporations*. New York: Palgrave Macmillan.

Browne, Katherine E. 2009. "Economics and Morality: Introduction." In *Economics and Morality: Anthropological Approaches*, edited by Katherine E. Browne and B. Lynne Milgram, 1–40. Lanham, MD: AltaMira Press.

Brutt-Griffler, Janina. 2002. *World English: A Study of Its Development*. Clevedon: Multilingual Matters.

Bucholtz, Mary, and Kira Hall. 2016. "Embodied Sociolinguistics." In *Sociolinguistics: Theoretical Debates*, edited by Nikolas Coupland, 173–98. Cambridge: Cambridge University Press.

Butler, Yuko Goto. 2015. "English Language Education among Young Learners in East Asia: A Review of Current Research (2004–2014)." *Language Teaching* 48 (3): 303–42. https://doi.org/10.1017/S0261444815000105.

Byean, Hyera. 2015. "English, Tracking, and Neoliberalization of Education in South Korea." *TESOL Quarterly* 49 (4): 867–82.

Cameron, Deborah. 2000. *Good to Talk?: Living and Working in a Communication Culture*. London: Sage.

Cameron, Deborah. 2005. "Communication and Commodification: Global Economic Change in Sociolinguistic Perspective." In *Language, Communication and the Economy*, edited by Guido Erreygers, 9–23. Amsterdam: John Benjamins.

Campbell, Sarah, and Celia Roberts. 2007. "Migration, Ethnicity and Competing Discourses in the Job Interview: Synthesizing the Institutional and Personal." *Discourse & Society* 18 (3): 243–71. https://doi.org/10.1177/0957926507075474.

Canagarajah, A. Suresh. 1999. *Resisting Linguistic Imperialism in English Teaching*. Oxford: Oxford University Press.

Cavanaugh, Jillian R, and Shalini Shankar, eds. 2017. *Language and Materiality: Ethnographic and Theoretical Explorations*. Cambridge: Cambridge University Press.

Cho, Donmoon. 2006. "Haebang 60 nyeon hanguksahoe gyegeupgujo byeonhwawa nodonggyegeup gyegeupguseong byeonhwa." In *Gwangbok 60 Nyeon: Hangukui Byeonhwawa Seongjang Geuligo Huimang*. Seoul: Guksapyeonchanwiwonhoe.

Cho, Hae-joang. 2015. "The Spec Generation Who Can't Say 'No': Overeducated and Underemployed Youth in Contemporary South Korea." *Positions* 23 (3): 437–62. https://doi.org/10.1215/10679847-3125823.

Cho, Jinhyun. 2012. "Campus in English or Campus in Shock?" *English Today* 28 (2): 18–25. https://doi.org/10.1017/S026607841200020X.

Cho, Jinhyun. 2017. *English Language Ideologies in Korea: Interpreting the Past and Present*. New York: Springer.

Choi, Chul Woong. 2013. "Ilsangui geumyunghwawa taljeongchihwaui jeongchi." *Munhwagwahak* 74: 284–311.

Choi, Jinsook. 2016. "'Speaking English Naturally': The Language Ideologies of English as an Official Language at a Korean University." *Journal of Multilingual and Multicultural Development* 37 (8): 783–93. https://doi.org/10.1080/01434632.2016.1142550.

Choi, Lee Jin. 2014. "Fragile Bilinguals: Rescaling 'Good' and 'Bad' South Korean Bilinguals." PhD dissertation, University of Illinois at Urbana-Champaign.

Choi, Lee Jin. 2016. "Revisiting the Issue of Native Speakerism: 'I Don't Want to Speak like a Native Speaker of English.'" *Language and Education* 30 (1): 72–85. https://doi.org/10.1080/09500782.2015.1089887.

Choi, Lee Jin. 2021. "'English Is Always Proportional to One's Wealth': English, English Language Education, and Social Reproduction in South Korea." *Multilingua* 40 (1): 87–106. https://doi.org/10.1515/multi-2019-0031.

Choi, Saetbyeol. 2007. "Hanguksahoeeseo yeongeosillyeokeun munhwajaboninga: Daehaksaengdeurui yeongeohakseup siltaewa yeongeo neungtongjae daehan insikeul jungsimeuro." In *Yeongeo, nae maeumui sikminjuui*, edited by Jigwan Yun, 105–30. Seoul: Dangdae.

Chu, Wang-hun. 2006. "'Yeongeokkwang'eun samseonggeulup ipsa pogihaeya." *Hangyoreh*, February 3, 2006. http://www.hani.co.kr/arti/economy/working/99672.html.

Chun, Christian W. 2017. *The Discourses of Capitalism: Everyday Economists and the Production of Common Sense*. New York: Routledge.

Chun, Jennifer Jihye, and Ju Hui Judy Han. 2015. "Language Travels and Global Aspirations of Korean Youth." *Positions* 23 (3): 565–93. https://doi.org/10.1215/10679847-3125913.

Cohen, Susanne. 2015. "The New Communication Order: Management, Language, and Morality in a Multinational Corporation." *American Ethnologist* 42 (2): 324–39. https://doi.org/10.1111/amet.12133.

Colebrook, Claire. 2002. *Understanding Deleuze*. Crows Nest, N.S.W: Allen & Unwin.

Comaroff, John L., and Jean Comaroff. 2009. *Ethnicity, Inc*. Chicago: University of Chicago Press.

Curran, Nathaniel Ming. 2018. "Learned Through Labour: The Discursive Production of English Speakers in South Korea." *English Today* 34 (3): 30–35. https://doi.org/10.1017/S0266078417000608.

Curran, Nathaniel Ming. 2021. "English, Gatekeeping, and Mandarin: The Future of Language Learning in South Korea." *International Journal of Bilingual Education and Bilingualism* 24 (5): 723–735. https://doi.org/10.1080/13670050.2018.1501332.

Dardot, Pierre, and Christian Laval. 2013. *The New Way of the World: On Neoliberal Society*. London: Verso.

De Costa, Peter I. 2015. "Reenvisioning Language Anxiety in the Globalized Classroom Through a Social Imaginary Lens." *Language Learning* 65 (3): 504–32. https://doi.org/10.1111/lang.12121.

De Costa, Peter, Joseph Sung-Yul Park, and Lionel Wee. 2016. "Language Learning as Linguistic Entrepreneurship: Implications for Language Education." *The Asia-Pacific Education Researcher* 25 (5–6): 695–702. https://doi.org/10.1007/s40299-016-0302-5.

Deleuze, Gilles, and Félix Guattari. 1983. *Anti-Oedipus: Capitalism and Schizophrenia*. Minneapolis: University of Minnesota Press.

Dor, Daniel. 2004. "From Englishization to Imposed Multilingualism: Globalization, the Internet, and the Political Economy of the Linguistic Code." *Public Culture* 16 (1): 97–118.

Duchêne, Alexandre, and Monica Heller, eds. 2012. *Language in Late Capitalism: Pride and Profit*. New York: Routledge.

Duménil, Gérard, and Dominique Lévy. 2004. *Capital Resurgent: Roots of the Neoliberal Revolution*. Cambridge, MA: Harvard University Press.

Dunn, Bill. 2017. "Against Neoliberalism as a Concept." *Capital & Class* 41 (3): 435–454. https://doi.org/10.1177/0309816816678583.

Ehrenreich, Barbara. 1989. *Fear of Falling: The Inner Life of the Middle Class*. New York: Pantheon.

Enever, Janet. 2018. *Policy and Politics in Global Primary English*. Oxford: Oxford University Press.

Enever, Janet, and Jayne Moon. 2009. "New Global Contexts for Teaching Primary ELT: Change and Challenge." In *Young Learner English Language Policy and Implementation: International Perspectives*, edited by Janet Enever, Jayne Moon, and Uma Raman, 5–18. Reading: Garnet Education.

Enever, Janet, Jayne Moon, and Uma Raman, eds. 2009. *Young Learner English Language Policy and Implementation: International Perspectives*. Reading: Garnet Education.

Erling, Elizabeth J. 2017. "Language Planning, English Language Education and Development Aid in Bangladesh." *Current Issues in Language Planning* 18 (4): 388–406. https://doi.org/10.1080/14664208.2017.1331496.

Ertman, Martha M., and Joan C. Williams, eds. 2005. *Rethinking Commodification: Cases and Readings in Law and Culture*. New York: New York University Press.

Ferguson, James. 2009. "The Uses of Neoliberalism." *Antipode* 41 (S1): 166–84. https://doi.org/10.1111/j.1467-8330.2009.00721.x.

Fishman, Joshua A., Andrew W. Conrad, and Alma Rubal-Lopez, eds. 1996. *Post-Imperial English: Status Change in Former British and American Colonies, 1940–1990*. Berlin: Mouton de Gruyter.

Flores, Nelson, and Jonathan Rosa. 2015. "Undoing Appropriateness: Raciolinguistic Ideologies and Language Diversity in Education." *Harvard Educational Review* 85 (2): 149–71. https://doi.org/10.17763/0017-8055.85.2.149.

Flubacher, Mi-Cha. 2020. "'Selling the Self': Packaging the Narrative Trajectories of Workers for the Labour Market." *International Journal of Multilingualism* 17 (1): 30–45. https://doi.org/10.1080/14790718.2020.1682249.

Flubacher, Mi-Cha, and Alfonso Del Percio, eds. 2017. *Language, Education and Neoliberalism: Critical Studies in Sociolinguistics*. Bristol: Multilingual Matters.

Flubacher, Mi-Cha, Alexandre Duchêne, and Renata Coray. 2018. *Language Investment and Employability*. Cham: Palgrave Macmillan.

Foucault, Michel. 1978. *The History of Sexuality*. Volume 1. New York: Pantheon Books.

Foucault, Michel. 1980. *Power/Knowledge: Selected Interviews and Other Writings, 1972–1977*. Edited by Colin Gordon. New York: Pantheon Books.

Foucault, Michel. 1982. "The Subject and Power." *Critical Inquiry* 8: 777–95.

Foucault, Michel. 1993. "About the Beginning of the Hermeneutics of the Self: Two Lectures at Dartmouth." *Political Theory* 21 (2): 198–227. https://doi.org/10.1177/0090591793021002004.

Foucault, Michel. 1997. *Ethics: Subjectivity and Truth*. New York: The New Press.

Foucault, Michel. 2008. *The Birth of Biopolitics: Lectures at the Collège de France, 1978–79*. Basingstoke: Palgrave Macmillan.

Gal, Susan, and Kathryn A. Woolard. 2001. "Constructing Languages and Publics: Authority and Representation." In *Languages and Publics: The Making of Authority*, edited by Susan Gal and Kathryn A. Woolard, 1–12. Manchester: St. Jerome.

Ganti, Tejaswini. 2014. "Neoliberalism." *Annual Review of Anthropology* 43 (1): 89–104. https://doi.org/10.1146/annurev-anthro-092412-155528.

Gao, Shuang. 2012. "Commodification of Place, Consumption of Identity: The Sociolinguistic Construction of a 'Global Village' in Rural China." *Journal of Sociolinguistics* 16 (3): 336–57. https://doi.org/10.1111/j.1467-9841.2012.00534.x.

Gao, Shuang. 2019. *Aspiring to Be Global: Language and Social Change in a Tourism Village in China*. Bristol: Multilingual Matters.

Gao, Shuang, and Joseph Sung-Yul Park. 2015. "Space and Language Learning under the Neoliberal Economy." *L2 Journal* 7 (3): 78–96.

Gaudio, Rudolf P. 2003. "Coffeetalk: Starbucks™ and the Commercialization of Casual Conversation." *Language in Society* 32 (5): 659–91. https://doi.org/10.1017/S0047404503325035.

Gee, James Paul, Glynda A. Hull, and Colin Lankshear. 1996. *The New Work Order: Behind the Language of the New Capitalism*. St. Leonards: Allen & Unwin.

Gershon, Ilana. 2016. "'I'm Not a Businessman, I'm a Business, Man': Typing the Neoliberal Self into a Branded Existence." *HAU: Journal of Ethnographic Theory* 6 (3): 223–46. https://doi.org/10.14318/hau6.3.017.

Giddens, Anthony. 1984. *The Constitution of Society: Outline of the Theory of Structuration*. Cambridge: Polity Press.

Gordon, Colin. 1991. "Governmental Rationality: An Introduction." In *The Foucault Effect: Studies in Governmentality*, edited by Graham Burchell, Colin Gordon, and Peter Miller, 1–51. London: Harvester Wheatsheaf.

Gowan, Peter. 1999. *The Global Gamble: Washington's Faustian Bid for World Dominance*. London: Verso.

Gramling, David. 2016. *The Invention of Monolingualism*. New York: Bloomsbury Academic.

Gray, John. 2010. "The Branding of English and The Culture of the New Capitalism: Representations of the World of Work in English Language Textbooks." *Applied Linguistics* 31 (5): 714–33. https://doi.org/10.1093/applin/amq034.

Gumperz, John. 1982. *Discourse Strategies*. Cambridge: Cambridge University Press.

Habermas, Jürgen. 1989. *The Structural Transformation of the Public Sphere: An Inquiry into a Category of Bourgeois Society*. Cambridge, MA: MIT Press.

Hamid, M. Obaidul. 2010. "Globalisation, English for Everyone and English Teacher Capacity: Language Policy Discourses and Realities in Bangladesh." *Current Issues in Language Planning* 11 (4): 289–310. https://doi.org/10.1080/14664208.2011.532621.

Harvey, David. 2005. *A Brief History of Neoliberalism*. Oxford: Oxford University Press.

Heller, Monica. 2003. "Globalization, the New Economy, and the Commodification of Language and Identity." *Journal of Sociolinguistics* 7 (4): 473–92.

Heller, Monica. 2010. "The Commodification of Language." *Annual Review of Anthropology* 39 (1): 101–14. https://doi.org/10.1146/annurev.anthro.012809.104951.

Heller, Monica, and Alexandre Duchêne. 2016. "Treating Language as an Economic Resource: Discourse, Data and Debate." In *Sociolinguistics: Theoretical Debates*, edited by Nikolas Coupland, 139–56. Cambridge: Cambridge University Press.

Heller, Monica, Joan Pujolar, and Alexandre Duchêne. 2014. "Linguistic Commodification in Tourism." *Journal of Sociolinguistics* 18 (4): 539–66. https://doi.org/10.1111/josl.12082.

Henry, Eric Steven. 2010. "Interpretations of 'Chinglish': Native Speakers, Language Learners and the Enregisterment of a Stigmatized Code." *Language in Society* 39 (5): 669–88. https://doi.org/10.1017/S0047404510000655.

Hillman, Sara, and Emilio Ocampo Eibenschutz. 2018. "English, Super-Diversity, and Identity in the State of Qatar." *World Englishes* 37 (2): 228–47. https://doi.org/10.1111/weng.12312.

Hiramoto, Mie, and Joseph Sung-Yul Park. 2014. "Anxiety, Insecurity, and Border Crossing: Language Contact in a Globalizing World." *Journal of Asian Pacific Communication* 24 (2): 141–51. https://doi.org/10.1075/japc.24.2.001int.

Hochschild, Arlie Russell. 2003. *The Managed Heart: Commercialization of Human Feeling*. Berkeley: University of California Press.

Holborow, Marnie. 2015. *Language and Neoliberalism*. New York: Routledge.

Holborow, Marnie. 2018a. "Language Skills as Human Capital? Challenging the Neoliberal Frame." *Language and Intercultural Communication* 18 (5): 520–32. https://doi.org/10.1080/14708477.2018.1501846.

Holborow, Marnie. 2018b. "Language, Commodification and Labour: The Relevance of Marx." *Language Sciences* 70: 58–67. https://doi.org/10.1016/j.langsci.2018.02.002.

Holliday, Adrian. 2005. *The Struggle to Teach English as an International Language*. Oxford: Oxford University Press.

Hsu, Funie. 2015. "The Coloniality of Neoliberal English: The Enduring Structures of American Colonial English Instruction in the Philippines and Puerto Rico." *L2 Journal* 7 (3): 123–45.

Huer, John. 2009. "Psychology of Korean Han." *The Korea Times*, March 22, 2009. https://www.koreatimes.co.kr/www/news/opinon/2012/08/272_41770.html.

Hwang, Bo-yeon. 2005. "Banjjokjjali yeongeo injaeneun gala!" *Hangyoreh*, July 8, 2005. http://www.hani.co.kr/arti/economy/economy_general/48579.html.

Hwang, Gyu-jin. 2006. *Pathways to State Welfare in Korea: Interests, Ideas and Institutions*. Aldershot: Ashgate.

Iedema, Rick, and Hermine Scheeres. 2003. "From Doing Work to Talking Work: Renegotiating Knowing, Doing, and Identity." *Applied Linguistics* 24 (3): 316–37. https://doi.org/10.1093/applin/24.3.316.

Inoue, Miyako. 2006. *Vicarious Language: Gender and Linguistic Modernity in Japan*. Berkeley: University of California Press.

Irvine, Judith T., and Susan Gal. 2000. "Language Ideology and Linguistic Differentiation." In *Regimes of Language: Ideologies, Polities, and Identities*, edited by Paul V. Kroskrity, 35–83. Santa Fe, NM: School of American Research Press.

Ives, Peter. 2010. "Cosmopolitanism and Global English: Language Politics in Globalisation Debates." *Political Studies* 58 (3): 516–35. https://doi.org/10.1111/j.1467-9248.2009.00781.x.

Jahan, Iffat, and M. Obaidul Hamid. 2019. "English as a Medium of Instruction and the Discursive Construction of Elite Identity." *Journal of Sociolinguistics* 23 (4): 386–408. https://doi.org/10.1111/josl.12360.

Jang, Gwiyeon. 2013. "Sinjayujuui Sidae Hangukui Gyegeupgujo." *Mareukeuseujuui Yeongu* 10 (3): 12–40.

Jang, In Chull. 2015. "Language Learning as a Struggle for Distinction in Today's Corporate Recruitment Culture: An Ethnographic Study of English Study Abroad Practices among South Korean Undergraduates." *L2 Journal* 7 (3): 57–77.

Jang, In Chull. 2017. "Consuming Global Language and Culture: South Korean Youth in English Study Abroad." PhD dissertation, Toronto: University of Toronto.

Jenks, Christopher J. 2017. *Race and Ethnicity in English Language Teaching: Korea in Focus*. Bristol: Multilingual Matters.

Jenks, Christopher J., and Jerry Won Lee. 2020. "Native Speaker Saviorism: A Racialized Teaching Ideology." *Critical Inquiry in Language Studies* 17 (3): 186–205. https://doi.org/10.1080/15427587.2019.1664904.

Jeon, Mihyon. 2012a. "Globalization of English Teaching and Overseas Koreans as Temporary Migrant Workers in Rural Korea." *Journal of Sociolinguistics* 16 (2): 238–54.

Jeon, Mihyon. 2012b. "English Immersion and Educational Inequality in South Korea." *Journal of Multilingual and Multicultural Development* 33 (4): 395–408. https://doi.org/10.1080/01434632.2012.661438.

Jeon, Mihyon, and Jiyoon Lee. 2006. "Hiring Native-Speaking English Teachers in East Asian Countries." *English Today* 22 (4): 53–58. https://doi.org/10.1017/S0266078406004093.

Jeong, Lakin. 2018. "Jukeumui jakeopjange naemollin 'cheongnyeon Gim Yonggyun.'" *Sisajeoneol*, December 21, 2018. https://www.sisajournal.com/news/articleView.html?idxno=179247.

Jessop, Bob. 2002. "Liberalism, Neoliberalism, and Urban Governance: A State-Theoretical Perspective." *Antipode* 34 (3): 452–72. https://doi.org/10.1111/1467-8330.00250.

Ji, Juhyeong. 2011. Hanguk Sinjayujuuiui giwongwa hyeongseong. Seoul: Chaekseang.

Johnstone, Barbara. 2009. "Pittsburghese Shirts: Commodification and the Enregisterment of an Urban Dialect." *American Speech* 84 (2): 157–75. https://doi.org/10.1215/00031283-2009-013.

Jonna, R. Jamil, and John Bellamy Foster. 2015. "Marx's Theory of Working-Class Precariousness—and Its Relevance Today." *Alternate Routes: A Journal of Critical Social Research* 27: 21–45.

Jordan, Agnes Sohn. 2019. "Making an Exit: Millennials, Place-Making, and Exodus at South Korea's Edge." PhD dissertation, Urbana: University of Illinois at Urbana-Champaign.

Kachru, Braj B. 1985. "Standards, Codification and Sociolinguistic Realism: The English Language in the Outer Circle." In *English in the World: Teaching and Learning the*

Language and Literature, edited by Randolph Quirk and H. G. Widdowson, 11–30. Cambridge: Cambridge University Press.

Kachru, Braj B. 1997. "World Englishes and English-Using Communities." *Annual Review of Applied Linguistics* 17: 66–87.

Kalleberg, Arne L., and Steven P. Vallas. 2018. "Probing Precarious Work: Theory, Research, and Politics." In *Precarious Work: Causes, Characteristics, and Consequences*, edited by Arne L. Kalleberg and Steven P. Vallas, 1–30. Bingley: Emerald.

Kang, Hyeon-Seok. 2017. "Is English Being Challenged by Mandarin in South Korea?" *English Today* 33 (4): 40–46. https://doi.org/10.1017/S0266078417000220.

Kang, Inkyu. 2014. "It All Started with a Bang: The Role of PC Bangs in South Korea's Cybercultures." In *The Korean Popular Culture Reader*, edited by Kyung Hyun Kim and Youngmin Choe, 56–75. Durham, NC: Duke University Press.

Kang, Jiyeon, and Nancy Abelmann. 2011. "The Domestication of South Korean Pre-College Study Abroad in the First Decade of the Millennium." *Journal of Korean Studies* 16 (1): 89–118. https://doi.org/10.1353/jks.2011.0001.

Kang, Junman. 2007. "Yeongeogwangpungeun haplijeok haengwida." *Hangyore 21*, 668, July 21, 2007. http://legacy.h21.hani.co.kr/section-021128000/2007/07/021128000200707120668029.html.

Kang, M. Agnes. 2003. "Negotiating Conflict within the Constraints of Social Hierarchies in Korean American Discourse." *Journal of Sociolinguistics* 7 (3): 299–320. https://doi.org/10.1111/1467-9481.00226.

Kang, Myung-koo. 2005. "The Struggle for Press Freedom and Emergence of 'Unelected' Media Power in South Korea." In *Asian Media Studies: Politics of Subjectivities*, edited by John Nguyet Erni and Siew Keng Chua, 75–90. Oxford: Blackwell.

Kang, Sejun. 1995. "Toik dolpung: Eoje yukmanyeomyeong eungsi." *Hangyoreh*, September 25, 1995.

Kang, Yoonhee. 2012. "Singlish or Globish: Multiple Language Ideologies and Global Identities among Korean Educational Migrants in Singapore." *Journal of Sociolinguistics* 16 (2): 165–83. https://doi.org/10.1111/j.1467-9841.2011.00522.x.

Kang, Yoonhee. 2015. "Going Global in Comfort: The South Korean Educational Exodus in Singapore." In *South Korea's Education Exodus: The Life and Times of Early Study Abroad*, edited by Adrienne Lo, Nancy Abelmann, Soo Ah Kwon, and Sumie Okazaki, 125–46. Seattle: University of Washington Press.

Kang, Yoonhee. 2018. "A Pathway to 'Constant Becoming': Time, Temporalities and the Construction of Self among South Korean Educational Migrants in Singapore." *Discourse: Studies in the Cultural Politics of Education* 39 (5): 798–813. https://doi.org/10.1080/01596306.2018.1435584.

Keat, Russell, and Nicholas Abercrombie, eds. 1991. *Enterprise Culture*. New York: Routledge.

Kelsky, Karen. 2001. *Women on the Verge: Japanese Women, Western Dreams*. Durham, NC: Duke University Press.

Kim, Boksun, and Hyeonsang Jeong. 2016. "Choegeun bijeonggyujik nodongsijangui byeonhwa: 2015nyeon 8wol geunlohyeongtaebyeol bugajosaleul iyonghayeo." *Nodongribyu* 130: 91–108. https://www.kli.re.kr/kli/downloadPodFile.do?pdicalOrginlDwldNo=3346.

Kim, Heesam. 2011. Yeongeogyoyuk tujaui hyeongpyeongseonggwa hyoyulseonge gwanhan yeongu. Report no. 2011–04. Korea Development Institute.

Kim, Hyejin. 2017. "'Spoon Theory' and the Fall of a Populist Princess in Seoul." *The Journal of Asian Studies* 76 (4): 839–49. https://doi.org/10.1017/S0021911817000778.

Kim, Jaegon. 2005. "Malmundadhin yeongeoneun no! Toik sidae kkeutnana?" *Jugan Chosun*, September 28, 2005.

Kim, Jeehun. 2010. "'Downed' and Stuck in Singapore: Lower/Middle Class South Korean Wild Geese (Kirogi) Children in Singapore." In *Globalization, Changing Demographics, and Educational Challenges in East Asia*, edited by Emily Hannum, Hyunjoon Park, and Yuko Goto Butler, 271–311. Bingley: Emerald Group Publishing.

Kim, Jeehun, and Sumie Okazaki. 2017. "Short-Term 'Intensive Mothering' on a Budget: Working Mothers of Korean Children Studying Abroad in Southeast Asia." *Asian Women* 33 (3): 111–39.

Kim, Jeongyeon, Jinsook Choi, and Bradley Tatar. 2017. "English-Medium Instruction and Intercultural Sensitivity: A Korean Case Study." *Journal of Studies in International Education* 21 (5): 467–82. https://doi.org/10.1177/1028315317720767.

Kim, Miso, Duk-In Choi, and Tae-Young Kim. 2018. "A Political Economic Analysis of Commodified English in South Korean Neoliberal Labor Markets." *Language Sciences* 70: 82–91. https://doi.org/10.1016/j.langsci.2018.05.011.

Kim, Nadia Y. 2008. *Imperial Citizens: Koreans and Race from Seoul to LA*. Stanford, CA: Stanford University Press.

Kim, Sandra So Hee Chi. 2017. "Korean Han and the Postcolonial Afterlives of 'The Beauty of Sorrow.'" *Korean Studies* 41: 253–79. https://doi.org/10.17613/M6WN61.

Kim, Stephanie K. 2016. "English Is for Dummies: Linguistic Contradictions at an International College in South Korea." *Compare: A Journal of Comparative and International Education* 46 (1): 116–35. https://doi.org/10.1080/03057925.2014.922409.

Kim, Stephanie K. 2018. "Illegitimate Elites and the Politics of Belonging at a Korean University." *Journal of Korean Studies* 23 (1): 175–202. https://doi.org/10.1215/21581665-4339107.

Kim, Yeonjeong. 2019. "Jinanhae hanguk jayeongeopja bijung 25.1%: OECD 5wi." *Yonhap News*, September 30, 2019. https://www.yna.co.kr/view/AKR20190929059600002.

Kim, Yong Cheol. 1998. "Industrial Reform and Labor Backlash in South Korea: Genesis, Escalation, and Termination of the 1997 General Strike." *Asian Survey* 38 (12): 1142–60.

Kim, Young Chun. 2016. *Shadow Education and the Curriculum and Culture of Schooling in South Korea*. New York: Palgrave Macmillan.

Kim, Yundeok. 1995. "'Yeongeolo deudgo malhala' Kaempeoseu samkineun 'toik yeol-pung.'" *Kyunghyang Sinmun*, September 5, 1995.

Kim, Yuseon. 2018. "Bijeonggyujik gyumowa siltae." *KLSI Issue Paper* 101. Hanguknodongsahoeyeonguso.

Kipnis, Andrew B. 2008. "Audit Cultures: Neoliberal Governmentality, Socialist Legacy, or Technologies of Governing?" *American Ethnologist* 35 (2): 275–89.

Koo, Hagen. 2000. "The Dilemmas of Empowered Labor in Korea: Korean Workers in the Face of Global Capitalism." *Asian Survey* 40 (2): 227–50. https://doi.org/10.2307/3021131.

Krais, Beate. 1993. "Gender and Symbolic Violence: Female Oppression in the Light of Pierre Bourdieu's Theory of Social Practice." In *Bourdieu: Critical Perspectives*, edited by Craig Calhoun, Edward LiPuma, and Moishe Postone, 156–77. Chicago: University of Chicago Press.

Kramsch, Claire. 2006. "The Traffic in Meaning." *Asia Pacific Journal of Education* 26 (1): 99–104. https://doi.org/10.1080/02188790600608091.

Kramsch, Claire. 2009. *The Multilingual Subject: What Foreign Language Learners Say about Their Experience and Why It Matters*. Oxford: Oxford University Press.

Kroskrity, Paul V. 2004. "Language Ideologies." In *A Companion to Linguistic Anthropology*, edited by Alessandro Duranti, 496–517. Malden, MA: Blackwell.

Kroskrity, Paul V., ed. 2000. *Regimes of Language: Ideologies, Polities, and Identities*. Santa Fe, NM: School of American Research Press.

Kubota, Ryuko. 2011a. "Questioning Linguistic Instrumentalism: English, Neoliberalism, and Language Tests in Japan." *Linguistics and Education* 22 (3): 248–60. https://doi.org/10.1016/j.linged.2011.02.002.

Kubota, Ryuko. 2011b. "Learning a Foreign Language as Leisure and Consumption: Enjoyment, Desire, and the Business of *Eikaiwa*." *International Journal of Bilingual Education and Bilingualism* 14 (4): 473–88. https://doi.org/10.1080/13670050.2011.573069.

Kubota, Ryuko. 2013. "'Language Is Only a Tool': Japanese Expatriates Working in China and Implications for Language Teaching." *Multilingual Education* 3 (4). https://doi.org/doi:10.1186/2191-5059-3-4.

Kubota, Ryuko. 2016. "The Multi/Plural Turn, Postcolonial Theory, and Neoliberal Multiculturalism: Complicities and Implications for Applied Linguistics." *Applied Linguistics* 37 (4): 474–94. https://doi.org/10.1093/applin/amu045.

Kumaravadivelu, B. 2016. "The Decolonial Option in English Teaching: Can the Subaltern Act?" *TESOL Quarterly* 50 (1): 66–85. https://doi.org/10.1002/tesq.202.

Kwon, Giseok, and Yun Heo. 2005. "'Jeomsu nopado oegukingwa daehwa an doede-ola': Toik manjeomjado chwieop nakbang." *Kookmin Ilbo*, July 6, 2005.

Kwon, Oryang, and Jeonglyeol Kim. 2010. *Hangukyeongeogyoyuksa*. Seoul: Hangukmunhwasa.

Labov, William. 1966. *The Social Stratification of English in New York City*. Washington, D.C.: Center for Applied Linguistics.

Labov, William. 1972a. *Language in the Inner City: Studies in the Black English Vernacular*. Philadelphia: University of Pennsylvania Press.

Labov, William. 1972b. *Sociolinguistic Patterns*. Philadelphia: University of Pennsylvania Press.

Labov, William. 2001. *Principles of Linguistic Change, Vol 2: Social Factors*. Malden, MA: Blackwell.

Lee, Hakyoon. 2010. "'I Am a Kirogi Mother': Education Exodus and Life Transformation Among Korean Transnational Women." *Journal of Language, Identity & Education* 9 (4): 250–64. https://doi.org/10.1080/15348458.2010.503915.

Lee, Hikyoung, and Kathy Lee. 2013. "Publish (in International Indexed Journals) or Perish: Neoliberal Ideology in a Korean University." *Language Policy* 12 (3): 215–30. https://doi.org/10.1007/s10993-012-9267-2.

Lee, Jaeyoon. 2015. "Jogiyuhaksaengsu chui." *Yonhap News*, November 17, 2015. http://m.yna.co.kr/kr/contents/?cid=GYH20151117000300044.

Lee, Jamie Shinhee. 2016. "'Everywhere You Go, You See English!': Elderly Women's Perspectives on Globalization and English." *Critical Inquiry in Language Studies* 13 (4): 319–50. https://doi.org/10.1080/15427587.2016.1190654.

Lee, Junhyeop. 2016. Cheongnyeon goyongbojojipyoui hyeonhwanggwa gaeseon-bangan. VIP Report 658. Hyundai Research Institute. http://hri.co.kr/board/reportView.asp?numIdx=25772&firstDepth=1&secondDepth=1.

Lee, Mun Woo. 2010. "The Issues and Self-Perceptions of Korean Early Study-Abroad Undergraduates in the U.S." *Ijungeoneohak* 43: 301–24.

Lee, Mun Woo. 2016. "'Gangnam Style' English Ideologies: Neoliberalism, Class and the Parents of Early Study-Abroad Students." *International Journal of Bilingual Education and Bilingualism* 19 (1): 35–50. https://doi.org/10.1080/13670050.2014.963024.

Lee, Sook-Jong, and Taejoon Han. 2006. "The Demise of 'Korea, Inc.': Paradigm Shift in Korea's Developmental State." *Journal of Contemporary Asia* 36 (3): 305–24. https://doi.org/10.1080/00472330680000191.

Lee, Yoonkyung. 2015a. "Sky Protest: New Forms of Labour Resistance in Neo-Liberal Korea." *Journal of Contemporary Asia* 45 (3): 443–64. https://doi.org/10.1080/00472336.2015.1012647.

Lee, Yoonkyung. 2015b. "Labor after Neoliberalism: The Birth of the Insecure Class in South Korea." *Globalizations* 12 (2): 184–202. https://doi.org/10.1080/14747731.2014.935087.

Leeman, Jennifer, and Glenn Martínez. 2007. "From Identity to Commodity: Ideologies of Spanish in Heritage Language Textbooks." *Critical Inquiry in Language Studies* 4 (1): 35–65. https://doi.org/10.1080/15427580701340741.

Lemke, Thomas. 2001. "'The Birth of Bio-Politics': Michel Foucault's Lecture at the Collège de France on Neo-Liberal Governmentality." *Economy and Society* 30 (2): 190–207. https://doi.org/10.1080/03085140120042271.

Lemke, Thomas. 2011a. "Beyond Foucault: From Biopolitics to the Government of Life." In *Governmentality: Current Issues and Future Challenges*, edited by Ulrich Bröckling, Susanne Krasmann, and Thomas Lemke, 165–84. New York: Routledge.

Lemke, Thomas. 2011b. *Biopolitics: An Advanced Introduction*. New York: New York University Press.

Lie, John. 1998. *Han Unbound: The Political Economy of South Korea*. Stanford, CA: Stanford University Press.

Lim, Jae Hoon. 2012. "South Korea's 'School Collapse' Debates." In *No Alternative?: Experiments in South Korean Education*, edited by Nancy Abelmann, Jung-Ah Choi, and So Jin Park, 28–43. Berkeley: University of California Press.

Liyanage, Indika, and Suresh Canagarajah. 2019. "Shame in English Language Teaching: Desirable Pedagogical Possibilities for Kiribati in Neoliberal Times." *TESOL Quarterly* 53 (2): 430–55. https://doi.org/10.1002/tesq.494.

Lo, Adrienne. 2004. "Evidentiality and Morality in a Korean Heritage Language School." *Pragmatics* 14 (2/3): 235–56.

Lo, Adrienne. 2009. "Lessons about Respect and Affect in a Korean Heritage Language School." *Linguistics and Education* 20 (3): 217–34. https://doi.org/10.1016/j.linged.2009.07.002.

Lo, Adrienne. 2020. "Race, Language, and Representations." *International Journal of the Sociology of Language* 263: 77–83. https://doi.org/10.1515/ijsl-2020-2085.

Lo, Adrienne, Nancy Abelmann, Soo Ah Kwon, and Sumie Okazaki, eds. 2015. *South Korea's Education Exodus: The Life and Times of Early Study Abroad*. Seattle: University of Washington Press.

Lo, Adrienne, and Lee Jin Choi. 2017. "Forming Capital: Emblematizing Discourses of Mobility in South Korea." *Language in Society* 46 (1): 77–93. https://doi.org/10.1017/S0047404516000816.

Lo, Adrienne, and Jenna Kim. 2011. "Manufacturing Citizenship: Metapragmatic Framings of Language Competencies in Media Images of Mixed Race Men in

South Korea." *Discourse & Society* 22 (4): 440–57. https://doi.org/10.1177/0957926510395834.

Lo, Adrienne, and Jenna Kim. 2012. "Linguistic Competency and Citizenship: Contrasting Portraits of Multilingualism in the South Korean Popular Media." *Journal of Sociolinguistics* 16 (2): 255–76.

Lo, Adrienne, and Jenna Kim. 2015. "Early Wave Returnees in Seoul: The Dilemmas of Modernity and Morality." In *South Korea's Education Exodus: The Life and Times of Early Study Abroad*, edited by Adrienne Lo, Nancy Abelmann, Soo Ah Kwon, and Sumie Okazaki, 168–88. Seattle: University of Washington Press.

López-Gopar, Mario E., and William Sughrua. 2014. "Social Class in English Language Education in Oaxaca, Mexico." *Journal of Language, Identity & Education* 13 (2): 104–10. https://doi.org/10.1080/15348458.2014.901822.

Lorente, Beatriz P. 2012. "The Making of 'Workers of the World': Language and the Labor Brokerage State." In *Language in Late Capitalism: Pride and Profit*, edited by Alexandre Duchêne and Monica Heller, 183–206. New York: Routledge.

Lorente, Beatriz P. 2017. *Scripts of Servitude: Language, Labor Migration and Transnational Domestic Work*. Bristol: Multilingual Matters.

Luhrmann, T. M. 2006. "Subjectivity." *Anthropological Theory* 6 (3): 345–61. https://doi.org/10.1177/1463499606066892.

Lutz, Catherine, and Lila Abu-Lughod, eds. 1990. *Language and the Politics of Emotion*. Cambridge: Cambridge University Press.

Maldonado-Torres, Nelson. 2007. "On the Coloniality of Being: Contributions to the Development of a Concept." *Cultural Studies* 21 (2–3): 240–70. https://doi.org/10.1080/09502380601162548.

Martín Rojo, Luisa, and Alfonso Del Percio, eds. 2020. *Language and Neoliberal Governmentality*. London: Routledge.

Martín Rojo, Luisa. 2020. "The 'Self-Made Speaker': The Neoliberal Governance of Speakers." In *Language and Neoliberal Governmentality*, edited by Luisa Martín Rojo and Alfonso Del Percio, 162–89. London: Routledge.

Marx, Karl. 1964. *Economic and Philosophic Manuscripts of 1844*. New York: International Publishers.

Matear, Ann. 2008. "English Language Learning and Education Policy in Chile: Can English Really Open Doors for All?" *Asia Pacific Journal of Education* 28 (2): 131–47. https://doi.org/10.1080/02188790802036679.

May, Stephen. 2014. "Contesting Public Monolingualism and Diglossia: Rethinking Political Theory and Language Policy for a Multilingual World." *Language Policy* 13 (4): 371–93. https://doi.org/10.1007/s10993-014-9327-x.

Mbembe, Achille. 2003. "Necropolitics." *Public Culture* 15 (1): 11–40.

McElhinny, Bonnie. 2010. "The Audacity of Affect: Gender, Race, and History in Linguistic Accounts of Legitimacy and Belonging." *Annual Review of Anthropology* 39 (1): 309–28. https://doi.org/10.1146/annurev-anthro-091908-164358.

McGill, Kenneth. 2013. "Political Economy and Language: A Review of Some Recent Literature." *Journal of Linguistic Anthropology* 23 (2): E84–101.

Mignolo, Walter, and Catherine E. Walsh. 2018. *On Decoloniality: Concepts, Analytics, and Praxis*. Durham, NC: Duke University Press.

Millar, Kathleen M. 2014. "The Precarious Present: Wageless Labor and Disrupted Life in Rio de Janeiro, Brazil." *Cultural Anthropology* 29 (1): 32–53. https://doi.org/10.14506/ca29.1.04.

Mincer, Jacob. 1958. "Investment in Human Capital and Personal Income Distribution." *Journal of Political Economy* 66 (4): 281–302.

Ministry of Education [Gyoyukbu]. 1995. "Gukminhakkyo gyoyukgwajeong: Chonglon, Yeongeo." Gyoyukbu Gosi 1995-7.

Ministry of Education, Science, and Technology [Gyoyukgwahakgisulbu]. 2011. "Yeongeogwa Gyoyukgwajeong." Gyoyukgwahakgisulbu Gosi 2011-361, Supplement 14. http://ncic.kice.re.kr/nation.kri.org.

Mirchandani, Kiran. 2012. *Phone Clones: Authenticity Work in the Transnational Service Economy*. Ithaca, NY: ILR Press.

Mirowski, Philip, and Dieter Plehwe, eds. 2009. *The Road from Mont Pèlerin: The Making of the Neoliberal Thought Collective*. Cambridge, MA: Harvard University Press.

Motha, Suhanthie. 2014. *Race, Empire, and English Language Teaching: Creating Responsible and Ethical Anti-Racist Practice*. New York: Teachers College Press.

Motha, Suhanthie, and Angel Lin. 2014. "'Non-Coercive Rearrangements': Theorizing Desire in TESOL." *TESOL Quarterly* 48 (2): 331–59. https://doi.org/10.1002/tesq.126.

Muth, Sebastian. 2018. "'The Ideal Russian Speaker Is No Russian': Language Commodification and Its Limits in Medical Tourism to Switzerland." *Language Policy* 17 (2): 217–37. https://doi.org/10.1007/s10993-017-9434-6.

Muth, Sebastian, and Alfonso Del Percio. 2018. "Policing for Commodification: Turning Communicative Resources into Commodities." *Language Policy* 17 (2): 129–35. https://doi.org/10.1007/s10993-017-9441-7.

Nam, Taehyeon. 2012. Yeongeogyegeupsahoe. Paju: Owolui Bom.

Nelson, Laura. 2000. *Measured Excess: Status, Gender, and Consumer Nationalism in South Korea*. New York: Columbia University Press.

Niño-Murcia, Mercedes. 2003. "'English Is Like the Dollar': Hard Currency Ideology and the Status of English in Peru." *World Englishes* 22 (2): 121–41. https://doi.org/10.1111/1467-971X.00283.

Oak, Cheol. 2016. "10dae jaebeolgamun sangjangsa jusikgachi jeungsi sigachongaek jeolban chaji." *Yonhap News*, August 3, 2016. https://www.yna.co.kr/view/AKR20160802167700003.

Ochs, Elinor, and Bambi B. Schieffelin. 1989. "Language Has a Heart." *Text* 9 (1): 7–25.

OECD. 2017. "Poverty Rate (Indicator)." https://data.oecd.org/inequality/poverty-rate.htm.

Ong, Aihwa. 2006. *Neoliberalism as Exception: Mutations in Citizenship and Sovereignty*. Durham, NC: Duke University Press.

Ortner, Sherry. 2005. "Subjectivity and Cultural Critique." *Anthropological Theory* 5 (1): 31–52. https://doi.org/10.1177/1463499605050867.

Park, Byeonglyul. 2017. "Hanguk nodongja mog bosang OECD choehawigwon." *Kyunghyang Sinmun*, October 10, 2017. http://biz.khan.co.kr/khan_art_view.html?code=920100&artid=201710100600065.

Park, Joseph Sung-Yul. 2009. *The Local Construction of a Global Language: Ideologies of English in South Korea*. Berlin: Mouton de Gruyter.

Park, Joseph Sung-Yul. 2012. "English as Border-Crossing: Longing and Belonging in the South Korean Experience." In *English Language as Hydra: Its Impacts on Non-English Language Cultures*, edited by Vaughan Rapatahana and Pauline Bunce, 208–20. Bristol: Multilingual Matters.

Park, Joseph Sung-Yul. 2013a. "English, Class and Neoliberalism in South Korea." In *The Politics of English: South Asia, Southeast Asia and the Asia Pacific*, edited by Lionel Wee, Robbie B. H. Goh, and Lisa Lim, 287–302. Amsterdam: John Benjamins.

Park, Joseph Sung-Yul. 2013b. "Metadiscursive Regimes of Diversity in a Multinational Corporation." *Language in Society* 42 (5): 557–77. https://doi.org/10.1017/S0047404513000663.

Park, Joseph Sung-Yul. 2014. "Cartographies of Language: Making Sense of Mobility among Korean Transmigrants in Singapore." *Language & Communication* 39: 83–91. https://doi.org/10.1016/j.langcom.2014.09.001.

Park, Joseph Sung-Yul. 2015. "Structures of Feeling in Unequal Englishes." In *Unequal Englishes: The Politics of Englishes Today*, edited by Ruanni Tupas, 59–73. New York: Palgrave Macmillan.

Park, Joseph Sung-Yul. 2017. "English as the Medium of Instruction in Korean Higher Education: Language and Subjectivity as Critical Perspective on Neoliberalism." In *Language, Education and Neoliberalism: Critical Studies in Sociolinguistics*, edited by Mi-Cha Flubacher and Alfonso Del Percio, 82–100. Bristol: Multilingual Matters.

Park, Joseph Sung-Yul. 2018. "Mediatizing Neoliberalism: The Discursive Construction of Education's 'Future.'" *Language and Intercultural Communication* 18 (5): 478–89. https://doi.org/10.1080/14708477.2018.1501843.

Park, Joseph Sung-Yul. 2020a. "Emotion, Language, and Cultural Transformation." In *The Routledge Handbook of Language and Emotion*, edited by Sonya E. Pritzker, Janina Fenigsen, and James Wilce, 100–113. New York: Taylor and Francis.

Park, Joseph Sung-Yul. 2020b. "Translating Culture in the Global Workplace: Language, Communication, and Diversity Management." *Applied Linguistics* 41 (1): 109–28. https://doi.org/10.1093/applin/amz019.

Park, Joseph Sung-Yul. Forthcoming. "Figures of Personhood: Time, Space, and Affect as Heuristics for Metapragmatic Analysis." *International Journal of the Sociology of Language*.

Park, Joseph Sung-Yul, and Sohee Bae. 2009. "Language Ideologies in Educational Migration: Korean Jogi Yuhak Families in Singapore." *Linguistics and Education* 20 (4): 366–77. https://doi.org/10.1016/j.linged.2009.09.001.

Park, Joseph Sung-Yul, and Sohee Bae. 2015. "School Choice in the Global Schoolhouse: How Korean Education Migrants Calibrate 'Success' in Singapore." In *South Korea's Education Exodus: The Life and Times of Early Study Abroad*, edited by Adrienne Lo, Nancy Abelmann, Soo Ah Kwon, and Sumie Okazaki, 85–102. Seattle: University of Washington Press.

Park, Joseph Sung-Yul, and Adrienne Lo. 2012. "Transnational South Korea as a Site for a Sociolinguistics of Globalization: Markets, Timescales, Neoliberalism." *Journal of Sociolinguistics* 16 (2): 147–64. https://doi.org/10.1111/j.1467-9841.2011.00524.x.

Park, Joseph Sung-Yul, and Lionel Wee. 2012. *Markets of English: Linguistic Capital and Language Policy in a Globalizing World*. New York: Routledge.

Park, So Jin, and Nancy Abelmann. 2004. "Class and Cosmopolitan Striving: Mothers' Management of English Education in South Korea." *Anthropological Quarterly* 77 (4): 645–72.

Pavlenko, Aneta. 2005. *Emotions and Multilingualism*. Cambridge: Cambridge University Press.

Peck, Jamie. 2013. "Explaining (with) Neoliberalism." *Territory, Politics, Governance* 1 (2): 132–57. https://doi.org/10.1080/21622671.2013.785365.

Peck, Jamie, and Nik Theodore. 2012. "Reanimating Neoliberalism: Process Geographies of Neoliberalisation." *Social Anthropology* 20 (2): 177–85. https://doi.org/10.1111/j.1469-8676.2012.00194.x.

Pennycook, Alastair. 1994. *The Cultural Politics of English as an International Language*. London: Longman.

Pennycook, Alastair. 1998. *English and the Discourses of Colonialism*. London: Routledge.

Pennycook, Alastair. 2007a. *Global Englishes and Transcultural Flows*. London: Routledge.

Pennycook, Alastair. 2007b. "The Myth of English as an International Language." In *Disinventing and Reconstituting Languages*, edited by Sinfree Makoni and Alastair Pennycook, 90–115. Clevedon: Multilingual Matters.

Phan, Le Ha. 2017. *Transnational Education Crossing Asia and the West: Adjusted Desire, Transformative Mediocrity, Neo-Colonial Disguise*. London: Routledge.

Phan, Le Ha, and Osman Z. Barnawi. 2015. "Where English, Neoliberalism, Desire and Internationalization Are Alive and Kicking: Higher Education in Saudi Arabia Today." *Language and Education* 29 (6): 545–65. https://doi.org/10.1080/09500782.2015.1059436.

Phillipson, Robert. 1992. *Linguistic Imperialism*. Oxford: Oxford University Press.

Piller, Ingrid, and Jinhyun Cho. 2013. "Neoliberalism as Language Policy." *Language in Society* 42 (1): 23–44. https://doi.org/10.1017/S0047404512000887.

Piller, Ingrid, and Kimie Takahashi. 2006. "A Passion for English: Desire and the Language Market." In *Bilingual Minds: Emotional Experience, Expression, and Representation*, edited by Aneta Pavlenko, 59–83. Clevedon: Multilingual Matters.

Piller, Ingrid, and Kimie Takahashi. 2013. "Language Work Aboard the Low-Cost Airline." In *Language, Migration and Social Inequalities: A Critical Sociolinguistic Perspective on Institutions and Work*, edited by Alexandre Duchêne, Melissa Moyer, and Celia Roberts, 95–117. Bristol: Multilingual Matters.

Pirie, Iain. 2008. *The Korean Developmental State: From Dirigisme to Neo-Liberalism*. London: Routledge.

Prendergast, Catherine. 2008. *Buying into English: Language and Investment in the New Capitalist World*. Pittsburgh, PA: University of Pittsburgh Press.

Prentice, Michael M. 2017. "Ranks & Files: Corporate Hierarchies, Genres of Management, and Shifting Control in South Korea's Corporate World." PhD dissertation, Ann Arbor: University of Michigan.

Price, Gareth. 2014. "English for All? Neoliberalism, Globalization, and Language Policy in Taiwan." *Language in Society* 43 (5): 567–89. https://doi.org/10.1017/S0047404514000566.

Proctor, Lavanya Murali. 2014. "English and Globalization in India: The Fractal Nature of Discourse." *Journal of Linguistic Anthropology* 24 (3): 294–314. https://doi.org/10.1111/jola.12056.

Quijano, Anibal. 2000. "Coloniality of Power, Eurocentrism, and Latin America." *Nepantla: Views from South* 1 (3): 533–80.

Rahman, Tariq. 2009. "Language Ideology, Identity and the Commodification of Language in the Call Centers of Pakistan." *Language in Society* 38 (2): 233–58. https://doi.org/10.1017/S0047404509090344.

Rajan-Rankin, Sweta. 2016. "The 'Authentic Cybertariat'? Commodifying Feeling, Accents, and Cultural Identities in the Global South." In *Intimate Economies*, edited by Susanne Hofmann and Adi Moreno, 33–56. New York: Palgrave Macmillan. https://doi.org/10.1057/978-1-137-56036-0_2.

Ramanathan, Vaidehi. 2005. *The English-Vernacular Divide: Postcolonial Language Politics and Practice*. Clevedon: Multilingual Matters.

Rehmann, Jan. 2013. *Theories of Ideology: The Powers of Alienation and Subjection*. Leiden: Brill.

Reyes, Angela. 2017. "Inventing Postcolonial Elites: Race, Language, Mix, Excess." *Journal of Linguistic Anthropology* 27 (2): 210–31. https://doi.org/10.1111/jola.12156.

Ricento, Thomas, ed. 2015. *Language Policy and Political Economy: English in a Global Context*. Oxford: Oxford University Press.

Roberts, Celia. 2012. "Translating Global Experience into Institutional Models of Competency: Linguistic Inequalities in the Job Interview." *Diversities* 14 (2): 49–71.

Rosa, Jonathan, and Nelson Flores. 2017. "Unsettling Race and Language: Toward a Raciolinguistic Perspective." *Language in Society* 46 (5): 621–47. https://doi.org/10.1017/S0047404517000562.

Rose, Nikolas. 1990. *Governing the Soul: The Shaping of the Private Self*. London: Routledge.

Rose, Nikolas. 1996. *Inventing Our Selves: Psychology, Power, and Personhood*. Cambridge: Cambridge University Press.

Ryu, Hyeonseong. 2014. Hanguk jasaljeunggayul 12nyeongan 109.4%: Segye 2wi." *Yonhap News*, September 4, 2014. http://www.yonhapnews.co.kr/international/2014/09/04/0601140000AKR20140904172051088.HTML.

Sayer, Peter. 2015. "'More & Earlier': Neoliberalism and Primary English Education in Mexican Public Schools." *L2 Journal* 7 (3): 40–56.

Sayer, Peter. 2018. "Does English Really Open Doors? Social Class and English Teaching in Public Primary Schools in Mexico." *System* 73: 58–70. https://doi.org/10.1016/j.system.2017.11.006.

Schieffelin, Bambi B., Kathryn A. Woolard, and Paul V. Kroskrity, eds. 1998. *Language Ideologies: Practice and Theory*. New York: Oxford University Press.

Schmid, Andre. 2002. *Korea between Empires, 1895–1919*. New York: Columbia University Press.

Schultz, Theodore. 1971. *Investment in Human Capital: The Role of Education and of Research*. New York: Free Press.

Seilhamer, Mark. 2019. *Gender, Neoliberalism, and Distinction through Linguistic Capital: Taiwanese Narratives of Struggle and Strategy*. Bristol: Multilingual Matters.

Sennett, Richard. 2006. *The Culture of the New Capitalism*. New Haven, CT: Yale University Press.

Seo, Dongjin. 2009. *Jayuui Uiji Jagigyebalui Uiji: Sinjayujuui Hanguksahoeeseo Jagigyebalhaneun Jucheui Tansaeng*. Paju: Dolbegae.

Seth, Michael J. 2002. *Education Fever: Society, Politics, and the Pursuit of Schooling in South Korea*. Honolulu: University of Hawai'i Press.

Shin, Dongil. 2018a. "Geullobeol injaewa yeongeoneunglyeoke gwanhan damlonjeok silcheongwa sinjayujuui jucheseongui ihae." *Yeongeohak* 18 (3): 349–80. https://doi.org/10.15738/kjell.18.3.201809.349.

Shin, Dongil. 2018b. "Yeongeosiheome gwanhan damlon jeongchiui yeoksaseong bunseok: Sinjayujuuiwa pyeonggagukgaui nonjeomeulobuteo." *Eungyongeoneohak* 34 (3): 65–106.

Shin, Giseop. 2014. "Hanguk sanjae samangja 10manmyeongdang 18myeongeulo segye choego." *Hangyoreh*, April 30, 2014. http://www.hani.co.kr/arti/society/society_general/635146.html.

Shin, Gi-Wook, and Joon Nak Choi. 2015. *Global Talent: Skilled Labor as Social Capital in Korea*. Stanford, CA: Stanford University Press.

Shin, Hyunjung. 2006. "Rethinking TESOL from a SOL's Perspective: Indigenous Epistemology and Decolonizing Praxis in TESOL." *Critical Inquiry in Language Studies* 3 (2 & 3): 147–67.

Shin, Hyunjung. 2012. "From FOB to Cool: Transnational Migrant Students in Toronto and the Styling of Global Linguistic Capital." *Journal of Sociolinguistics* 16 (2): 184–200. https://doi.org/10.1111/j.1467-9841.2011.00523.x.

Shin, Hyunjung. 2014. "Social Class, Habitus, and Language Learning: The Case of Korean Early Study-Abroad Students." *Journal of Language, Identity & Education* 13 (2): 99–103. https://doi.org/10.1080/15348458.2014.901821.

Shin, Hyunjung. 2016. "Language 'Skills' and the Neoliberal English Education Industry." *Journal of Multilingual and Multicultural Development* 37 (5): 509–22. https://doi.org/10.1080/01434632.2015.1071828.

Shin, Hyunjung, and Byungmin Lee. 2019. "'English Divide' and ELT in Korea: Towards Critical ELT Policy and Practices." In *Second Handbook of English Language Teaching*, edited by Xuesong Gao. Cham: Springer International Publishing. https://doi.org/10.1007/978-3-319-58542-0_5-1.

Shin, Hyunjung, and Joseph Sung-Yul Park. 2016. "Researching Language and Neoliberalism." *Journal of Multilingual and Multicultural Development* 37 (5): 443–52. https://doi.org/0.1080/01434632.2015.1071823.

Shin, Jang-Sup, and Ha-Joon Chang. 2003. *Restructuring Korea Inc.* New York: Routledge.

Shore, Cris, and Susan Wright. 2015. "Governing by Numbers: Audit Culture, Rankings and the New World Order." *Social Anthropology* 23 (1): 22–28. https://doi.org/10.1111/1469-8676.12098.

Silverstein, Michael. 1979. "Language Structure and Linguistic Ideology." In *The Elements: A Parasession on Linguistic Units and Levels*, edited by Paul R. Clyne, William F. Hanks, and Carol L. Hofbauer, 193–247. Chicago Linguistic Society 15. Chicago: Chicago Linguistic Society.

Simpson, William, and John P. O'Regan. 2018. "Fetishism and the Language Commodity: A Materialist Critique." *Language Sciences* 70: 155–66. https://doi.org/10.1016/j.langsci.2018.05.009.

Song, Jae Jung. 2011. "English as an Official Language in South Korea: Global English or Social Malady?" *Language Problems and Language Planning* 35 (1): 35–55. https://doi.org/10.1075/lplp.35.1.03son.

Song, Jesook. 2009. *South Koreans in the Debt Crisis: The Creation of a Neoliberal Welfare Society*. Durham, NC: Duke University Press.

Song, Jesook. 2014. *Living on Your Own: Single Women, Rental Housing, and Post-Revolutionary Affect in Contemporary South Korea*. Albany: SUNY Press.

Song, Juyoung. 2010. "Language Ideology and Identity in Transnational Space: Globalization, Migration, and Bilingualism among Korean Families in the USA." *International Journal of Bilingual Education and Bilingualism* 13 (1): 23–42. https://doi.org/10.1080/13670050902748778.

Song, Juyoung. 2012. "The Struggle over Class, Identity, and Language: A Case Study of South Korean Transnational Families." *Journal of Sociolinguistics* 16 (2): 201–17. https://doi.org/10.1111/j.1467-9841.2011.00525.x.

Song, Juyoung. 2018. "English Just Is Not Enough!: Neoliberalism, Class, and Children's Study Abroad among Korean Families." *System* 73: 80–88.

Spivak, Gayatri. 2002. "Postcolonial Literature." Paper presented at the Graduate Seminars on Postcolonial Literature, July 2002. University of Hong Kong, Pokfulam, Hong Kong.

Spolsky, Bernard, and Young-in Moon, eds. 2012. *Primary School English-Language Education in Asia: From Policy to Practice*. New York: Routledge.

Spowage, Kate. 2018. "English and Marx's 'General Intellect': The Construction of an English-Speaking Elite in Rwanda." *Language Sciences* 70: 167–78. https://doi.org/10.1016/j.langsci.2018.04.003.

Standing, Guy. 2011. *The Precariat: The New Dangerous Class*. London; New York: Bloomsbury.

Statistics Korea. 2015. *2015nyeon chojunggo sagyoyukbijosa gyelgwa*. Seoul: Statistics Korea.

Strathern, Marilyn, ed. 2000. *Audit Cultures: Anthropological Studies in Accountability, Ethics, and the Academy*. New York: Routledge.

Takahashi, Kimie. 2013. *Language Learning, Gender and Desire: Japanese Women on the Move*. Bristol: Multilingual Matters.

Tan, Peter K. W., and Rani Rubdy, eds. 2008. *Language as Commodity: Global Structures, Local Marketplaces*. London: Continuum.

Tupas, Ruanni. 2019. "Entanglements of Colonialism, Social Class, and Unequal Englishes." *Journal of Sociolinguistics* 23 (5): 529–42. https://doi.org/10.1111/josl.12384.

Tupas, Ruanni, and Aileen Salonga. 2016. "Unequal Englishes in the Philippines." *Journal of Sociolinguistics* 20 (3): 367–81. https://doi.org/10.1111/josl.12185.

Urciuoli, Bonnie. 2008. "Skills and Selves in the New Workplace." *American Ethnologist* 35 (2): 211–28.

Urciuoli, Bonnie. 2011. "Neoliberal Education: Preparing the Student for the New Workplace." In *Ethnographies of Neoliberalism*, edited by Carol J. Greenhouse, 162–76. Philadelphia: University of Pennsylvania Press.

Urciuoli, Bonnie, and Chaise LaDousa. 2013. "Language Management/Labor." *Annual Review of Anthropology* 42 (1): 175–90. https://doi.org/10.1146/annurev-anthro-092412-155524.

Urla, Jacqueline. 2019. "Governmentality and Language." *Annual Review of Anthropology* 48 (1): 261–78. https://doi.org/10.1146/annurev-anthro-102317-050258.

Van Parijs, Philippe. 2011. *Linguistic Justice for Europe and the World*. Oxford: Oxford University Press.

Venugopal, Rajesh. 2015. "Neoliberalism as Concept." *Economy and Society* 44 (2): 165–87. https://doi.org/10.1080/03085147.2015.1013356.

Walkerdine, Valerie. 2006. "Workers in the New Economy: Transformation as Border Crossing." *Ethos* 34 (1): 10–41.

Walkerdine, Valerie. 2011. "Neoliberalism, Working-Class Subjectivities and Higher Education." *Contemporary Social Science* 6 (2): 255–71.

Warriner, Doris S. 2007. "'It's Just the Nature of the Beast': Re-Imagining the Literacies of Schooling in Adult ESL Education." *Linguistics and Education* 18: 305–24.

Warriner, Doris S. 2016. "'Here, without English, You Are Dead': Ideologies of Language and Discourses of Neoliberalism in Adult English Language Learning." *Journal of Multilingual and Multicultural Development* 37 (5): 495–508. https://doi.org/10.1080/01434632.2015.1071827.

Weber, Max. 2001[1930]. *The Protestant Ethic and the Spirit of Capitalism*. London: Routledge.

Wee, Lionel, and Ann Brooks. 2010. "Personal Branding and the Commodification of Reflexivity." *Cultural Sociology* 4 (1): 45–62. https://doi.org/10.1177/1749975509356754.

Wilce, James M. 2009. *Language and Emotion*. Cambridge: Cambridge University Press.

Wilce, James M., and Janina Fenigsen. 2016. "Emotion Pedagogies: What Are They, and Why Do They Matter?" *Ethos* 44 (2): 81–95. https://doi.org/10.1111/etho.12117.

Williams, Raymond. 1977. *Marxism and Literature*. Oxford: Oxford University Press.

Woo, Suk-hoon, and Park Il-kwon. 2007. *88Manwon Sedae*. Seoul: Redian.

Woolard, Kathryn A. 1998. "Introduction: Language Ideology as a Field of Inquiry." In *Language Ideologies: Practice and Theory*, edited by Bambi B. Schieffelin, Kathryn A. Woolard, and Paul V. Kroskrity, 3–47. Oxford: Oxford University Press.

World Health Organization. 2016. *World Health Statistics 2016*. http://www.who.int/gho/publications/world_health_statistics/2016/en/.

Wortham, Stanton E. F., and Angela Reyes. 2015. *Discourse Analysis beyond the Speech Event*. London: Routledge.

Yi, Wonseok. 2013. *Geodaehan Sagigeuk: Jagigyebalseo Gwonhaneun Sahoeui Heowa Sil*. Seoul: Book by Book.

Yoon, Kyong. 2014. "Transnational Youth Mobility in the Neoliberal Economy of Experience." *Journal of Youth Studies* 17 (8): 1014–28. https://doi.org/10.1080/13676261.2013.878791.

Yu, Taeyeong, and Nam Hyejeong. 2016. "Jasallyul 1wi uulhan hanguk: Anjeonmang jeolsil." *Segye Ilbo*, February 2, 2016. http://www.segye.com/newsView/20160202003880.

Zamora, Daniel, and Michael C. Behrent, eds. 2015. *Foucault and Neoliberalism*. London: Polity Press.

Zimmermann, Martina, and Sebastian Muth. 2020. "Entrepreneurial Visions of the Self: Language Teaching and Learning under Neoliberal Conditions." *Multilingua*. https://doi.org/10.1515/multi-2020-0045.

INDEX

For the benefit of digital users, indexed terms that span two pages (e.g., 52–53) may, on occasion, appear on only one of those pages.